I0623083

THE LAST DINOSAUR BOOK

THE

Last

DINO

BOOK

The Life and Times
of a Cultural Icon

W.J.T. Mitchell

The University of Chicago Press

Chicago and London

Riverside Community College
NOV '99   Library
4800 Magnolia Avenue
Riverside, CA 92506

E169.04 .M58 1998
Mitchell, W. J. T. (William
John Thomas), 1942–
The last dinosaur book : th
life and times of a cultura
icon

W.J.T. MITCHELL is the Gaylord Donnelley
Distinguished Service Professor in the Department
of English Language and Literature and in the
Department of Art at the University of Chicago.
He is author or editor of eight books published by
the University of Chicago Press, including *Picture
Theory*, which won the Charles Rufus Morey Award
in the history of art of the College Art Association.
He is also editor of *Critical Inquiry*.

The University of Chicago Press, Chicago 60637
The University of Chicago Press, Ltd., London
© 1998 by W.J.T. Mitchell
All rights reserved. Published 1998
Printed in Hong Kong

07 06 05 04 03 02 01 00 99 98   1 2 3 4 5

The images on pages iii, iv, and v are reproduced
here with permission. They are also presented,
discussed, and attributed in the text as, respectively,
figures 15.1, 32.5, and 5.1.

ISBN 0-226-53204-6 (cloth)

Library of Congress Cataloging-in-Publication Data

Mitchell, W. J. Thomas, 1942–
    The last dinosaur book : the life and times of a
cultural icon / W. J. T. Mitchell.
        p.   cm.
    Includes bibliographic references and index.
    ISBN 0-226-53204-6 (alk. paper)
    1. Popular culture—United States—History—
20th century. 2. Dinosaurs—Social aspects—United
States. 3. Dinosaur paraphernalia—United States.
4. Signs and symbols—United States—History—20th
century. I. Title.
E169.04.M58   1998
306'. 0973—DC21   98–16676
                                        CIP

Design: Joan Sommers Design

This book is printed on acid-free paper.

For my mother and my sisters

Leona Gaertner Mitchell Maupin
Sandra Maupin Ryan
Marylee Mitchell Tyler
Kathleen Mitchell Ombry (1936–1994)

Salamander Starship, Captain's Log, Stardate 3324. Have discovered relics of vanished civilization on Terra, 3rd planet in solar system Los. Preliminary survey indicates typical phase-3 evolutionary failure: advanced technologies, rudimentary eco-sociopolitical arrangements leading to irreversible environmental degradation and premature extinction of higher vertebrate life-forms. Terra now a desert planet with toxic atmosphere populated by micro-organisms. Only notable anomaly: traces of primitive Salamandrean life-forms found among the ruins of late Terran civilization. Recommend dispatch of interdisciplinary archaeological team to investigate.

TRACES, TALES, AND THEORIES

Reptilicus erectus

1.1

Aliens in the form of erect reptilian bipeds visit the earth. They hold a conference to discuss the fossil remains of an extinct mammalian biped known as *Homo sapiens*. These intelligent dinosauroids might find us as puzzling to them as they (or their ancient ancestors) are to us. (Cartoon by William Stout, © 1986.)

IMAGINE A DISTANT FUTURE in which the iron law of Darwinian necessity has taken effect, and human life has vanished from the earth. Visitors from another galaxy (erect reptilian bipeds, naturally) arrive on this planet and try to reconstruct a picture of human civilization from fragmentary fossil remains. They hold a symposium in which they attempt to make sense of this strange race of bipedal mammals, *Homo sapiens,* and reconstruct their culture.

Given the aliens' own reptilian characteristics, they would no doubt find the traces of the dinosaur especially fascinating. It would not be surprising, in fact, if they saw the dinosaur figure as absolutely central to human civilization, especially in the late twentieth century. If they dug up the ruins of a major metropolitan natural history museum, they might imagine that the giant figures were animal deities erected for public worship like the Golden Calf of biblical fame. The resemblance of these giant reptiles to the physiognomy of the visitors themselves might lead them to conclude that human beings worshipped the visitors' own primitive ancestors, *Reptilicus erectus,* as an obviously superior life-form. If they happened upon the ruins of a first-grader's bedroom, they might regard dinosaur images as fetish objects associated with a private cult. The rarest specimens by far would be the relics of that ritual practice that human beings called "scientific research." The authentic bones and fossils housed in paleontological archives would not just be relatively few in number compared with the replicas and reproductions. They would also be quite fragile

1.2

This is not an alien, but a paleontologist's image of what dinosaurs might have become if they had not died out. It is not a fantasy image, but a rigorous scientific speculation based in the laws of evolutionary adaptation that favor erectness, bipedalism, frontal eye sockets, and opposable thumbs. The *Stenonychus inequalis,* the most highly evolved dinosaur known to scientists, stands next to the dinosauroid. (Sculpture by Dale Russell and Ron Séguin, *Model of Stenonychosaurus and Dinosauroid,* from "Reconstructions of the Small Cretaceous Theropod *Stenonychosaurus inequalis* and a Hypothetical Dinosauroid" [Syllogeus, no. 37], 1982. Reproduced with permission of the Canadian Museum of Nature, Ottawa, Canada.)

when excavated from their protective matrix of earth. By contrast, the plastic models and bronze statues and laser discs would be relatively intact.

The alien visitors would discover similar proportions if they dug up a library. For every book on the scientific study of dinosaurs, they would find a hundred for children or for popular consumption. Among these books, they will find one that was written with them in mind, in anticipation of their visit. It is a book that attempts to look at the dinosaur in a rearview mirror, that treats both the real and the imaginary, the scientific and the popular dinosaur as fossils in a common archaeological dig. It is called *The Last Dinosaur Book*.

The Last Dinosaur Book begins by acknowledging the inevitable certainty that a time will come when there will be no more books about dinosaurs; when all the dinosaur images in the world, like the real creatures they stand for, will exist only as relics of a lost world. It recognizes that the very idea of the dinosaur depends on our ability to conceive of what the historian Martin Rudwick calls "deep time," an unimaginably distant past measured in hundreds of millions of years. *The Last Dinosaur Book* is written in anticipation of an equally deep *future,* a time when our present will have become the remote past and we will have gone the way of the dinosaurs. The cultures, indeed, the whole species that produced images of the dinosaur will be as extinct as the dinosaurs themselves.

This may sound like a gloomy prospect, but *The Last Dinosaur Book* need not be an exercise in melancholy predictions of doom. It could also be a kind of cosmic comedy, the entire human species seen as nature's way of introducing absurdity into the world. And we can take some comfort from the assurance that it will certainly not be the last book about dinosaurs, much less a book about the death of the last dinosaur. Thousands of books about dinosaurs will continue to appear, and *The Last Dinosaur Book* might even produce a few sequels. But the future visitors from outer space will recognize this book as the first one written with their interests and questions in mind. This book will not assume that the meaning of the dinosaur is fully explained by the science of paleontology, or that it is just a matter of common sense. From the point of view of the alien visitors, the ordinary behavior of human beings toward erect reptiles will probably look strange, contradictory, exotic—perhaps even ridiculous. Things that seem obvious to us will have to be explained to them. Jokes and clichés we understand without a second thought will require interpretation, the same way we excavate, assemble, and decipher the fragmentary remains of a buried city. Things we see as normal will look very strange, and vice versa.

The biggest problem facing *The Last Dinosaur Book* will be the question of what to include. Dinosaur paleontologists have the opposite problem: they have to construct their picture of the dinosaur from extraordinarily skimpy evidence. The fossil record is so fragmentary that many questions about dinosaurs may never be answered. For scholars who study dinosaur images, on the other hand, the problem is overabundance. There is simply too much material. Written at the end of the twentieth century in the midst of the greatest dinosaur craze the world has ever seen, *The Last Dinosaur Book* will be a kind of "Jurassic Ark," preserving only enough examples to give some glimpse of the variety of species. There is no possibility of encyclopedic comprehensiveness. The world is overrun with dinosaurs—or rather, with dinosaur images, which are what this book is really about: pictures, descriptions, narratives, models, toys, replicas of bones, footprints, and skeletons. There are probably more dinosaur images on the earth during the late twentieth century than there were real creatures in ancient times. They have escaped from the laboratory and the museum, cropping up in shopping malls, theme parks, movies, novels, advertisements, sitcoms, cartoons and comic books, metaphors and everyday language.[1] "They are," as one eminent paleontologist recently said to me, "a disease." Whether they are a curable disease, a self-limiting epidemic, or a symptom of an irreversible catastrophe is yet to be determined. First we need a basic description of the phenomenon itself.

So a limited historical and geographic sample will have to do. The history of the dinosaur

1.3

This is not a child's bedroom, but an artist's installation displaying the dinosaur collectibles available to middle-class children today. From a perspective in the distant future, we might think of this as an archaeological site revealing the late twentieth century as the period when "dinosaurs ruled the earth."

(Mark Dion, multimedia installation, *When Dinosaurs Ruled the Earth: Toys 'R' U.S.*, 1994.)

image, from its invention in the 1840s to its emergence as a media superstar in global popular culture at the end of the twentieth century, will have to be framed within a bare-bones outline of the story of modern culture from the Enlightenment through the Industrial Revolution to the postmodern era of biocybernetic reproduction. And the story of the global, international distribution of dinosaur images will have to be focused mainly on the United States. This will be partly a consequence of the limitations of the author, who (as it happens) will write as a North American White Male Academic (NAWMA), a citizen of the United States, about an image that has a special, peculiar role in American cultural history. The author is aware that dinosaur fascination is as strong in Japan as it is in the United States, that England and France pioneered the early research in paleontology, and that many other countries have made notable contributions to the scientific understanding of dinosaurs. Nevertheless, he feels that it makes sense to concentrate on a specific "cultural dig" in the archive of dinosaur images he knows best, and leave the bigger picture to be filled in later. The United States was the site of the first major "bone rush" during the golden age of dinosaur discovery in the late nineteenth century. The excavation and display of big fossil bones had been connected to national pride and prestige since the era of Thomas Jefferson. And the United States continued in the late twentieth century to be the world's largest producer and exporter of dinosaur images, most notably in *Jurassic Park*.

The Last Dinosaur Book will have to be written by someone rather like the alien visitors themselves, someone who finds the human obsession with dinosaurs strange and puzzling, not at all self-evident. It is unlikely, therefore, that this book would be written by a dinosaur scientist, or by one of the amateur dinophiles who collects dinosaur images and keeps up with the latest paleontological discoveries. These kinds of people are too close to the subject to take such a perspective on it. Their testimony is crucial, and their knowledge of the subject is frequently vast, but for that very reason they may not be in a good position to take seriously the sort of naive questions that the alien visitors will have. Most scientists, for instance, are not concerned with popular images of the dinosaur, except as a hobby, or as a distraction and an irritating source of popular misunderstanding. Scientists, quite rightly, feel that their job is to construct correct, true images of *real* dinosaurs, not to speculate about imaginary ones. The dinophiles, on the other hand, approach the subject with passion: they love dinosaur images, are drawn to them, collect them, and converse about them obsessively. Their participation in a common passion makes them disinclined to analyze the meaning of the whole phenomenon in which they participate, any more than one would want to analyze any other love object.

The Last Dinosaur Book will have to be written, then, by an outsider to both dinosaur science and dinomania. The author's viewpoint will be rather like that of an anthropologist interviewing native informants, a cultural historian combing the archives, an art critic poring over an array of images.

Neither dinophile nor dino-scientist, the author will approach his subject as an iconologist, an analyst of *images*—representations, pictures, descriptions, figures, imprints, traces, metaphors—a scientist whose object is not nature, but culture, or nature as it is constructed within culture (see appendix B, "Science and Culture," for more on this issue). But this author, being human, will not be a total outsider to dino-fascination. The author will play the double role of "participant-observer," serving as a contemporary witness to the dinosaur phenomenon of the late twentieth century who finds it alternately strange and familiar, exotic and banal, sublime and ridiculous. The author (like many of his fellow human beings and all NAWMAs) may even feel, at times, like a dinosaur himself. His book may read like a message in a bottle, cast adrift on the sea of time and space, drifting toward an unknown destination.

His book is the one you are reading now.

BIG, FIERCE, EXTINCT

WHY DO PEOPLE LIKE to look at dinosaurs? Why are children especially fascinated with them, and what about the ones who are not? How and where did the popular interest in dinosaurs originate, and how has it changed in the 150 years since the "terrible lizards" made their first public appearance? How is it that a creature that seems like mere background noise to most people, ubiquitous but unremarkable, emerged as the star attraction in one of the greatest Hollywood moneymakers of all time? How can something be utterly familiar, a universally intelligible commonplace, and yet also be regarded as an enigma, a riddle, and a haunting mystery?[1]

The scientific puzzles surrounding the dinosaur are, by comparison, relatively straightforward: What were the dinosaurs? How did they live? Why did they die out? What we do not yet understand is the *cultural* function of the dinosaur, its strange, chameleonlike status as a scientific wonder, a children's toy, a corporate logo, a voracious monster, a civic monument, and a synonym for obsolescence. We find an extraordinary proliferation of cultural images of the dinosaur, and some amazing collections of these images—dinosaur scrapbooks, fanzines, dictionaries, data books, television specials—but very few attempts to understand the underlying meaning of all these images, the basis for their fascination.[2]

How is the dinosaur able to play all these roles? How can it be an object of both public display and private obsession, rigorous scientific research and unbridled fantasy? What lessons are children learning when they learn about dinosaurs, and why have adults made dinosaurs a regular fixture of modern elementary education? What is the dinosaur's role in social identification and differentiation? Are dinosaurs, as is generally assumed, appreciated mainly by males of the human species? If so, why does the most popular dinosaur fiction of the late twentieth century *(Jurassic Park)* represent them as females? Do attitudes toward dinosaurs have some connection with racial or ethnic identity? With social, economic, or professional class? With nationality? How has the meaning of the dinosaur changed since its invention in the 1840s?

The most succinct explanation of dinosaur fascination is provided by the evolutionary biologist Stephen Jay Gould: "I know of no better response than the epitome proposed by a psychologist colleague: big, fierce, extinct—in other words, alluringly scary, but sufficiently safe."[3] This explanation of what Gould calls the "archetypal fascination" with dinosaurs is an excellent starting point, but it is (as Gould himself notes) not the last word. To begin with, every term of this explanation begs for further explanation. Why are bigness, ferocity, and extinction fascinating? Why are they not simply terrifying and repulsive? What makes human beings crave spectacles of gigantic violence? What makes us interested in imagining scenes of unspeakable terror involving creatures that have been dead for 65 million years? Is this a universal human desire—what Gould calls an "archetypal fascination"—or something specific to certain cultures and historical epochs? If we assume that power, violence, and death are always inherently interesting to human beings (already a questionable assumption), there are plenty of ways to gratify this desire without dinosaurs. Spectacles of animal violence, especially against human beings, have been a staple of human fascination at least since the Romans pitted lions against Christians, and possibly since God expelled Adam and Eve from the Garden of Eden, ending humanity's peaceable, utopian relationship with the animal kingdom.

Nor does the formula of "big, fierce, extinct" distribute itself consistently over the group of animals called dinosaurs. Some were big but not fierce; some were fierce but not especially big (perhaps this is why *Tyrannosaurus rex* dominates the popular imagery of dinosaurs, as the single example that fulfills this ideal formula). And if contemporary paleontologists are correct, they are not extinct either: some of them simply evolved into birds. If human fascination with dinosaurs depends on extinction (along with size and ferocity), then that fascination may be about to lose one of its crucial components.

It seems clear, then, that the promising formula of giantism, ferocity, and extinction is not by itself going to explain dinosaur fascination; it is only a starting point for our inquiry. The most difficult problem with the cultural meaning of the dinosaur, in fact, is resisting the temptation to settle for quick and easy answers, no matter how initially persuasive they may seem. People assume, quite rightly, that it takes a great deal of special training and knowledge to interpret the fossil remains of a dinosaur. But they assume, quite wrongly, that the traces of popular fascination with dinosaurs can be explained with a bit of common sense. As we shall see, it takes more than this.

One problem with Gould's explanation, which Gould himself notes, is that it is completely ahistorical. It doesn't explain why dinomania breaks out at certain times and places and not others, or why there seem to be "boom and bust" cycles of dinosaur fascination. Gould thinks that the answer must lie in a "quintessentially American source," namely, "commercialization" (224). Every so often a clever entrepreneur figures out a way to "turn the Jungian substrate into profits." *Jurassic Park* (both novel and film), with its multitude of commercial products, tie-ins, and spin-offs, is simply the latest and most powerful joining of the eternal fascination with bigness, ferocity, and extinction with the (equally eternal?) urge to make money.

Gould immediately concedes that this explanation needs still further explanation. He is not at all sure how these periodic outbursts of dinomania get started.

> Should we look to the great expansion of museum gift shops from holes-in-the-wall run by volunteers to glitzy operations crucial to the financial health of their increasingly commercialized parent institutions? Or did some particular product, or character, grip enough youthful imaginations at some point? Should we be looking for an evil genius, or just for an initial chaotic fluctuation, then amplified by cultural loops of positive feedback? (224)

Gould admits that he doesn't really have the answer to these questions. He suggests that they belong properly to "cultural historians"—which is where we come in.

Two basic questions about dinosaur fascination emerge in Gould's account: the why and the when. These two questions belong (roughly) to the disciplines of psychology and history, respectively. The first investigates the human fascination with big, fierce, extinct creatures; the second gives an account of the historical conditions that make this fascination change over time and become commercially exploitable in certain specific forms. From the standpoint of cultural history, however, these two disciplines cannot be sharply separated. The why is inseparable from the when. The "archetypal fascination" with dinosaurs, for instance, cannot be a universal, essential feature of the human psyche, because there were no dinosaurs to be fascinated with before the nineteenth century. There were plenty of large, fierce creatures, an abundance of real and mythical monsters, but there was no idea of the extinction of animal species before Cuvier, the great French paleontologist, conceived it in the 1790s, and no creatures called "dinosaurs" before the English paleontologist Richard Owen coined the word and concept in the 1840s. One might, of course, argue that dinosaurs just moved into the cultural niche formerly occupied by dragons and other monsters, but then one would be faced with a host of new questions. Dinosaurs clearly do not occupy *exactly* the same cultural niche as dragons (see chapter 13, "The Way of Dragons," for more on this). Dragons are generally thought to be mythical creatures. Modern people think that dragons never existed except in the popular superstitions of premodern cultures. Dinosaurs, by contrast, really did exist, and may still exist (as birds). They are thoroughly modern monsters, formerly living beings whose real existence has been scientifically proven beyond a shadow of doubt. Any psychological explanation, then, will have to take into account the historically modern and scientific character of the dinosaur. It will not be able to rely on assumptions about eternal archetypes.

As for the idea that extinction makes dinosaurs "sufficiently safe" for human beings, this seems like overkill. Cages and bars would do the trick just as well, as would the "fourth wall" of representation in movies, paintings, and other representational media. We don't need extinction to feel safe with dinosaurs; a little distance, domestication, or miniaturization is enough. That is why the most popular dinosaurs exist in the form of toys or cuddly, toothless figures like Barney. In any case, the fact that dinosaurs are extinct is not necessarily reassuring. It might just as easily awaken feelings of anxiety or guilt: we humans may be on the same endangered species list to which we add new names every day.[1]

There is a similar problem with grounding the history of dinosaur fascination in "commercialization." The desire for wealth is surely as eternal as the fascination with monsters. The real question is why this desire attaches itself to the dinosaur, why it works at some times (resulting in an outbreak of dinomania) and not at others, and why it takes different forms at different historical moments. The idea that dinosaurs are a surefire commercial attraction is not so reliable as it might at first appear. After all, the dinosaur is also a synonym for failure and obsolescence, the exact opposite of success. To be called a dinosaur in a rapidly changing, competitive market economy is hardly a prescription for commercial attractiveness. For anyone trying to capitalize on the dinosaur, then, the question of when (and how) cannot so easily be separated from the question of why.

Still, Gould's intuition that the secret of dinosaur fascination lies in the conjunction of monsters and money is a good starting point.[5] We need, however, a more precise sense of exactly what sort of monster the dinosaur is, and a more fully articulated framework for thinking about money, one that sees it as inseparable from the monstrous global system we call modern capitalism. We need a way of linking the dinosaur, not just to individual entrepreneurs such as Waterhouse Hawkins, Barnum Brown, and Stephen Spielberg who have "cashed in" on its public fascination, but also to the larger economic cycles that provide a setting for the speculation in dinosaur images. The history of these images is inseparable from the larger story of modern banking, fossil fuels, the oil and steel industries, and advancements in technology such as the railroad, the automobile, nuclear weapons, the computer, and biogenetic engineering.

The dinosaur is also linked to business cycles and surplus speculative capital in a fairly straightforward way. As a symbol of failure in a competitive world, it epitomizes the obsolete business strategy, the unsalable commodity, or even the unemployable worker whose skills are no longer needed in a "survival of the fittest" economy. The image of the dinosaur as a homeless beggar who is willing to hunt for food captures perfectly the slightly pathetic and contemptuous overtones that accompany any reference to a person as a dinosaur. And yet the image carries something more as well, something that qualifies the pity and contempt. Suppose hunting for food were to come back as a survival strategy? The pathetic dinosaur would still have his big teeth and claws. He might still be dangerous. And what if he were not headed for extinction, but growing in numbers, appearing more frequently on street corners in large cities? If the inner city becomes a jungle, what sort of creature is likely to survive there? Teeth and claws might turn out to have a use after all.

"Will Hunt for Food" makes at least one thing clear about the dinosaur as metaphor and cultural icon: it cannot be explained by a one-sided char-

2.1

One key to our fascination with dinosaurs is ambivalence. They are like us, yet unlike us. They are terrifying monsters, yet safely extinct. We look at the dinosaur as we look at the homeless or unemployed with mixed feelings of superiority and anxiety, pity, and apprehension. After all, we are not obsolete, homeless, or on the road to extinction . . . are we? And they can't hurt us . . . can they?

(Cartoon by Dave Lowery, ©1993 by Universal Studios, Inc. Courtesy of Universal Studios Publishing Rights. All rights reserved.)

acterization as "big, fierce, and extinct." Giantism, ferocity, and extinction all have to be seen in relation to antithetical scenarios—the dinosaur as a small, pathetic, contemptible failure, or a creature that may, in some mysterious way, be still with us, or coming back to new life and resumed dominance. The only term we have to summarize these complex and contradictory associations is "ambivalence," the tendency to hold opposite feelings, to be "of two minds" about a single thing. This word does not itself explain anything, but it may help us to resist the urge to settle for simple, one-sided explanations, and to pause for reflection over a cultural icon whose meaning at first seems completely transparent.

The dinosaur of "Will Hunt for Food," like the homeless person on the street, like the *T. rex* of *Jurassic Park,* may be closer than he appears in our rearview mirrors. In an age of speculation and capital surplus, he could make a dramatic comeback. Big money has always had a special fondness for extinct giants. Since the practical payoff of scientific dinosaur research is not all that obvious, a great deal of the early work in American paleontology was sponsored by wealthy individuals such as George Peabody, J. P. Morgan, and Andrew Carnegie. Relatively little public money was spent on the early scientific study of dinosaurs. (Spielberg's *Jurassic Park* cost more to make—and earned more—than all the money ever expended on paleontology.)[6] Dinosaurs are an "extra," and during the Depression, they almost disappeared as a scientific object, though they thrived in popular culture. Today they are hot items in both the scientific and popular imagination, a situation that echoes earlier eras of dinomania (the high Victorian moment of the 1850s, the Gilded Age in the United States after the Civil War, the period of American economic ascendancy before and after World War I). A *Megalosaurus* strolls up the road in Dickens's *Bleak House,* and one of the most popular children's films of the nineties in America, called *We're Back! A Dinosaur's Story,* features the return of the dinosaurs to suburban America, where *T. rex,* far from being homeless, is found playing a round of golf.[7]

A STEGOSAURUS MADE OF MONEY

CONSIDER A SYMPTOMATIC ANECDOTE about a dinosaur display at the Smithsonian Institution's National Museum of Natural History in Washington, DC:

> This dinosaur exhibit provides an excellent example of display recycling. The papier-mâché Stegosaurus now on the south side of the hall had been on view in both preceding dinosaur exhibits. The life-size beast was originally made for the 1904 St. Louis Exposition and paid for with funds appropriated for displays there. Somehow a wild rumor got started in the 1960s that the papier-mâché was made from worn money withdrawn from circulation. The staff knew better, but to resolve the point, several people from the Bureau of Printing and Engraving did an "autopsy" and determined that ordinary paper was involved.[1]

We will probably never know exactly how this "wild rumor" got started. The interesting question is what gives rumors like this currency. How does a perfectly ordinary, rational scientific object get recycled in popular culture as the subject of an urban legend? Why would people want to believe, despite authoritative denials, in a *Stegosaurus* made of money? Why does it seem so crucial to the story that the money was, as it were, "obsolete," withdrawn from circulation? Why was a forensic "autopsy" required to lay the rumor to rest? What is this story really about?[2]

One possibility is that the *Stegosaurus* made of money is one of those "wild rumors" (like

We're going to make a fortune on this place!

—LAWYER, on first seeing Jurassic Park

Reproduced by special permission of *The Saturday Evening Post.*
Copyright 1940 by the Curtis Publishing Company

"I don't mind you boosting your home state, Conroy, but stop telling the children that dinosaur is a California jack rabbit!"

UFOs) that signify public indifference, or even resistance, to scientific and governmental authority. The story is partly about popular distrust of science and the state, about the suspicion that deep secrets are in the possession of government scientists and being kept from the public with bland denials. It is also about the public recognition that scientific and governmental expertise is not monolithic; scientists and bureaucrats can disagree among themselves, and different kinds of expertise need to be checked against one another. The rumor is finally laid to rest not by the paleontologists, but by the experts from the Bureau of Printing and Engraving, who know real paper money—"authentic specie"—when they see it.

Above all, the story is about desire. For some reason, the public wanted to believe in a *Stegosaurus* made of money. What that reason is will take some time to unfold. Is it the same

3.1
The dinosaur is a popular subject of the tall tales adults tell to children. In the Middle Ages, fossil bones were thought to be a hoax played by God to test the faith of Christians. In the modern world, they have become Barnumesque attractions and monuments to the prestige of nations and states.

lure that draws spectators to such spectacles of wealth as the U.S. Mint or the Crown Jewels? Is it the familiar mystique of what Marx called the "commodity fetish," the irrational attachment to money that causes Donald Duck's Uncle Scrooge to bask in his swimming pool full of currency and coins? Is it the paper equivalent of the "Midas complex," a wish to transform the giant lizard's flesh into greenbacks?

The *Stegosaurus* made of money surely builds on our traditional fascination with wealth, but it transforms that fascination in important ways. First, it converts it to animal form. Like the biblical Golden Calf, which was made from the golden jewelry the Israelites brought out of Egypt, the *Stegosaurus* is a cross between an idol and a cash cow. Unlike the Golden Calf, the *Stegosaurus* is not worshipped as a religious object, but is the product of a self-reinforcing mass fascination.[3] Once the rumor is unleashed, a feedback loop between dinomania and the love of money is set in motion, and official denials are unable to slow it down. It is a perfect example of what has been called "mimetic desire," the accelerated demand for an object triggered by the perception that many other people already desire that object.[4]

But there is a second transformation that is crucial. Unlike the gold specie that constitutes the Golden Calf, the currency of the *Stegosaurus* is not current. It is paper money withdrawn from circulation. There is a congruence, in other words, between the status of the extinct animal and the extinct, obsolete money. What people are coming to see, then, is *dead* money, that which used to be living, productive, and valuable, but no longer is. The attraction is not quite like the fascination with Confederate or even counterfeit money. It is the attraction of lost or stolen value, of buried treasure, of something that was enormously valuable in its proper time and place, and which might (like the dinosaur) be brought back to life. The National Museum's papier-mâché *Stegosaurus* was originally put on display at the St. Louis World's Fair of 1904, during the first wave of public dinosaur displays in the great natural history museums of the United States. Its second resurrection, or "recycling," in the 1960s corresponds to a period of massive suspicion about the credibility of the U.S. government, and the beginning of a "dinosaur renaissance" that has now reached its peak in the *Jurassic Park* phenomenon. Perhaps public desire was, with the aid of new research paradigms and funding for new displays, willing the dinosaur back to life, putting its value back into circulation. Perhaps it was also a symptom of the widespread suspicion that the U.S. government in the 1960s was an institution that sought to withhold wealth from its own people and invest it in death and extinction. The perception that the U.S. treasury was pouring money into a genocidal war in Southeast Asia, a war that decimated a whole generation of Americans and Vietnamese, might underlie the suspicion that the United States had withdrawn money from living circulation to invest in the production of death, literally depositing that money in the body of an extinct animal.

This interpretation is, admittedly, about as wild as the rumor itself. It helps us to see in the *Stegosaurus* made of money a lesson about dinosaur lessons. It will no doubt have occurred to you that this story may have no meaning at all; that it is just a trivial anecdote, a wild rumor. I have been mining it for significance, and (like any competent cultural historian) I have been finding what I have been looking for. But for many people, this story—and the dinosaur more generally—has no special significance or importance. They may recognize that dinosaurs are important to certain kinds of scientists and amateur dinophiles. They may acknowledge that many children find dinosaurs a fascinating subject for a brief period. But my guess is that most adults regard dinosaurs, if they think of them at all, as a curiosity, a passing fad, or as a scientific object that is somebody else's business. The affirmation that dinosaurs are "deep" cultural symbols, with complex meanings and profound social importance, is just as likely to provoke suspicion toward cultural experts like myself as are the expert denials that the *Stegosaurus* is made of money.

Disavowal of the cultural significance of the dinosaur can come from several quarters: from scientists who see cultural explanations as threatening to their own expertise, and who want to keep the dinosaur a "purely" scientific object; from dinophiles who, like the scientists, want to keep their passions pure and unexamined; from those who think that "common sense" is enough, and that cultural experts are just "reading into" things that are perfectly obvious and require no interpretation.

Our alien visitors from the future are not likely to buy these sorts of disclaimers. They will be committed on principle to the notion that all the data, no matter how trivial or seemingly insignificant, have to be interpreted and deciphered. Given their own reptilian physiognomy, they will be strongly inclined to see the dinosaur image as deeply significant, all the more so when accompanied by disavowals or expressions of indifference. They will see such disavowals as simply another symptom of the ambivalence and paradox that seems so invariably associated with the dinosaur image. They will recognize the dinosaur, like so many other modern superstitions (from rabbit's feet to broken mirrors to walking under ladders), as a figure that shuttles between belief and skepticism, monumental importance and triviality.

They will be alert to the tensions in Stephen Jay Gould's "archetypal fascination" account. The dinosaur is fascinating because it is large, fierce, and extinct; and yet its popularity is also dependent on its miniaturization as a harmless toy, and its resurrection in "lifelike" restorations. The dinosaur is supposed to be a surefire commercial attraction, a magnet for money; and yet it is a synonym for failure and obsolescence, a money-monster that is nothing but worthless paper. It is supposed to be a scientific object, a modern invention; and yet it attracts myths and fantasies that remind us of archaic superstition.

The alien visitors will also see a parallel between the paradoxes of the dinosaur and a whole series of crises in modern history, a linkage between this image and controversies in politics, science, and culture. They will quickly discover that dinosaur bones have been put on display to make arguments for and against evolution; to express anxieties about uncontrolled migration and racial mixing, and to illustrate the consequences of failure to migrate and adapt to new conditions. They will observe that the greatest epidemic of dinosaur images occurs in the late twentieth century, just at the moment when widespread public awareness of ecological catastrophe is dawning, and the possibility of irreversible extinction is becoming widely evident. But they will also note the curious way in which the dinosaur image serves as a monument to the prestige of modern states and nations. Why, they will ask, does the United States have a "Dinosaur National Monument," and why does every state in the union want its own dinosaur? (The New Jersey state legislature declared *Hadrosaurus* its "state dinosaur" in 1994; New Mexico claims *Seismosaurus,* the biggest dinosaur in the world, of which only a few tail bones have been found; Texas brags about its "Lone Star Dinosaurs" that "roamed where jumbo jets now roll down runways"[5]; California has no real dinosaurs to brag about, but it displays them "in response to public demand" at the La Brea tar pits and Universal Studios.) We presume that Theodor Adorno's famous remark that the appearance of the dinosaur is a symptom of the "monstrous total State" was directed at the fascist regimes of Europe.[6] But suppose it has an unintended significance, an application to places like New Jersey and (of course) California? Or simply to that "state of affairs" we call the modern world?

4.1

The first glimpse of the Jurassic Park
dinosaurs. The immediate reaction of Dr.
Grant (Sam Neill): "We're out of a job."
Paleontology depends for its life upon the
extinction of its object. If dinosaurs come
back to life, paleontologists are doomed.
The paleontologist Jack Horner (the
model for Dr. Grant) has expressed anxiety about the technical perfection of animated dinosaur restorations in *The Lost
World,* Spielberg's sequel to *Jurassic
Park.* "There is no mystery left,"
remarked Horner. "Now that we know
exactly how they looked, sounded, and
moved, the fascination may be lost."
(Film still, *Jurassic Park.*)

THE END OF DINOSAUROLOGY

OUR ALIEN VISITORS from the future might conclude at this point that the behavior of the extinct *Homo sapiens* was simply too complex, irrational, and unpredictable to admit of any explanation. They might be tempted to turn away from rumors, myths, and superstitions and concentrate strictly on scientific accounts of dinosaurs, hoping thereby to find calm order, clearly defined terms, and cool rationality. Unfortunately, they will find things no better within the realm of science. Paleontology turns out to be less a refuge from dinomania than its storm center. The study of dinosaurs is not like any other branch of science. Dinosaurs are accorded special treatment totally out of proportion to their practical or theoretical importance. New discoveries are routinely treated as front-page news, and are mounted as marquee attractions in major cities. Natural history museums install picture windows in their laboratories so the public can watch the scientists at work. Star dinosaurologists become media celebrities, Hollywood consultants, and culture heroes. Lesser lights, and non-dinosaur paleontologists who focus on less popular organisms, labor on in obscurity, vacillating between resentment at this absurd dinosaur cult and

> For several decades in the mid twentieth century . . . the field of dinosaur research seemed fossilized itself. Dinosaurs were considered so terminally extinct, and were so stigmatized by their irrevocable disappearance, that there seemed little to be learned about them or from them that was worth knowing.
>
> —JOHN NOBLE WILFORD,
> *The Riddle of the Dinosaur*

relief that they can work undisturbed. Debates over the names and classification of dinosaurs have raged in the technical journals and spilled over into public awareness, from the famous "fossil feuds" and "bone wars" of the nineteenth century to the current argument about birds as descendants of dinosaurs.

When money is short and public attention slackens, on the other hand, "the field of dinosaur research," as John Noble Wilford notes, seems to become "fossilized itself."[1] But that does not mean that there is some simple, direct relation between popularity and scientific interest. Sometimes the relation seems to be inverted, as Gregory Paul points out.

> By the 1930s, dinosaurology had another problem besides the Depression. Dinosaurs had become so popular with the public that the subject had taken on something of a circus air, and paleontologists shied away from studying the creatures. They became reptilian curiosities, good for drawing crowds into the museum, but evolutionary dead ends of little theoretical importance.[2]

Many scientists would be uncomfortable with Paul's suggestion that there is (or ever was) a field called "dinosaurology." They would prefer to be called "paleontologists," steering clear of overidentification with such a controversial and volatile object. Paul is an artist-scientist-author who straddles the gap between the amateur dinophile and the professional scientist, which may explain why he is comfortable with the term.[3]

But the "circus air" surrounding dinosaurs may not be the deepest reason for scientists' discomfort with dinosaurology. Their anxiety also has reasons internal to paleontology. For much of the dinosaur's short life as a biological concept, it has been under a cloud of suspicion.[4] Although there is no doubt that giant creatures

> It became clear that, as for all major taxa, the term *dinosaur* has a significant arbitrary component. . . . where we choose to draw the boundary between dinosaurs and non-dinosaurs is a subjective matter, not a given fact of nature.
>
> —*The Dinosauria*

with some reptilian features walked the earth (and swam the seas and clove the air) millions of years ago, there has been considerable debate about whether it makes sense to call them dinosaurs.[5] The distinguished Yale paleontologist John Ostrom notes that "the term 'Dinosauria' was abandoned as an official formal label many years ago, but the general public never gave up on it."[6] "Dinosaur" is really a term in folk taxonomy (like "creeping things"), not an indisputable scientific category. As John Noble Wilford explains the situation:

> Dinosauria is not, strictly speaking, a recognized scientific grouping of animals. Almost nothing learned about them suggests that they form a single natural group. Indeed, since the late nineteenth century, most scientists have come to believe that the so-called dinosaurs consisted of two separate groups that were rather distantly related. These are the Saurischia, or "lizard hips," and Ornithischia, "bird hips." As the names suggest, saurischians and ornithischians have quite different anatomies that mark them as being perhaps no more related to each other than they are to other members of the reptilian family tree, such as crocodiles and pterosaurs. (60)

The word "dinosaur," unlike "mammal," may not denote a natural group of animals with a coherent group of derived characteristics; it may instead be an artificial, arbitrary construct that encompasses two radically different animal groups. (The saurischians include most of the predatory bipeds like *T. rex* and *Velociraptor;* the ornithischians are exemplified by heavily armored quadrupeds like *Stegosaurus* and *Triceratops.*) A similar mistake about us could be made by the alien visitors in the deep future. They could assemble specimens of all the birds and mammals currently living on earth and lump them together in a class called "birmals," postulating a common ancestor to make sense of the whole thing.

What difference would it make if the concept of the dinosaur became as obsolete as the notions of "phlogiston" and "the ether" are in physics? Suppose the dinosaur was discarded as an outmoded notion, going the way of hysteria in psychoanalysis, race in biology, or totemism in anthropology? What if the very idea of the dinosaur turned out to be a dinosaur?

Most working scientists will say that names are irrelevant to the research they do. They are interested in things, not words. Biological taxonomy is just a filing system, and all the names are artificial and arbitrary. The organisms would still exist no matter what they were called. This cheerfully nominalistic attitude fades rapidly, however, when it is suggested that the name and concept "dinosaur" should be retired from scientific nomenclature. Arguments are mustered to prove that dinosaurs *were* a natural grouping with a common ancestor and shared features (these are now clearly in the ascendancy, and I have been assured by more than one expert that Wilford and Ostrom are mistaken, and that dinosaurs are definitely "monophyletic," not "polyphyletic," though the missing links required for definite proof have yet to be found).[7] Traditions and precedents are invoked to support the maintenance of the disputed name and concept. The exigencies of fund-raising and public support of science are offered as a clinching argument for keeping the dinosaur in play. And of course the dinophiles can be counted on to rally in support of the endangered name and the cult object that goes with it.

I'm not especially interested in who is right in the debate over the scientific coherence of the dinosaur concept. What is interesting here is that there *is* a debate—a long-standing suspicion that the term doesn't really pick out a natural group of animals—and yet the term survives (like the *Stegosaurus* made of money), more because of popular demand than scientific certainty. What would happen if paleontologists publicly declared the term "dinosaur" to be obsolete? Would it make any difference in the public fascination with and belief in the terrible lizards? What would happen if they announced tomorrow that a common ancestor had definitively established the monophyletic status of the group? Dinosaurs flourished in popular culture for nearly a century (1866–1960s) during which scientists (quietly) regarded the name and concept with suspicion; they existed (as images and words) independently of their scientific status. They became a "folk taxon," a new category in the popular understanding of the natural order, one that did not exist before the 1840s.[8]

The concept of the dinosaur may have already gone through its period of scientific obsolescence, only to make a comeback in the 1960s, the dawn of the famous "dinosaur renaissance." The dinosaur's revival from the dustbin of the history of science has been one of the big stories of paleontology in what cultural historians call the postmodern era. The new-model dinosaur of the late twentieth century is warm-blooded, birdlike, clever, agile, adaptive, and sociable. *We're Back! A Dinosaur's Story* is the title of a popular children's film about the return of the dinosaurs as benevolent companions. "The Dinosaurs Return. A New Era Begins" is the slogan on the poster for the new dinosaur hall at the American Museum of Natural History. "They never went away" might be the appropriate sound bite for the current proposal that dinosaurs evolved into birds.

If the dinosaur is no longer in danger of being dumped by science, however, it may still be in some peril from its own success as a cultural icon. Gould concludes his meditation on dinomania by lamenting the "commercial flood that may truly extinguish dinosaurs by turning them from sources of awe into clichés and commodities. Will we have strength to stand up to this deluge?" (237). Perhaps not. The deluge of commodities and clichés has been ebbing and flowing since the first "spin-off" replicas and toys based on the 1854 Crystal Palace sculptures of Waterhouse Hawkins.[9] The vacillation between sublime awe and clichéd commodification has been built into the creature from the beginning. Dinosaurs have been starring in movies since their debut in Winsor McCay's 1914 classic, *Gertie the Dinosaur*, and they have been linked with big money since the Sinclair dinosaur became an emblem of corporate giantism in the thirties.

If Gould is right that giantism, ferocity, and extinction are the keys to dinomania, then it may be a self-limiting malady. The more the dinosaur proliferates, the more it is diminished in stature, pacified, and domesticated, and the less interesting its extinction becomes. Every first-grader knows that the name of the dinosaur ("terrible lizard") is a misnomer: very few of them were terrible (many, we now know, were nurturing, caring creatures with family values, just like us),[10] and none of them were lizards. As for the haunting "riddle of extinction," it has now been solved, or even more ominously, *dis*-solved. The general public thinks it knows why the dinosaurs died out (a large meteorite produced a global nuclear-style winter), even if scientists do not agree on this scenario. Or the survival of the dinosaurs as birds simply makes the whole question of extinction disappear, taking a considerable quotient of mystery along with it. How much mystique will remain when the creatures formerly known as dinosaurs take on their proper name of "early birds," and dinosaurology disappears to be replaced by paleo-ornithology?

It would be a fitting irony if *The Last Dinosaur Book* heralded a second extinction, a story of the dinosaur killed off by its own success, dying from overproduction, runaway inflation, and consumer glut. The *Stegosaurus* made of money could then be withdrawn from circulation for good. The theoretical interest of the dinosaur would shift from the natural to the cultural and social sciences. And the last dinosaurologist could sit down to write its history.

5.1

The dinosaur was at home on the range in the Wild West, and paleontologists were on the frontier alongside the cowboys, Indians, trappers, traders, outlaws, and miners. A "Bone Rush" accompanied the Gold Rush in the West after the Civil War. If there had been any living dinosaurs in "them thar hills," they would have quickly gone the way of the buffalo.

(Painting by Bob Walters illustrating Sharon Farber's short story, "The Last Thunder Horse West of the Mississippi," © 1988 Robert F. Walters.)

THE LAST THUNDER HORSE WEST OF THE MISSISSIPPI

IF NEITHER PALEONTOLOGY nor popular rumors and fantasies can give us a clear, unequivocal account of dino-fascination, then perhaps we should turn to the realm of literature, to deliberately constructed fictions about dinosaurs that make no claim to scientific truth. Since the question of extinction seems central to the mystique of the dinosaur, and is obviously a structural issue in the closure of the "total" dinosaur narrative, stories of extinction are the obvious place to start. I will discuss the evolution of scientific stories about dinosaur extinction later (see chapter 34, "Catastrophe, Entropy, Chaos"), but for now let us look at a few versions of what might be called "the last dino-story"—fictional narratives about the end of the line for the dinosaur. We may never know what killed off the real dinosaurs, but we can be sure that where uncertainty reigns, fabulous stories will thrive.

> Indians believe fossilized bones to be the remnant of an extinct race of giants. They consider me a man of great wisdom, and call me "Bone Medicine Man" and "Big Bone Chief." Chief Red Cloud is my personal friend, as is Buffalo Bill.
>
> —O. C. MARSH

In 1996, the National Film Board of Canada produced an animated film for children that explains how dinosaurs nearly went extinct, but instead evolved into birds (*How Dinosaurs Learned to Fly*, 1996, directed by Munro Ferguson).[1] Dinosaurs, we are told, had extremely small brains, and so could think of only one idea at a time. This idea generally involved having a good time—smoking, drinking, dancing to loud rock and roll music—habits that were clearly bad for dinosaurian health. Then one dinosaur had a new idea about how to have a good time. He began to enjoy the Jurassic equivalent of bungee jumping. This dinosaur would jump off a cliff for the pure pleasure of the free fall. The only problem was the sudden, violent stop at the bottom (since the bungee cord had not yet been invented) and the ensuing bodily damage. This dinosaur's bright new idea (which was widely copied by all his friends) was turning him into an endangered species. Then another dinosaur had another bright idea: if you flapped your short little arms wildly on the way down, the impact of the fall would be moderated. This idea was copied, and steadily improved, until dinosaurs gradually evolved into the birds we know today.

The remarkable thing about this story is not so much its fabulous, improbable character as its successful combination of a series of ideas that have all been taken as true or probable by scientists at some point. The idea that small brains had something to do with extinction is a commonplace in what might be called the "classic" model of the dinosaur—the slow, stupid giant that is incapable of adapting to any sort of change. The notion that species evolve by trying out new tricks (flapping the arms) that are then passed on to their descendants is a basic principle of Lamarckian "progressive evolution," a dominant paradigm in natural history before Darwin.[2] And the idea that dinosaurs evolved into birds is now regarded as a scientific truth by most paleontologists (though there are many ornithologists who dissent from this position).[3] In short, this children's story is not just a fantasy, but a specific combination of ideas from different periods in the history of science. Two of these ideas (progressive evolution and extinction through stupidity) are now widely regarded as obsolete, while the third (the bird hypothesis) enjoys widespread acceptance. In short, this "fiction" of the dinosaur isn't mere invention: it is an assemblage of scientific "truths" from three different periods of paleontological science, an assemblage that adds up to a wild, implausible fable that makes perfect sense. Anyone watching this film will have to conclude, at a minimum, that the relation between science and fantasy is a very complicated one—that facts and fictions cannot be segregated neatly in different compartments, but weave into one another in very strange ways.

Sharon Farber's "The Last Thunder Horse West of the Mississippi" (in *Isaac Asimov's Science Fiction Magazine*, 1988) is a combination of science fiction, historical romance, and cowboy adventure. It is loosely based on the bitter, widely publicized rivalry between the two greatest American paleontologists of the nineteenth century, Othniel Charles Marsh of Yale and Edward Drinker Cope, a Quaker from Philadelphia. Cope and Marsh are legendary figures in the history of the quest for American dinosaurs. They were the pioneers in the "bone rush" that accompanied the gold rush in the western United States after the Civil War.[4] They have also come to epitomize contrasting styles of the scientist as a cultural figure. Marsh was a plodding, careful scholar, a skillful administrator, and a master of public relations who parlayed his Uncle Peabody's fortune into the first professorship of paleontology at Yale. Marsh may well have been the most famous scientist in America in the late nineteenth century, and he further inflated his reputation with exaggerated stories about his frontier heroism and his friendship with the Indians. Cope, by contrast, was a brilliant, moody prodigy who made hundreds of original discoveries and exhausted his family's modest fortunes in his insatiable quest for fossils. Cope and Marsh's "fossil feud" was waged over priorities in naming, describing, and classifying new species, and over the bones themselves, which often became as hotly contested as mining claims. Marsh ultimately got the upper hand with his superior financial and institutional support. He circulated stories that Cope was mad, and did his best to destroy Cope's reputation as a scientist.

Farber has transformed this story into a Western yarn, complete with cowboys, Indians, and a living dinosaur—the last thunder horse west of the Mississippi. When Cope and Marsh hear the news that a real, live dinosaur is in captivity in a secret location out there in the wilderness, they set out with teams of cowboys and Indian guides to get there first and put down the highest bid on the beast. To prevent the dinosaur from falling into the hands of the wrong party, one of Marsh's hirelings straps sticks of dynamite onto its body. During the gunfight over the hapless beast, it is blown to bits.

There is nothing particularly obscure about the moral of this story. Greed and ruthless competition lead to the destruction of an endangered species. The pristine wilderness is corrupted and then destroyed by the invasion of white men, modern science, and capitalism. Marsh, in particular, is portrayed as a ruthless competitor, able to top any bid. He shows off his frontier prowess by shooting buffalo from a moving wagon just to demonstrate his marksmanship. Bob Walters' illustration for the story captures this theme nicely, showing the last dinosaur rearing up on its hind legs, under attack by a pair of cowboys brandishing their shooting irons.

The real interest of this story, however, is not the inventive transformation of a true piece of scientific history into a Western romance, but the fact that so little invention or transformation is required. Like the story of Jurassic bungee jumping, this fiction is an assemblage of historical facts and theories that have, at one time or another, enjoyed the status of scientific doctrine. The true history was already a cowboy yarn. Marsh really was a braggart who portrayed himself as a frontier hero, a friend of Buffalo Bill, General Custer, and Chief Red Cloud. He really was a ruthless entrepreneur who collected far more fossils than he knew how to describe, and who exploited the work of his students and colleagues. Cope really was a Quaker mystic who believed that his scientific work would ultimately vindicate his religious beliefs in perfectibility and progress. In his nightmares, the creatures he looked for had come back to life. He clung to the obsolete Lamarckian concept of progressive evolution, with its emphasis on individual improvements passed on as inherited characteristics, at a time when the Darwinian consensus was taking over. He really was a brilliant interpreter of fossils who traveled unarmed and with a single guide into Indian country (in contrast to Marsh's U.S. Cavalry escorts and gangs of hirelings). The only major invention in Farber's story is the living dinosaur. And this dinosaur, the *Josaurus,* fits right into the frontier romance, the world of dime novels, hoaxes, Indian princesses, snake-oil salesmen, varmints, gunslingers, and nineteenth-century American paleontology. One might expect that an image of a dinosaur with cowboys would have a surrealistic weirdness, but the surprise is how natural it looks. No matter how insistently science reassures us that Walters' picture of dinosaurs and cowboys together is impossible, the rightness and plausibility of that picture are overwhelming.

This plausibility may be partly a result of a natural extension of Gould's dinomania formula into a new domain: the "big, fierce, extinct" triad applies to cowboys as well as to dinosaurs. Cowboys are always shown as big, strong, tough, and dangerous in a fight. They are also shown as a vanishing breed. From Natty Bumppo to the Road Warrior, the frontiersman is an endangered species, always about to disappear over the western horizon into the sunset. Equally important, however, is the frontiersman's role as a deliberate or unwitting danger to other species. The western plains in the 1870s were littered with the bones of buffalo, slaughtered by cowboys and professional hunters as a deliberate strategy for destroying the Indian way of life and replacing it with the civilized pursuits of cattle ranching and mining. From the corpse-strewn battlefields of the Civil War, to the bones left by the great cattle drives, to the whitening buffalo skeletons along the transcontinental railroad lines, to the trainloads of dinosaur fossils returning to the East Coast, the landscape of the American West was a veritable boneyard. The mythic period of the American frontier in the second half of the nineteenth century might well be called "the age of bones," and the landscape of this period could be portrayed as "the valley of dry bones."

So dinosaurs rightly belong in the picture with cowboys and Indians and buffalo and outlaws and railroads and cavalry—in short, in the world of the American frontier, understood as a blend of fact and fantasy, a real place and a Hollywood invention. There is a natural truth in this image that is not the truth of natural science, but of a cultural, social science, the study of the history of images. In that history, paleontologists are cowboys fighting over livestock or buried treasure. They are determined to bring it back, dead or alive, like bounty hunters, Indian fighters, buffalo hunters, wranglers rounding up a stray calf, or desperadoes in search of a mining claim. *Josaurus,* like the *Stegosaurus,* is worth a lot of money. Marsh bids $500 for it. The cowboys who have penned it up are treating it already as a potential cash cow. If it isn't sold to the scientists, it could be valuable breeding stock, or become a monster attraction in P. T. Barnum's circus.

Sadly, the *Josaurus* doesn't get the opportunity to evolve, reproduce, or make money as a public attraction. It is blown to smithereens by a drunken cowboy. The story ends with the two disappointed paleontologists catching the train back east. "The Last Thunder Horse West of the Mississippi," like so many Western romances of the quest for hidden treasure in a primeval wilderness, turns out to be an ironic tale of disappointment. Instead of the "seek and ye shall find" moral of the traditional quest, this story suggests that the quest destroys the very object that it is seeking.

DINOTOPIA: THE NEWT WORLD ORDER

LIKE BEAST FABLES of any kind, dinosaur stories are really about human beings. Either the dinosaurs must be treated as if they were human, or they must be brought into some kind of encounter with human beings as an alien, hostile life-form. Dinosaurs, in short, are "us," or they are "not-us." As erect bipeds, they resemble us; as reptiles, they are the "other," the exotic, strange, and sinister alien, loaded down with satanic associations, from the serpent who tempts Eve to the Great Red Dragon of the Apocalypse. "It's hard to believe we're built like that inside!" comments the lady in the natural history museum standing face to face with her bony counterpart.

Dinosaur stories like "The Last Thunder Horse West of the Mississippi" treat the dinosaur as a "vanishing race," a marginal victim, doomed to extinction. But there is an equally powerful strain in dinosaur narratives that treats them in just the opposite way, as a "master race" or dominant life-form. These alternative worlds, or "dinotopias," have their scientific basis in the notion of a 170-million-year "Age of Reptiles" extending from the Devonian to the Triassic.[1] Science and narrative fiction thus converge on the common goal of bringing the dinosaurian "world order" into some relation to our human world. These dinotopias can be visited in fiction by such pretexts

> **As our flesh is warm, so is theirs cold. We have hair upon our heads and a hunter will grow a proud beard, while the animals that we hunt have warm flesh and fur or hair, but this not true of Yilane. They are cold and smooth and scaled, have claws and teeth to rend and tear, are large and terrible, to be feared. And hated.**
>
> —HARRY HARRISON,
> *West of Eden*

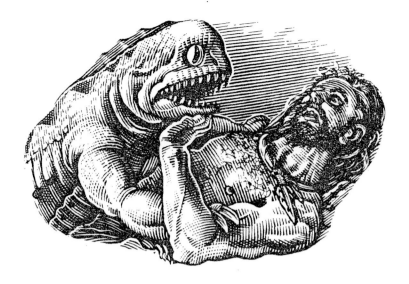

6.1

As monstrous double, the dinosaur is both our twin and our antagonist. Despite the scientific certainty that dinosaurs and human beings never walked the earth at the same time, people and dinosaurs often appear together, typically in stories about a world where savage men are locked in a life-and-death struggle with the ruling reptiles. (Bill Sanderson, woodcut illustration from Harry Harrison's *West of Eden*.)

as time or space travel (the journey back in time to the Jurassic era; the journey through space to a "lost world" where that era still survives), or brought to life for us by the technological re-creation of the dinosaurian world, as in *Jurassic Park*. Sometimes the dinotopia is *dystopic*, a vicious, Hobbesian "state of nature" where life is nasty, brutish, and short. Other times it is *eutopic*, a "happy place" like the CD-ROM world of *Dinotopia* (a romantic land of adventures where most of the dinosaurs are benign helpers) or the sitcom suburbia of *The Flintstones* (where dinosaurs serve as household appliances and heavy equipment).[2]

6.2

One basis for human fascination with dinosaurs is anatomical and ecological similarity—that is, their stature and status. Dinosaurs are the "monstrous doubles" of human beings, with many of them resembling us in their erect, bipedal stature and in their status as "rulers of the earth" in the Age of Reptiles.

Reproduced by special permission from *The Saturday Evening Post*.
Copyright 1939 by the Curtis Publishing Company
"It's hard to believe we're made like that inside!"

The most interesting dinotopias of the modern era elude these simple classifications, presenting complex imaginary worlds complete with politics, history, economics, and a social order. Karel Capek, one of the greatest modern Czech writers and the coiner of the word "robot" (from the Czech *robota,* meaning "heavy labor"), produced what is arguably the best dinotopian novel just before World War II. *War with the Newts* (1937) is a speculative, utopian fiction about the "evolutionary resurrection" of "Miocene salamanders."[3] The Newts are amphibious, erect, bipedal saurians, evolutionary throwbacks that survive in the cove of an isolated tropical island near Sumatra, and are regarded superstitiously as "devils" by the islanders despite their complete lack of aggressiveness. A Czech sea captain accelerates their evolutionary progress when he begins trading with them (knives for pearls) and teaching them language in the bargain. When the pearls are exhausted, he transports them to other islands to establish colonies in the vicinity of fresh oyster beds. The Newts rapidly progress from the status of colonized natives to exotic zoo or carnival animals, to familiar domestic drudges, to commodities traded by the "Salamander Syndicate" as slave

6.3

When early dinosaur artists such as Benjamin Waterhouse Hawkins attempted to portray the erect reptiles, one obvious model was the figure of the erect serpent in the Garden of Eden. The pictorial ancestor of the Hadrosaurus in the swamps of New Jersey is the guileful, Satanic serpent, the tempter of Eve, the talking salamander with the human face.

(Hawkins, *Cretaceous Life of New Jersey;* PP36 oil on canvas, 80.2 x 221.5 cm. Princeton University Department of Geology and Geophysical Sciences, Guyot Hall. Photo by Bruce M. White.)

6.4

Hugo van der Goes, *The Fall of Man*, Kunsthistorisches Museum, Vienna.

6.5

Hieronymus Bosch, (imitator of),
Netherlandish, c. 1450–1516,
Garden of Paradise. (Oil and
tempera on panel, c. 1509,
27 x 40.6 cm, Robert A. Waller
Memorial Fund, 1936.239, photo-
graph © 1997, The Art Institute of
Chicago. All rights reserved.)

labor, to a kind of maritime industrial prole-
tariat, employed in harbor and coastal recla-
mation projects. The Newts breed like rabbits
and adapt to all climates. The world economy
rapidly becomes dependent on this invisible reptilian empire (it is the number one consumer of
munitions, food, and industrial commodities,
especially metals).[4] Unified resistance to the
Newts becomes impossible because it is in each
nation's interest to maintain its own Newt-based
economy. The population of Newts rapidly out-
strips that of human beings, and their need for
new coastal breeding grounds leads them to
undermine and flood the major landmasses of
the world. As the novel ends, they are well on
their way to flooding the entire earth and erad-
icating the human species. Capek ends the
novel with some (admittedly wishful) speculation that the Newts might begin to fight among
themselves as they take over the earth, unleashing a plague that would wipe them all out and
leave a human remnant to rebuild civilization
after the deluge.

Harry Harrison's *West of Eden* (1984) is a speculative "alternative history" that poses the question, what would the world be like if the dinosaurs had not died out, but evolved into an advanced civilization with complex social organization and sophisticated technology? Harrison portrays the dinosaurs as a rigid matriarchal society with male "drones" involved in a kind of quasi-marsupial child rearing. Their technology is based on biogenetic engineering and completely lacking in fire and metallurgy. They have an agrarian, peasant economy presided over by an aristocratic, feudal hierarchy. Their cities are "grown" rather than "built," and they travel across the sea on genetically altered leviathans that serve as ocean liners. Their weapons are reptilian tubes, modified to shoot poison darts a considerable distance.

Against this ancient civilization of ruling reptiles, Harrison imagines the earliest ancestors of the human species, hunter-gatherer "cave men" living in small tribal groups with a patriarchal organization. Forced into increasing contact by the onset of an ice age, each species regards the other with instinctive, militant hatred as a threat to its very existence. The civilized reptiles, with their superior technology and centralized military organization, have the upper hand, easily wiping out the nomadic humans when they come upon them. In a replay of the American frontier "captivity narrative," the dinosaurs take a young boy prisoner and teach him their language and customs. He is thus able, after escaping, to lead the humans in a successful war

> There's no mistake, with the coming of the Newts gigantic prosperity has descended on the world, an ideal that is called Quantity. "We people of the Newt Age," the people say with just pride, where would the obsolete Human Age have got to with its slow, finicky, and useless fuss called culture, art, pure science, or what not? Real self-respecting men of the Newt Age will no longer waste their time pondering about the substance of things; they will only be concerned with their quantity and mass production.
>
> —KAREL CAPEK, *War with the Newts*

against the reptiles. Fire turns out to be the decisive factor, and the burning of the reptiles' new colonial capital suggests that the human species will finally triumph over the erect reptiles.

Both of these novels exhibit the double logic of dinotopia. They treat the dinosaur as the "other" or antagonist to the human species, yet at another level, the reptiles are exactly like human beings (cp. figure 1.2). Capek's Newts are an allegory of mass society, an enormous, proliferating mob of faceless, interchangeable creatures who live only to work (in the case of the males) or to reproduce (in the case of the females). The Newts' power comes not from their aggressiveness, but from their industriousness, insatiable appetite, and fertility. They raise the specter of overpopulation, racist fears of a "Yellow Peril," and the modern anxiety that the colonized and proletarian masses of the Third World will breed their way into world dominance. (The anxieties about "uncontrolled reproduction" in *Jurassic Park* betray a similar concern.) Capek situates these anxieties in Europe on the verge of World War II, and depicts the inability of human beings to contend with the Newts as a consequence of their inability to transcend nationalist self-interest.

Harrison's novel, similarly, undercuts any simple perception of the reptiles as "other." Their ancient, aristocratic civilization is no more (or less) alien to a modern reader than is the tribal life of the cave men. And Harrison quite explicitly models the war between the humans and the reptiles on popular images of the Indian wars in North America after the Civil War. The men are armed with only spears, axes, and bows and arrows against the serpentine "rifles" of the saurians. Their small tribal units are no match for the highly organized military machine of the dinosaurs, which includes shock troops, cavalry, fortifications, rapid transport of supplies, and even aerial surveillance (with genetically modified eagles and owls). *West of Eden* is a dinotopia, in short, that reverses the outcome of the nineteenth-century Indian wars. The dinosaurs are the imperial, colonizing civilization waging a genocidal war of extermination against a "primitive" aboriginal population. The cave men are the heroic guerilla fighters, waging a war of retreat and survival that turns (in a miracle of wishful thinking) into a decisive destruction of the reptiles' army and their colonial capital. Dinotopia seems to require a happy ending for mammals, no matter how arbitrary: the cold-blooded logic of the narrative is simply unacceptable to warm-blooded authors and readers.

Ridley Scott's *Alien* films are an exception to this rule in their adherence to the most pessimistic logic of dinotopia. The initial discovery of the petrified alien creature is presented as a paleontological find. The space travelers descend into the fossilized belly of an ancient subterranean dragon, a vaulted, cavernous labyrinth supported by enormous ribs. Their presence revives the dormant eggs waiting in the giant womb, and unleashes the rebirth of a monster whose blood is not merely cold, but composed of metal-eating acid. The reborn monsters are "body-snatchers" who breed by using human bodies as temporary wombs until they are ready for their ghastly and deadly "birth." The monsters are regarded as a potentially valuable military technology by the intergalactic corporation financing the expedition. The alien, it becomes clear, is actually the "monstrous double" of the very corporate state that wants to exploit its power. The only way to destroy the creature, finally, is the self-immolation of the human host, the scene that concludes the trilogy. ("Resurrection," however, and a fourth *Alien* film, were not long in arriving.)

These dinotopias assemble many of the features we have already seen in dinosaur tales. Capek's Newts, like the *Stegosaurus* made of money, make the link between dinosaurs and capitalism central. The Newts are a "cash cow," both a commodity to be traded by the "Salamander Syndicate" and a source of cheap labor and mass consumption. They also become the object of a dinomaniac-style cult, modeled on "the worship of Moloch, whom they pictured as a huge Newt with a human head," represented in "tremendous submarine idols made of cast iron" (226). Harrison's reptiles occupy the same terrain of frontier warfare, colonization, and aboriginal extermination that we have seen in "The Last Thunder Horse" and will encounter repeatedly in the history of American paleontology. Dinotopias elaborate these themes as world historical events on a global stage (the *Alien* films take the theme to an interplanetary realm). Capek's Newts make sense in a European context of impending world war, mass destruction, and genocide as viewed from a small, vulnerable country (Czechoslovakia), within a temporal framework that projects modern civilization into a speculative future. Harrison gives us the world as North America, and world history as an overlay of paleolithic dreamtime on the nineteenth-century "golden age" of imperialism.

7

THE LAST DINOSTORY: AS TOLD BY HIMSELF

> I continued
> looking at the
> skeleton, the Father,
> the Brother, my
> Counterpart, my Self;
> I recognized my fleshless
> limbs, my lineaments
> carved in stone, everything
> we had been and were no
> longer, our majesty, our
> faults, our ruin.
>
> —ITALO CALVINO,
> "The Dinosaurs"

ALL THE STORIES about dinosaurs that we have looked at so far are told about an alien, exotic, and monstrous beast from a human point of view, which is of course understandable. But there are some stories that attempt to re-create a dinosaurial point of view. Many children's books tell stories about dinosaurs in the ancient mode of the animal fable. In these stories animals are given personal, human attributes, talk to one another, tell jokes and stories, and have adventures, just like human beings. Gary Larson's brilliant animal cartoons have made us realize the extent to which all stories and images of the animal as "other" are really about ourselves. The formula of the *Three Little Pigs* can be extended quite easily to the *Triceratops;* Chicken Little might as well be a Large Duck—the Good Mother *Maiasaura;* and the *T. rex* named Sue is already the subject of rumors and folklore. The eminent paleontologist Robert Bakker has even taken a holiday from science to weave a gripping adventure novel called *Raptor Red* that gives us a year in the life of a wily, courageous hunter and her family.

Nevertheless, most dinosaur tales, like other animal fables, take only a proximate look at the dinosaurial point of view. They tend, like Bakker's, to be narrated in the third person, telling us from an omniscient perspective what Raptor Red is thinking about as she closes in on

7.1

When we look at the dinosauroid, we are looking in the mirror, seeing ourselves. What would it mean to look back from the other side of the mirror, to see things from the dinosaur's point of view, to hear his story as he would tell it? (Detail of figure 1.2.)

a dangerously large herbivore. It is relatively rare for the dinosaur to tell his or her own story in the first person. It is equally rare for dinosaur stories to deal directly with extinction. Most are like the children's story called *The Last Dinosaur:* they simply tell the story of the death of an individual, not of a species or larger biological group. The extinction scene in Walt Disney's *Fantasia,* showing multitudes of dinosaurs perishing in a drought, is really only about a local catastrophe, not a global extinction. Even *Josaurus,* "The Last Thunder Horse West of the Mississippi," may not literally be the last of its kind. Its parents and siblings could be hiding somewhere in the badlands. Gary Larson's pictorial stories of extinction tend to deal with dinosaurial premonitions of trouble ahead, not with actual representations of the dying and disappearance, or its aftermath. They show the familiar narratives of creatures endangered by their stupidity or failure to adapt to changing conditions. (A typical Larson scenario shows a *Stegosaurus* lecturer addressing his audience: "The picture's pretty bleak, gentlemen. . . . The world's climates are changing, the mammals are taking over, and we all have a brain about the size of a walnut.") And of course they show these stories from outside, in accordance with the demands of pictorial representation.

To my knowledge, only one writer has tried to tell the story of the dinosaur and its disappearance from the dinosaur's point of view. That is Italo Calvino, arguably the greatest Italian storyteller of modern times. Calvino slips a story called "The Dinosaurs" into *Cosmicomics,* a book of tales told by Qfwfq (I pronounce this "kyoofkyew"), a participant eyewitness to the entire history of the universe, from the primal soup to the modern mollusk. Qfwfq has lived as a dinosaur for about 50 million years, well beyond the death of all his kinfolk. He prefers not to talk much about the good old days when dinosaurs ruled the earth, or the bad old days when the trouble began. He doesn't believe in the myths about dinosaur decadence or death wishes, and he has no wish to dwell on his memories of the great dying, or his centuries of lonely wandering through the cemeteries of his brethren.

What really interests the Last Dinosaur are the "New Ones," the beaver-like mammals who accept him into their village. They don't realize he's a dinosaur, mistaking him for a big, strong, ugly foreigner. They put him to work carrying trees in his mouth, and he lives among them as a kind of *gastarbeiter* or resident alien. The Last Dinosaur feels deeply strange among the New Ones, and he is especially sensitive to the ridiculous things they say about dinosaurs, who are regarded as terrifying monsters that ravish and devour their victims.

As the Last Dinosaur becomes a pillar of the community and falls in love with a New One named Fernflower, he notices that a new fashion in dinosaur stories is taking over. Rather than being feared and hated, the dinosaur is gradually becoming a figure of respect. But Qfwfq finds this overestimation of the dinosaurs' moral character just as wrong-headed as the earlier monster image. He tries to set the New Ones straight by revealing his own identity as a dinosaur, but of course no one believes him. Worst of all, Fernflower spurns him when he tries to take the dinosaur off its pedestal by abasing himself to her, telling her that she is better than any dinosaur.

Then a report arrives that "the dinosaurs are coming back." Everyone has mixed feelings about this, Qfwfq because the thrill of reuniting with his brothers is outweighed by his certainty that it will only renew the protracted dying, and the New Ones because they can't decide whether this will be a big thrill or a catastrophe. They settle this problem by putting Qfwfq in charge of defense. As a foreigner, he can be made the scapegoat if things go badly.

Unfortunately, the approaching dinosaurs turn out to be nothing but a herd of rhinoceroses. The New Ones are disappointed at this, and they blame Qfwfq for failing to deliver the expected sensation. The dinosaur stories change once again, from respect to contempt and ridicule. Fernflower dreams of comforting a funny green dinosaur who is teased until it cries. This makes the Last Dinosaur lose his temper. Once again he tells the New Ones the truth, that he is a dinosaur, and again they just laugh at him.

When an actual dinosaur's skeleton is discovered, none of the New Ones notice that it is the spitting image of Qfwfq. They just go on making up jokes and silly stories about the bones. That night the Last Dinosaur removes the skeleton and buries his dead, leaving the New Ones to ponder yet another dinosaur mystery. He determines never to reveal the secret of the dinosaur, which he alone possesses.

Then a band of vagabonds comes to the village, and Qfwfq notices among them an attractive half-breed female, a mixture of New One and dinosaur. When Fernflower tells him her current dinosaur dream of sadistic pleasure in watching a dinosaur dying, that is the last straw. Qfwfq runs off with the half-breed, and they spend the night dallying along the riverbank.

And that is basically the end of the story. The Last Dinosaur hangs around the village for a while, but nothing much happens. The New Ones begin to forget about dinosaurs; it is as if they never existed. Fernflower tells him a

7.2

"I continued looking at the skeleton, the Father, the Brother, my Counterpart, my Self; I recognized my fleshless limbs, my lineaments carved in stone, everything we had been and were no longer, our majesty, our faults, our ruin."—Italo Calvino, "The Dinosaurs." (Quarry Wall, Dinosaur National Monument, Vernal, Utah. Skull of *Camarasaurus*. Photo by the author.)

new dream, not of dinosaurs, but of "the sole survivor of a species whose name nobody remembered." The Last Dinosaur knows that she is dreaming of him, that now they can be lovers. He also understands that he has somehow conquered his situation by allowing the name of his species to disappear.

It's time for the Last Dinosaur to move on. He returns to his wandering ways, realizing that he can no longer even remember how the earth was when dinosaurs ruled it. He briefly crosses paths with his half-breed girlfriend and her newborn son, who is "full of his own Dinosaur essence," but completely unaware of it—which is just fine with him. And so he travels on until he comes to a station where he catches the first train, and is lost in the crowd.

The Irish have a saying about storytelling: A story is like a dead animal, and it's the basic job of the teller to assemble the bones of the story in the right order, but the real art comes when you put flesh on the bones and make the animal come to life. I have laid out the bones of

Calvino's story in so much detail because it assembles so many essential features of the dinosaur narrative into a single structure, features that tend to be dispersed and fragmented in most popular and scientific stories.

Calvino's story has a double skeleton, one in time, the other in space. The temporal sequence is basically that of the standard Hollywood Western (derived from the archetypal quest-romance), in which a wandering hero comes to town, falls in love, helps the community deal with its problems, and then rides off into the sunset. The central village segment of the story is subdivided into a series of episodes punctuated by the various challenges (work, rivalry, invasion, etc.) that the hero encounters, the villagers' changing attitudes toward dinosaurs that result from those encounters, and the sequence of Fernflower's dinosaur dreams. This central sequence also suggests a summary of the progression of popular stereotypes of the dinosaur, from its discovery in the mid-nineteenth century to a point well beyond its current status. The New Ones think of dinosaurs first as monsters, then as figures of respect, then as objects of ridicule, and finally they don't think of them at all, but lose interest in the whole subject. In this last phase, Calvino's story seems to extend beyond our own time of unprecedented worldwide dinomania to a period when the dinosaur has undergone a second extinction.

The spatial structure of Calvino's story is the layering of different levels of temporality, the deliberate confusion of personal, individual time (measured in days and hours), historical time (measured in the larger, rather amorphous periods of changing attitudes toward dinosaurs), and the "cosmic time" of natural history and paleontology, the 50 million years of the narrator's dinosaur life. Each level of time presents the characters at radically different levels of existence: as an individual, Qfwfq is simply an ordinary person whose narrative seems to span a few years at most; as a tribal, racial, species, or group representative, he is "the Last Dinosaur," and he lives on much longer than any historical individual possibly could, passing through periods whose shape he experiences and summarizes; in his role as the central figure of *Cosmicomics*, his 50-million-year dinosaur career is a mere episode in a much longer life. All these levels are co-present, and the narrative point of view functions like a kind of zoom lens that can slide from a macroscopic overview of cosmic history to a microscopic tale of two lovers.

At the same time, like all animal stories, this one continually presents a double face, both human and bestial. It is a story about animals who live and talk like human beings, or human beings who live and talk like animals. Calvino sustains the ambiguity of this double face by being very spare with his visual descriptions, providing only minimal details. We know that Qfwfq is ugly and large with a "little lizard's mouth" and a tail. The New Ones are visually indeterminate: we know only that they are fishermen who live by a river and cut down trees to dam it up. The animals, in short, are human stereotypes, the dinosaur playing the role of the loner, the outsider, and the New Ones typifying a sociable, chatty country village.

Calvino has grasped the fundamental features of every dinosaur story: first, the dinosaur must always be gendered, and male identity tends to dominate. Qfwfq recalls the glory days of the dinosaur as a "warrior brotherhood," but throughout this story he is a passive figure, rather like one of Capek's Newts. Harrison's Amazonian warrior matriarchy and Crichton's all-female cast of dinosaurs reflect the tendency to feminize the dinosaur in recent years, perhaps as part of the 1980s "backlash" against the "new women" of postmodern feminism.[1] Second, the dinosaur appears as an alien or stranger who is adopted and domesticated, going through a series of transformations in public perception. Just as Capek's Newts go from exotic attraction to tradable commodity, Calvino's dinosaur goes from terror to monument to joke (see figure 2.1 above).

Third, as in Capek's and Harrison's stories, the dinosaur is not magical or supernatural, but dwells in an intermediate, transitional space between modern science and myth. Calvino's weaving of modernity and myth is located in the zone that lies after memory and before history, the realm that is usually called "tradition." Like ourselves, none of the New Ones has ever seen a dinosaur. But Calvino's New Ones don't have any scientific account of dinosaurs. They treat them straightforwardly as the stuff of rumor and folklore, and thus as premodern, prehistoric, and pre-scientific, of the same order as the legendary dragon or the *Stegosaurus* made of money. On the other hand, Calvino understands that dinosaurs are modern, introducing his story with a scientific headnote about their 170-million-year life span and their mysterious extinction, and concluding it with a perfectly precise and incongruous detail. Instead of galloping off into the sunset, the Last Dinosaur catches a train and disappears into the crowd, just like the disappointed paleontologists at the end of "The Last Thunder Horse." The great vehicle of the nineteenth century arrives just as the legendary dinosaur disappears, to be absorbed into those other Victorian inventions, the scientific, paleontological dinosaur of natural history and that modern leviathan known as "the crowd." Could the New Ones be Newts in mammals' clothing?

The disappearance of the traditional dinosaur (fierce, gigantic) is thus actually an extension of its dominion. The figure of romance and legend goes underground, into the unconscious, into the "labyrinth of the survivors' thoughts." That is okay with Qfwfq, but it is clearly not okay with Calvino. The Last Dinosaur may have vowed never to tell his story to the New Ones, and to let the name of his race vanish from the world. But Calvino's story brings it all back to us, and makes us realize the extent to which it has "become one thing with the mute and anonymous molds of thought." The dinosaur becomes a thing to think *with*, not *of*. This, however, is a utopian state that we as readers have not yet reached. We still think far too much of dinosaurs. We are still like the New Ones, endlessly making up new myths and calling them the truth. We will not learn to think with dinosaurs, Calvino suggests, until we have learned to forget them.

7.3
Mark Hallett imagines the transitional moment
between the Age of Reptiles and the Age of
Mammals, a time when the remains of the last
dinosaurs are still fresh, and our warm-blooded
ancestors are new arrivals fighting among the
ruins of the old order. (*Dawn of a New Day*,
gouache, 11¼ x 14¼ inches. © 1984 Mark Hallett
Illustrations.)

seeing saurians

THERE IS NO LIMIT to the stories that can be made up about dinosaurs, and no limit to the ways of interpreting those stories. We may, at this point, feel less certain than ever about what it is that makes human beings so fascinated with these extinct giants. Perhaps the stories are just symptoms of our own inability to explain this phenomenon, an inability that has manifested itself as an infinite capacity for speculative invention. Rather than unraveling endless dinosaur tales, then, perhaps the best strategy is to look directly at the things themselves, the real bodies of the real creatures preserved in stone as fossils. These things are hard, concrete, definite, material objects: we can see and touch them. Surely the source of dinosaur fascination must ultimately lie in these things, which persist unchanged no matter how many stories are told about them.

We must begin, however, by thinking hard about what "real things" are, and what it means to see them firsthand or in representations. And here we encounter, I'm afraid, yet another paradox. No one has ever seen a dinosaur, but everyone knows what they look like. The generations of illustrators who have given us such vivid pictures, anatomical drawings, and sculptural reproductions of dinosaurs have made the images of dinosaurs as familiar as those of horses and cows. They are so familiar, in fact, that we tend to forget that fossil imprints and bones are the only real, natural traces of the dinosaur that

> The first subject matter for painting was animal. Probably the first paint was animal blood. Prior to that, it is not unreasonable to suppose that the first metaphor was animal.
>
> —JOHN BERGER, *About Looking*

8.1
Before dinosaurs appear as visual images, much less as cultural symbols, they manifest themselves as a chaotic jumble of fragments, a jigsaw puzzle in which many of the pieces are missing or broken.
(From a map of the Howe Quarry site, in *Bones for Barnum Brown* by Roland T. Bird. Negative #314524, courtesy Department of Library Services, American Museum of Natural History.)

anyone has ever seen. All dinosaurs are products of the creative imagination, assembled out of fragments and augmented with speculations about skin color, ornamentation, sounds, and movement.

I am not suggesting that scientific images of the dinosaur are false or inaccurate. On the contrary, they are the product of an impressive accumulation of detailed observations and long debate about the proper proportions and relations of parts. While we do not, of course, have any photographs of actual dinosaurs, the reproductions we do have probably approach the accuracy of anything that could have been made by a Jurassic eyewitness. The color of dinosaurs may be lost forever, but our representations of their lineaments and movements are probably quite true to life, and can approach the "look" of photographic and cinematic images, especially with the help of computer imaging and animation.[1]

Some dinosaur images are, of course, quite inaccurate and fanciful. The first reproductions, life-size cement and brick leviathans created by Waterhouse Hawkins for the Crystal Palace exhibition in 1854, reflected the best scientific knowledge of the time, but in the late twentieth century they look like Maurice Sendak's wild things. Many dinosaur images make no effort to be convincing or realistic. They simply evoke one of the prominent stereotypes (giantism, ferocity, reptilian features) and provide a recognizable summary, a generalized image. That is why the dinosaur image can be evoked by very minimal details, and serve as a corpo-

8.2

The first dinosaur reproductions, life-size cement, brick, and iron-reinforced leviathans exhibited at the Crystal Palace exhibition in 1854, reflected the best scientific knowledge of the time, but in the late twentieth century they look like Maurice Sendak's wild things. (Benjamin Waterhouse Hawkins, sculptural restoration of *Megalosaurus*. Crystal Palace Park, London. Photo © Steve McCarthy, 1994.)

4 Dinosaur Cookie Cutters

3557
MADE IN U.S.A.

8.3–8.4
The dinosaur image can be evoked with minimal details, which is why it can serve so well as an easily recognizable corporate logo. It is a "stereotyped" image in the exact sense of the word, with a limited repertoire of subtypes *(T. rex, Brontosaurus, Stegosaurus, Pterodactyl)* that can be captured by that crudest of all images, the cookie cutter. (8.3: Sinclair *Brontosaurus*; 8.4: Dinosaur Cookie Cutter, photo by John Butler-Ludwig.)

rate logo, a cartoon character, or a cookie cutter.[2] It is a stereotype in the most exact sense of the word, with a small repertoire of familiar sub-stereotypes *(T. rex, Brontosaurus, Triceratops, Stegosaurus, Pterodactyl,*[3] and now *Velociraptor)*. That is why the word "dinosaur" seems to specify an individual or concrete universal in a way that "mammal" does not. It's hard to imagine an interesting story with "the mammal" as the lead character, but "the dinosaur" (as Calvino makes clear) immediately suggests a concrete character, with a personality and (obviously) a destiny. The paradox here is that "mammal," which designates a real, coherent, natural kind, is much more vague in its general outlines than "dinosaur," which may be only an artificial umbrella term for radically different kinds of animals.

The point of all this is simply to make us pause and contemplate the obvious: the dinosaur is a constructed image—in fact, a whole repertoire of highly differentiated images—that must be fabricated in some medium or other. The dinosaur image is always accompanied by words, a whole lexicon of names, descriptive terms, narratives, and statements. We never *see* a dinosaur without *saying* something about it, naming or describing it, or telling its story. The dinosaur is thus a composite "imagetext,"[4] a combination of verbal and visual signs—what a semiologist would call "symbols" and "icons," a distinction related to what Jacques Lacan called the "Symbolic" and "Imaginary." The "real" dinosaur is available only in its traces or remains (bones, footprints, feces), what a semiologist would call "indices," signs of cause and effect or "existential connection," and in its imaginative restorations. When we see a dinosaur, then, we are seeing a constructed image with an assigned name and description. We never see the "real" dinosaur, but only an artifact, a visual-verbal-tactile construction based on its remains and an array of prototypes we use to make sense of those remains.

Natural historians work by comparison, differentiation, and genealogical derivation to classify living things and produce accurate accounts of them. Cultural historians do the same thing with the artifacts that human beings produce. Iconologists (like myself) are especially interested in the images that people produce and consume. Unlike art historians, we don't require that images have artistic status or merit, and we don't have to stick with a single medium like painting or sculpture, but tend to work comparatively across the visual and verbal media. Like natural historians, we are interested in classifying the variety of things in a specific domain and in tracing their evolution. How do images get produced? Where do they come from? How do they change over time? Do cultural images, like natural organisms, "evolve"?[5]

Natural historians are mainly concerned with classifying the things we see *in* dinosaur images: they want to differentiate carnivores and herbivores, "bird hips" and "lizard hips," juveniles and adults, *Apatosaurus* and *Triceratops*. Iconologists want to classify and differentiate the images themselves on the basis of things like form, function, style, intention, genre, effect, and content. The most straightforward classifications are based in content—what is represented by an image—so we distinguish genres such as landscape, portraiture, history painting, and images of animals. The very word "genre," with its echoes of "genetics" and "genus," suggests an analogy between images and organisms. Dinosaurs might be thought of, then, as members of a very large and diverse class of depicted animals, some real (lions), some imaginary (unicorns), and some perhaps in between (dinosaurs). From the standpoint of the iconologist, the differences between real and imaginary animal images are less important than the continuities among them, the fact that all of them are "imaginary" in the other sense of the word—that is, that they are all constructed visible images. When I use the word "imaginary" to describe dinosaur images, I am referring to this status as a constructed icon, a visual or verbal image, and I will reserve the word "fantasy" to refer to unreal (though not necessarily unscientific) images. The Dinosauroid (see figures 1.2 and 7.1) is clearly a fantastic, speculative image, not a representation of a real thing. Yet it is a scientific image through and through, constructed by a rational extrapolation of Darwinian principles.

Classification of images can proceed on many other principles. We might, for instance, consider intention and function, distinguishing images for scientific study from those for popular consumption or aesthetic contemplation. (Many dinosaur images clearly migrate back and forth across this border.) Sometimes the classifications are historical and evolutionary in character, grouping large numbers of images by style (classicism, romanticism) or medium (photography, cinema, painting, drawing, sculpture) or "movement" (cubism, impressionism, expressionism). It is also possible to classify images by their effect on beholders: images may deceive or enlighten, heal or induce sickness, attract or repel, elicit adoration or profanation, tell stories or describe states of affairs, illustrate ideas or arouse passions.

Classification by "artist" or author is one of the simplest and most reliably legitimate taxonomies, and probably comes closest to being the art historical equivalent of the "species" in natural history. A species is the basic classificatory unit or "taxon" for biological organisms (below it come race, breed, subspecies, population, and individual organism; above it are kingdoms, phyla, classes, orders, families, and genera).[6] All the members of a species share a "family resemblance" at two levels, one visible, the other invisible: they "look similar," and they maintain this similarity "through successive generations."[7] This sort of species concept discourages hybridization (at least among animals; plants are another story): apes and human beings cannot crossbreed even though they belong to the same order, family, and genus. Attempts to produce hybrids usually result in monstrous offspring who are sterile (see figure 10.2).[8] One might think of the artist as the "common ancestor" of all the images he or she produces, the artist's individual "style" as the visible family resemblance of an oeuvre, and the signature or documentation of authorship as evidence of genetic continuity and ancestry. The forgery or copy, by this analogy, becomes the sterile monster that satisfies only the external, visible requirement of similar appearance. The artistic connoisseur is then something like the taxonomist who classifies species by visible form and genetic lineage, tracing what is called a "chronospecies" in evolutionary biology.

But this analogy soon begins to feel rather far-fetched. The author of an image is its "progenitor" in some ways and not in others. How are we to transfer the sexual character of reproduction to the world of image production? (The myth of the male artist inspired by the female muse may be a trace of this analogy between the production of living beings and the creation of images, but this seems like a desperate way to save an analogy.) We must keep in mind, then, Yeats's intuition that images themselves have a reproductive capacity, and "beget" fresh images in a process that makes the human author or artist more like a vessel or vehicle or midwife. The great French art historian Henri Focillon called this "the life of forms in art" in his book by that title.[9] The "progenitor" of an image, for Focillon, is another image, and the principle of life that links images together is form. Focillon's idea, however, did something more radical than simply modeling the evolution of artistic forms on the development of biological organisms. Focillon turned the analogy around and modeled biology on the evolution of images, quoting Balzac's remark that "everything is form, and life itself is form" (10). He describes form as "a kind of fissure through which crowds of images aspiring to birth" are seen. This may sound mystical or metaphysical, but I think it is nothing more than a vivid intuition of a perfectly familiar and commonplace feature of the appearance of new images in the world. Artists consistently testify that they don't know where their images come from, that they come "unbidden" or from unconscious realms of memory and fantasy. When we ask "where images come from," we are like savages or children who don't know where babies come from.

We can illustrate the "life of forms" in dinosaur illustration by contrasting the first dinosaur images with the most recent. The Waterhouse Hawkins sculptures, based on Richard Owen's original conception of a "terrible lizard," are a kind of synthesis of the rhinoceros and the lizard, with mammalian, almost humanoid, five-fingered paws (see figures 8.2 and 18.1). The contemporary *T. rex* of Gregory Paul is a modern revival of T. H. Huxley's linkage of dinosaurs with the birds, and it looks very much like a large and rather dangerous plucked chicken (see figure 31.2).[10] The dinosaur illustrator doesn't just "copy" some visible model. The image has to be invented and constructed out of very scattered clues, assembled in relation to a concept. This is true of every image, of course, as Ernst Gombrich demonstrated long ago.[11] All seeing involves metaphor, or "seeing as," and so does all image making. But it is even more emphatically the case with the dinosaur, whose traces are so fragmentary and minimal. The production of vivid, colorful, lifelike images of dinosaurs in painting, sculpture, and cinema requires an arguably greater degree of imaginative activity than that of any other animal images, simply because there is such a large gap between the "real" creature (which no longer exists), the fragmentary traces and fossil remains, and the final image that we construct. Mythical creatures like the dragon or unicorn may require less imaginative work because there are no independent visual or nonvisual criteria of "rightness" to be observed, other than what appears in already existing images, and there is no imperative to correct and improve the truth-value of the image, as there is in scientific illustration.

Questions of "species," then, of classification and taxonomy, of origins and evolution and extinction, are just as complex and inescapable in the world of cultural images as they are in the world of nature and living organisms. And since we live every moment of our lives at the confluence of natural and cultural forces, the derivation of the model may go in either direction, as the etymology of the word *species* suggests. *Species* comes from the Latin word *specie,* meaning "appearance, form, kind, etc. from *specere,* to look, behold." In the seventeenth century, *species* came to mean "the outward appearance or aspect, the visible form or image of something, as constituting the proper object of vision."[12] The idea that things belong to a species if they "look similar" begins to have an unsuspected resonance. The classification of dinosaurs as animals and as images may actually be linked at some deeper level, particularly since no one has ever seen dinosaurs apart from some image of them.

The dinosaur image is not, then, *simply* a popularization of scientific understanding, a mere vehicle for reporting and representing scientific knowledge. The visual image is also a key element in the process of scientific thinking and discovery as such, not just as a descriptive afterthought or afterimage, but as a constitutive element, a speculative, theoretical construction.[13] The moment of scientific intuition is often a vivid insight, a daring projection of a visual or spatial model, and not merely a summing up of empirical data. This is especially true for paleontologists, who must turn fragments into wholes, skeletal structures into living, breathing, flesh-and-blood animals. Perhaps more than any of the other historical sciences, paleontology requires the aid of visual artists and illustrators to depict in concrete, visible form what the scientist conceives in the imagination. Many of the most gifted paleontologists have also had a gift for visualization and draftsmanship, the construction of models and sculptural forms. Among those who have turned their hand to dinosaurs, Paul Sereno, Robert Bakker, Gregory Paul, and Jack Horner all testify to the importance of visual perception and representation in their work. We should bear this in mind when we hear common-sense contrasts between science and "imagination," "speculation," or "fantasy."

9

SORTING SPECIES

The whole aim of theoretical science is to carry to the highest possible and conscious degree the perceptual reduction of chaos that began in so lowly and (in all probability) unconscious a way with the origin of life. In specific instances it can well be questioned whether the order so achieved is an objective characteristic of the phenomena or is an artifact constructed by the scientist. That question comes up time after time in animal taxonomy. . . . Nevertheless, the most basic postulate of science is that nature itself is orderly. . . . All theoretical science is ordering and, if systematics is equated with ordering, then systematics is synonymous with theoretical science.

—GEORGE GAYLORD SIMPSON,
Principles of Animal Taxonomy

WHEN HUMAN BEINGS TALK about "dinosaurs," they continually equivocate between reference to real, but extinct, creatures that existed millions of years in the past and the representations of those creatures that started to appear in the nineteenth century and began to proliferate rapidly in the late twentieth century. But the confusion between these two senses of the word is not just a negative condition to be overcome. It can also be a highly productive social, political, and cultural force. Human beings have fought wars and built civilizations on the basis of such confusions. They have founded religious institutions on the basis of puns and metaphors. They

57

are not rational creatures, but symbol-using animals who form all sorts of irrational attachments to images. The best we can hope for, then, is to describe very precisely the *kind* of image human beings are producing and consuming in the figure of the dinosaur.

We have seen that the cultural riddle of the dinosaur is not just about "the things themselves," but about the relation of these things to images. More precisely, it is about the relation between two *groups* or *series* of things: (1) the world of living things, of which dinosaurs are a particular group or class that happens to be extinct; and (2) the world of images, in which dinosaur images also appear as a particular group or class that is not only not extinct, but proliferating at a remarkable rate. The first group is commonly thought to be real, natural, scientifically coherent, and objective. The second is artificially constructed, though no less "real" and "objective," no matter how fantastic or subjective or rigorously accurate its content may be. But even the opposition between "natural" and "artificial" seems a bit fuzzy, since it seems clear that dinosaurs themselves are an artificial construction. For that matter, the whole "world of living things"—at least for human beings—is actually constituted as a world by acts of naming, image making, and classification. This goes for mammals as well as dinosaurs, though many scientists yearn for taxonomic classifications that "carve nature at the joints." Nature *is* culture; science *is* art. We don't ever "see nature" in the raw, but always cooked in categories and clothed in the garments of language and representation. Our two large groups (the images of artifice and the species of nature) are not radically different spheres, but something more like adjacent locations in culture, different places where images of different kinds are displayed.

> **The term totemism covers relations, posed ideologically, between two series, one natural, the other cultural.**
>
> —CLAUDE LÉVI-STRAUSS,
> *Totemism*

58

Our two "species" might be better thought of, then, as something like the collections of two juxtaposed museums. Think of the Metropolitan Museum of Art and the American Museum of Natural History on the east and west sides of Central Park in New York City. This juxtaposition is a study in contrasts between institutional constructions of nature and culture, of science and art.[1] It is also a study in the contrast between different generational audiences—children and adults. Perhaps most important, it exemplifies the contrast between two different cultures, or more precisely, a mythical and highly ideological division between cultures, "the West and the Rest." The natural history museum is full of non-Western cultural artifacts, "ethnographic" and "craft" objects that are generally classified as qualitatively different from the "aesthetic" objects in the art museum. All these contrasts are clearly rough, and are subject to numerous exceptions and crossovers. For that very reason, the contrast between the two actual, concrete places is likely to teach us more about the relation of nature and culture than any abstract consideration of the terms. Both places are archives filled with "species," in the double sense (organisms/images) we have now arrived at. Rather than producing binary oppositions between the two places, we can study the exchanges and traffic between them. We can notice that much of the visual and pictorial construction of natural history, for instance, is articulated in relation to painting styles that appear in the nineteenth-century galleries of the Metropolitan. We can notice that the "primitive" or ethnographic artifacts in the American Museum seem to have migrated into certain styles of modern art, particularly in the Cubist appropriation of African sculpture.

We must also be struck by a sharp disjunction between the two spaces. There is not, so far as I know, a single dinosaur image to be found in the Met, while dinosaurs are the marquee attraction of the American Museum, both the central exhibit in the main entrance hall and the main goal (in the Dinosaur Hall itself) of the majority of visitors. What is the meaning of this remarkable contrast? With all the traffic in images between these two spaces, why is the dinosaur image so rigorously confined to the space of natural history and prohibited from entering the space of "art"? The first answer that might come to mind is that dinosaur artists are not very good artists, certainly not good enough to get into the Met. One of my native informants from the world of paleontology puts it even more emphatically, suggesting that "dino-artists are not serious artists any more than most dino-scientists are serious scientists." They are mere illustrators, not even in the same ballpark with serious artists.

While I think this answer is too harsh as a judgment about "talent" or "skill," it certainly has some credibility at the level of perceived status. Dinosaur painting, in contrast to landscape, history painting, or portraiture, is not a recognized genre in that amorphous but very real institution called "the art world" (see the coda on "Paleoart," however, for qualification of this claim). In fact, it doesn't exist on the map of artistic genres in any textbook on the history of art that I have been able to find. You might think of this book as an effort to put it on that map, and to treat the makers of dinosaur images as artists. While art historians do recognize "animal painting" as a mainly nineteenth-century phenomenon in the history of oil painting (the work of the English painters George Stubbs and James Ward being particularly notable), dinosaurs came along too late to be part of this genre at its most attractive moment. Compare Charles Knight's "Dryptosauruses Fighting" (1900) with James Ward's "Bulls Fighting" (1800). The dinosaur painting is, in terms of artistic evolution, a "throwback" to this earlier style. It is not in step with the stylistic vanguard of early modernism, and the same thing could be said today, even though painters like John Gurche have employed the techniques of photorealism to make their images look contemporary.[2]

There are obvious practical reasons for the retrograde character of dinosaur painting. A cubist dinosaur would not be of much use, either to a paleontologist or to the public. Paleontological illustration clearly has to operate within the canons of pictorial realism, and the era of the visual arts that corresponds to the period of dinosaur image proliferation is vigorously anti-realist. It is not until the 1960s, and postmodernist work like Robert Smithson's, that there seems to be an opening for dinosaurs to "cross the park" and enter the art world.

The question is not just one of stylistic compatibility, however. There are also issues of cultural status that need to be faced. Dinosaur images suffer from a double stigma: they are both juvenilia and kitsch. They are an attraction for kids, and for that amorphous abstraction, "the masses." Capek's *War with the Newts* treats the erect reptilian biped as itself a figure of mediocre, mass society, and Calvino focuses on the dinosaur's role as mass attraction by rendering it as an object of rumor and mass hysteria in his cosmic comic village ("You look as if you'd seen a dinosaur!" "The dinosaurs are coming back!") Calvino's crowd eagerly awaits mass spectacle or mass destruction, or more likely both—as Walter Benjamin would argue, the uniquely modern pleasure of beholding one's own destruction as an aesthetic experience, a

9.1–9.2
Dinosaur painting often imitates the style of nineteenth-century realist and romantic landscape painting by depicting a savage world of animal violence with a dashing, expressionistic handling of paint. The style of Charles Knight's *Dryptosauruses Fighting* (1896) is a "throwback" to the manner of James Ward's *Bulls Fighting* (1800). (9.1: Negative #335199, photo by R. E. Logan. Courtesy Department of Library Services, American Museum of Natural History; 9.2: Victoria and Albert Picture Library, London.)

mass spectacle.[3] Dinosaurs are tailor-made for the link-up of the disaster film and the action-adventure flick. They thus epitomize everything that the modernist avant-garde in art struggled with: an aesthetics of spectacle, shock, mass consumption, and mass violence. One could hardly find a better exemplar of what Clement Greenberg called "kitsch" than the dinosaur's linking of commercial vulgarity with juvenile wonder and the imitation of past styles.[4] The art museum can find plenty of reasons to keep this kind of stuff out of its sacred precincts. The purism of high modernist abstraction would be utterly contaminated by the intrusion of the dinosaur. And since the dinosaur seems to have its "proper" place as the figurehead image of the natural history museum, it helps to reinforce the illusion of a strict separation between nature and culture, science and art. The truth is, this separation is one of cultural status and has absolutely nothing to do with nature, which in every culture is just as much the object of art as of science.

If the dinosaur is blocked at the portals of the art museum, however, it is welcomed with open arms by the movies. From the first animated dinosaur feature *(Gertie the Dinosaur)* to *Jurassic Park,* the dinosaur stands at the cutting edge of animation.[5] This is not, I think, because the figures of dinosaurs are more complex or difficult to animate than those of any other animal. It is because if no one has ever seen a dinosaur, it is even more emphatically the case that no one has ever seen one move. (*Gertie the Dinosaur* begins with the animator, Winsor McCay, wagering a group of artists that he can bring a dinosaur back to life in three months.) The novelty and wonder of "realist" or "live-action" animation (as contrasted with drawn cartoon animation) is superfluous with real animals. There would be no point in animating a horse or dog (except perhaps in a Philip K. Dick novel), unless one wanted to make it act like a human being—or a cyborg. King Kong is animated for reasons of scale and humanization: a model had to be used so that the illusion of gigantic appearance and human-like facial features could be achieved. But the cinematic image of the animated dinosaur shows us something that can be seen nowhere else (perhaps this is why the use of lizards and iguanas as live-action "stand-ins" for dinosaurs is so unsatisfactory).[6]

The "real" dinosaurs we see in museums are spectacles of death and stasis: they are fossils, bones, skeletons—ghastly sculptures.[7] But science and mass desire converge in the demand for their reanimation. Paleontology is full of metaphors of resurrection. The popular image of the dino-hunter is that of a new kind of big game hunter, one who seeks the biggest, most dangerous creature that ever stalked the earth.[8] The dino-hunter doesn't kill his prey, however, but raises it from the dead and brings it back as a living trophy. That is why two great modern narratives—the Big Game Hunt *(King Kong)* and scientific resurrection *(Frankenstein)*—converge in *Jurassic Park*'s narrative of the dinosaur's rebirth. Mass media, massive animals, mass destruction, mass consumption, and mass resurrection from the dead—all converge in the "animation" of the dinosaur.

All these dimensions of the dinosaur are linked with the authority and prestige of science and technology, the means by which all the forces of mass production and consumption are (we hope) both unleashed and kept under rational control. Human beings think they can deploy science and technology to unleash a "controlled" mass destruction. The figure of Godzilla, a mutant dinosaur spawned by the atomic bomb, is the Japanese response to, and representation of, this complacency. The same technology that destroys hundreds of thousands of people brings the dead reptile back to life, producing both destruction and creation as a spectacle for mass consumption. The dinosaur is not just "a" kitsch icon, then, but *the* epitome of kitsch in its condensation of all levels of modern mass culture into a single, authoritative natural form. In contrast to "mere" popular culture, it has the legitimacy of that modern secular religion we call science and a corresponding credibility as a respectable educational tool. At the same time, it is a kind of blank slate on which every kind of collective and individual fantasy can be projected.

The spectacular effect of the dinosaur thus depends upon a systematic betrayal or blurring of the actual scientific understanding on which it capitalizes. This betrayal is quite precise: it involves the confusion of a very large and diverse taxon (already of dubious coherence) with a "species"—none other than our own. That is why the prevailing metaphors in dinosaurology inevitably treat the terrible lizards as an extended allegory of the human species. Robert Bakker, the leading figure of the contemporary "dinosaur renaissance," weaves an epic tapestry of "dynasties" and "ruling clans" engaged in a triumphant imperial saga: "like the Mongol hordes sweeping across the old cities of eastern Europe, dinosaurs wasted little time in expelling . . . well-established kingdoms." This global conquest was not achieved without competition or opposition, and unlike the Mongols, it had staying power: "during their long reign, the dinosaurs faced potential threats from dozens of new clans that evolved even higher grades of teeth and claws, bodies and brains. Despite the evolutionary vigor of the potential opposition, dinosaurs kept their ecological frontiers intact."[9] Even more important, Bakker's imperial dinosaurs are a modernizing, progressive, dynamic "clan" of conquerors. He ridicules older imperial images of the dinosaur, their bodies "ornamented . . . like the decadent opulence of a Byzantine palace," (15) and insists that they "evolved quickly, changed repeatedly, and turned out wave after wave of new species with new adaptations through their long reign" (20). Bakker comes close to declaring that the "guiding principle of the modern age," namely, "Man is the measure of all things," should be replaced by a more comprehensive yardstick (18). If we measure "success" in terms of size, longevity, and dominance, dinosaurs are clearly the measure of all living things on earth. Like God and Man, if the Dinosaur did not exist, we would have invented him. In fact, we *have* invented him as the most spectacular animal image of the modern era. When Foucault wondered what would take the place of the Age of Man, he probably didn't suspect that it would be the Age of the Dinosaur.

Of course Bakker knows that his terminology of clans, dynasties, kingdoms, reigns, and conquests is only metaphoric. He is well aware that dinosaurs were not a species, but something much larger and more diverse, perhaps an order or suborder that contained many different species within it. Nevertheless, the fall into anthropomorphic and imperial metaphors, into the *image* of dinosaurs as world-conquering hordes of human beings, seems to be an unavoidable lapse, especially for any paleontologist who wants to write for a popular readership. The analogy between *Homo sapiens* and *Reptilicus erectus* is, as Mark Johnson and George Lakoff might put it, one of those "metaphors we live by." We cannot help falling into it, any more than we can encounter the look of animals without reflecting on ourselves.

monsters and dinomania

What can be said of . . . a creature with the nose of a *Macrauchenia* [an extinct South American mammal], the neck of a giraffe, the limbs of an elephant, the feet of a chalicothere [an extinct relative of the horse], the lungs of a bird, and the tail of a lizard?

—WALTER R. COOMBS (quoted in William Stout, *The Dinosaurs*)

IF WE ARE LOOKING for a general class of animals to place dinosaurs among, monsters are the obvious candidate. Brian Noble has shown convincingly that the gigantic size, ferocity, and "horror" of the dinosaur place it with the monsters.[1] The long association of monsters with hybrid combinations of different species and groups also makes a good fit with the dinosaur's ambiguous placement between the birds and the reptiles. (Dragons, for instance, are generally portrayed as composites of reptilian and avian characteristics, "plumed serpents" that live underground, but fly through the air.) The supposed sterility of monsters matches up with the stereotype of the dinosaur as an evolutionary dead end, a reproductive failure—a notion that Calvino's story sets out to subvert.[2] Finally, as Noble also suggests, the very word "monster" is linked to "demonstration," the "showing" of visible evidence in a scientific argument. In Catholic ritual, the "monstrance" is the vehicle in which the sacred host is held up for display to the congregation.

But a crucial feature of the "monstrosity" of the dinosaur is the ritual denial that it is a monster at all—the endless repetition of the claim that it is a real, natural kind, not an artificial or arbitrary class. Unlike the dragon, whose iconographic descendant it clearly is, the dinosaur is legitimated as real by modern science.

"THE EXTINCT ANIMALS" MODEL-ROOM, AT THE CRYSTAL PALACE, SYDENHAM.—(SEE PRECEDING PAGE.)

10.1

The extinct animal model room of Waterhouse Hawkins at the Crystal Palace, Sydenham. *Illustrated London News,* 31 December 1853. These early paleontological restorations portrayed extinct creatures as composites of familiar animal images: the *Iguanodon* in the center is a scaly rhino; the *Hyleosaurus* on the right is modeled on a dragon; the Tertiary mammal, *Anoplotherium,* on the left is an ancient pig-horse; the dicynodont (right foreground) is a walrus-turtle; the labyrinthodont amphibian (left foreground) is a toothy frog. (Photo courtesy of The Newberry Library, Chicago.)

Unlike real, scientific, natural monsters (Siamese twins, six-legged calves, hermaphrodites, elephant men), the dinosaur is not a deviation, anomaly, mutation, deformity, or hybrid, but a viable, "normal" animal. If we class the dinosaur among the monsters, then, we must put a whole row of asterisks after it, and answer a whole series of questions. What other monsters do we elevate to the position of public monuments? How many monsters can you think of that serve as hosts on children's TV programs, and as their first introduction to science?[3]

One answer to the puzzle of dinosaur image classification would be simply to declare that it is a "symbolic animal," one which, like lions, whales, sharks, bears, dragons, and unicorns, has been given a human significance. Like any other symbolic animal, it has a whole repertoire of metaphoric associations. Unlike the traditional bestiaries, however—those visual/verbal zoos filled with wily foxes, courageous lions, subtle serpents, and imitative apes—the dinosaur comprises a whole bestiary within itself, populated by gentle giant brontosauruses, fierce T. rexes, weird pterodactyls, shy stegosauruses, and (the latest invention) those "clever girls," the velociraptors of *Jurassic Park,* to say nothing of the whole cast of fictional dinosaurs from Gertie to Godzilla to Barney. The dinosaur provides, in short, a whole new "modern bestiary" (all "extinct," but all waiting to be resurrected). As such, it reflects the fate of nature—and specifically of animals—in the wake of that juggernaut we call "modernity," understood as the whole complex of man-made global forces that is leaving countless extinct species in its wake. The dinosaur is the animal emblem of the process of modernization, with its intertwined cycles of destruction and resurrection, innovation and obsolescence, expansive "giantism" and progressive "downsizing."[4]

The dinosaur also stands for the fate of the human species within the world system of modern capitalism, especially the "species anxieties" that are endemic to modernity, from decadence

10.2
Technically, a "monster" is not merely large, violent, or dangerous. It is a hybrid figure, a heterogeneous conjunction of incongruous parts in a single body. Here we see a more traditional monster, the "pope-ass," depicted as a hideous, obscene composite of animal and humanoid features.

to disaster to uncontrollable eco-suicide.[5] In this respect, it is the true descendant of the dragons, those "prodigies" whose appearance in traditional societies signified war, plague, natural disaster, or the wrath of God. (The association of the Chinese dragon with good luck and imperial nobility is the dialectical obverse of the disaster omen.) The dinosaur is a prestige symbol for modern nation-states, and a model for ideologies of world conquest and domination. It is associated with childhood, old age, and everything in between. It is associated with sexual differentiation and reproduction, and with the failure to reproduce. It is a figure of everything alien to human nature (cold-blooded, reptilian, rapacious) and of all that is most familiar in human nature (cold-blooded, reptilian, rapacious).

As you've probably noticed, the problem with this survey of the dinosaur as "cultural symbol" or symbolic animal is that it has too many meanings, and too many of them are contradictory. If one treats this subject as an anthropologist would, and interviews "native informants" about the meaning of dinosaurs and the reasons for their popularity, everyone seems to have a ready answer: it's their bigness, ferocity, rarity, antiquity, or strangeness; it's their uncanny appearance as erect reptiles, their commercial exploitability, or just because, as dinosaurologist Gregory Paul puts it, "dinosaurs look neat."[6] It's because we can admire them as a world-dominant species, or feel superior to them because they died out. It's because they are a riddle and an enigma, or because they are a universally intelligible symbol.

The contradictions in dino-fascination become ever more evident the closer one comes to the core of the dinosaur cult, what might be called "dinomania"—the occupational hazard of dinosaurology. Is dinomania more like affection toward a pet animal or fear of a monster? Is the collecting of bones a compulsive fetishistic activity or a scientific pursuit? Are dinosaurologists really serious scientists, or just big kids who never outgrew their childhood fascination? Are dinosaurs really as important and wonderful as the dinosaurologists and dinomaniacs think, or are they just the relatively uninteresting sideshow that most people see them as? Stephen Spielberg makes his own ambivalence explicit in the opening sequence of *The Lost World* when he segues from the face of a mother screaming at the attack on her daughter by tiny scavenger dinosaurs to the face of Jeff Goldblum yawning in boredom. Has the manufactured thrill of a sequel ever been signaled quite so overtly?

What are we to do with this mass of divergent and contradictory testimony about the significance of dinosaurs? Are we to scream or yawn? One answer would be to treat the dinosaur as basically an empty sign, a blank slate on which individuals can project any meaning they wish. But this would leave the basic question unanswered: why should that blank slate be imprinted with the name and image of the dinosaur? Why have dinosaurs been selected to play the role of an infinitely flexible cultural symbol? What makes their bones the "bones of contention" that surface in so many different public and private spheres? The mere accumulation of symbolic meanings would also prevent us from looking for any kind of logic or system in the variety of things that people actually say about dinosaurs. More important, it would prevent us from noticing the things people *do* with them, the rituals performed around them, the dances they are made to perform.

BIG MacDINO

CONSIDER A RECENT TELEVISION commercial for McDonald's Restaurants that uses the dinosaur as a central image. The scene opens at night in the spooky exhibition hall of a natural history museum. A giant *Tyrannosaurus rex* skeleton gleams in the moonlight. Suddenly, by the miracle of digital animation, it moves slightly and sniffs the air. It smells food. With a roar, it gallops through the museum hunting for the source. It finds the delicious bait to be nothing other than a packet of McDonald's french fries in the hands of a dozing guard. When the guard realizes what the creature wants, he teases it with the french fries, making it sit up and beg, roll over, and finally play dead, which it does with a sweeping bow, crashing into a heap of collapsing bones.[1]

The makers of this commercial intuited a basic feature of the human fascination with dinosaurs: its ambivalence or vacillation between contrary emotions (cp. figure 2.1). In the space of a minute, the McDonald's dinosaur goes from sublime to ridiculous. It is ghastly, impressive, and monumental one moment and the object of humiliation the next. Most dinosaur images don't make this transition between contrary emotions quite so explicit or rapid. But all dinosaur images, I want to suggest, function within a polarized logic of this sort. Even the monstrous *T. rex* of *Jurassic Park* is reduced, at a key moment, to a prop in a sight gag when it is framed in the rearview mirror of the jeep it is chasing with the textual legend, "Objects in Mirror Are Closer than They Appear." This diminution of the monster to a joke is reversed a few moments later when the diminutive and colorful *Dilophosaurus* is teased and ridiculed by the fat computer nerd, Nedry. Nedry asks the "little fellow" if it wants something to eat, tries unsuccessfully to make it fetch a stick, and then tells the dinosaur it's no wonder it's extinct, threatening to run over it with his jeep. But little *Dilophosaurus* turns out to be armed with a sticky poisonous venom, which it spits into

Nedry's eyes, reducing him to a blind and helpless prey in one of the more horrifying scenes in the film.

A similar ambivalence surrounds the whole question of whether the dinosaur is an important cultural symbol. On the one hand, we are told that dinosaurs are mainly for children, and that adults are bored with the whole subject. On the other hand, some adults have invested a great deal of time and money in the excavation and display of dinosaurs. When I've told people that I'm writing a book about dinosaurs, their reactions have ranged from enthusiasm to puzzlement, from an instant understanding of the importance of the topic to an amused and condescending smirk. The implication of the latter response is that I'm regressing to a second childhood in taking on this subject, or perhaps that I've become a kind of dinosaur myself in my dotage. My sense is that these contrasting reactions are not alternatives that we can choose between, as if we could decide once and for all whether dinosaurs are serious or trivial, sublime or ridiculous. The question is, how can we get beyond simply cataloguing these alternatives to some higher synthesis or deeper truth? The

11.1–11.4
The life cycle of a dinosaur in a frame sequence from a McDonald's commercial. First, the monumental dinosaur skeleton at the moment of coming back to life and pulling up its chains to go hunting for food. Second, its reduction to a domestic animal, sitting up and begging for a McDonald's french fry from the museum guard. Third, the moment when the french fry enters its mouth. Fourth, the dinosaur obeying the museum guard's order to perform a trick that "should be easy for you": "Play dead!" The dinosaur's transformations— from awesome monster to ridiculous pet—are here presented as a story of resurrection to life and return to a pretense of death.
(Film stills from McDonald's commercial by Leo Burnett & Co., "Fossil Fuels," 1994.)

11.5
Framed by a rearview mirror
inscribed with the words,
"Objects in Mirror Are Closer
than They Appear," the mighty
T. rex is reduced to a sight gag.
(Film still, *Jurassic Park*.)

dinosaur simply *is* the tension between these antithetical values and affects; it *is* a figure in constant symbolic motion, shuttling between science and fantasy, nature and culture, the image of the other and a mirror of the self. The question, then, is what sort of image, what sort of cultural figure, is capable of playing these antithetical roles? What *kind* of thing, finally, is the cultural image we call "the dinosaur"?

One final feature of the McDonald's commercial is worth lingering over. As the dinosaur makes it way through the hallways of the natural history museum in search of its prey, its ghastly, skeletal shadow passes over some other images that one would certainly expect to find in such a museum. These are Native American totem poles, whose carved animal and human faces glare out of the shadows as the *T. rex* passes by them. This unobtrusive transitional moment,[2] this image of passing from the role of impressive public monument to abject, humiliated pet, reveals, I think, the very special class of images to which the dinosaur belongs, and with which it is usually contrasted.

11.6–11.7
The shadow of the dinosaur passes over the silent faces of the Native American totem poles; its face is caught in profile peeking around the corner next to the profile of a totem mask. The dinosaur is, in fact, our modern totem animal—the most universally recognizable animal image of our era and the focus of distinctively modern rituals of resurrection and consumption. (Film stills from McDonald's commercial by Leo Burnett & Co., "Fossil Fuels," 1994.)

12.1 (Overleaf)
The dinosaur *Brachiosaurus* in the great hall of the Field Museum of Natural History, Chicago, with Native American totem poles in the distance. What is the relation between these two kinds of monumental figures? We routinely label totems as a "primitive" or "premodern" objects, in contrast to modern, scientific images of the dinosaur. What if we reversed the labels and thought about the totem pole as a reflection of real knowledge about the world and the dinosaur as the reflection of modern fantasy? (© Ted Lacey Photography, 1998.)

THE TOTEM ANIMAL OF MODERNITY

THE DINOSAUR IS THE TOTEM animal of modernity. By this I mean, first, that it is a symbolic animal that comes into existence for the first time in the modern era; second, that it epitomizes a modern time sense—both the geological "deep time" of paleontology and the temporal cycles of innovation and obsolescence endemic to modern capitalism; and third, that it functions in a number of rituals that introduce individuals to modern life and help societies to produce modern citizens. I call it *the* totem animal because it is unique, sui generis. The modern world has many symbolic animals and many monsters, but none of them function in precisely the way the dinosaur does. It is not just *a* totem animal of modernity, but *the* animal image that has, by a complex process of cultural selection, emerged as the global symbol of modern humanity's relation to nature.

The word "totem," as Claude Lévi-Strauss reminds us, "is taken from the Ojibwa, an Algonquin language of the region to the north of the Great Lakes of northern America. The expression *ototeman* . . . means roughly, 'he is a relative of mine.'" A totem (which is generally an animal, but can also be a plant, mineral, or even an artificial object) is thus a *social* symbol, a sign of the clan or collectivity.[1] In the world of sacred or superstitious objects and images, totems occupy a kind of middle ground between

> **Everything that concerned the true nature of the Dinosaurs must remain hidden. In the night, as the New Ones slept around the skeleton, which they had decked with flags, I transported it, vertebra by vertebra, and buried my Dead.**
>
> —ITALO CALVINO, "The Dinosaurs"

the fetish (a private object of devotion or obsession) and the idol (a collective projection of absolute power and divinity). Totems are more social than fetishes, less absolute and authoritarian—less religious—than idols. Fetishes, in psychoanalytic theory, are associated with severed body parts, idols with human sacrifice. The totem animal, by contrast, is itself the sacrificial object, a substitute for the human victim.

Totem animals in traditional, premodern societies played four basic roles. They served (1) as symbols of the social unit (tribe, clan, or nation); (2) as ancestor figures reminding the clan of its ancient origin and descent; (3) as "taboo" objects, both in the general sense of sacred or holy things, and in the more specific sense of a prohibition against touching or eating the totem animal or having sex with a member of the same clan;[2] and (4) as ritual objects, connected with the sacrifice of the animal followed by a "totem meal," in which the normally taboo animal is consumed. These functions are all independent of one another (it is relatively rare to find all of them present in traditional societies), and sometimes even contradictory: the forbidden object of sexual or culinary "consummation" may become the compulsory object of the sacrificial feast, the ritual meal or love object.

A moment's reflection reveals that the dinosaur plays all four of these roles, albeit in modified ways, in modern societies. The dinosaur is a "clan sign" for a wide range of social collectivities, from national to federal "states," from vanishing races to dominant, imperial civilizations, from warrior-hunter brotherhoods to dangerous new sisterhoods of "clever girls." As social symbol, moreover, the dinosaur is not merely a single, positive symbol for a specific tribe, nation, or species, but is itself a figure of collectivity, a group or series of species whose differences may be mapped onto any parallel set of differences in human society. Thus, the contrast between carnivorous and herbivorous dinosaurs can be encoded as a gender difference, equating "male with devourer and female with devoured"[3] (the dominant tendency in traditional societies), or inverted (as in *Jurassic Park,* in which all the dinosaurs are female, and all their human victims are male). The major "types" of dinosaurs in folk or vernacular taxonomy (the "cookie cutter" stereotypes of *T. rex, Brontosaurus, Triceratops, Stegosaurus,* and *Pterodactyl*) provide a ready-made bestiary for the differentiation of individuals and groups.[4] Elementary schoolchildren are routinely encouraged to select (and identify with) their "favorite" dinosaur, inspiring role-playing fantasies of flight, monstrous ferocity, gentle giantism, and armored invulnerability. It is a tribute to Spielberg and Crichton's inventiveness that they have actually succeeded in introducing a new member to the folk taxonomy of dinosaurs. *Velociraptor,* the pack-hunting, fast-moving, highly intelligent predator, has now entered the global vernacular, and has been adopted as the clan sign and emblem of Toronto's professional basketball team. These differentiated dinosaurial types may also, on the other hand, be dissolved into a generalized figure of homogeneous mass society, as Capek does with his "Newts" or "erect salamanders."

The ancestral function of the dinosaur is relatively straightforward: The Age of Reptiles precedes and makes way for the Age of Mammals in the master narrative of modern paleontology. Dinosaurs are the rulers of the earth before humankind. They must die out so that we can live; they must disappear or devolve into degenerate "creeping things" (or relatively harmless birds) so that we can appear and evolve into the dominant species. They are rather like the Chthonian (often reptilian) gods of the underworld in Greek mythology, the "giants of the earth" who had to be killed or imprisoned so that humanoid sky-gods, the Olympians, could assume dominance. This ancestral narrative is replayed, moreover, at the individual level in children's identification of their parents as dangerous dinosaurial giants who (fortunately) will inevitably make room for their offspring by becoming extinct (see "Lessons," the section on children and dinosaurs, below).

The most complex feature of the dinosaur totem is the cluster of taboos and rituals that surround its excavation and display. These form the core of public dinosaur fascination and "dinomania," the set of emotional and intellectual associations that give dinosaurs "magic" and "aura" in mass culture. Here we must note a few salient differences between dinosaurs and traditional totem animals. The traditional totem was generally a living, actually existing animal that had an immediate, familiar relation to its clan. The dinosaur is a rare, exotic, and extinct animal that has to be "brought back to life" in representations and then domesticated, made harmless and familiar. The traditional totem located power and agency in nature; totem animals and plants bring human beings to life and provide the natural basis for their social classifications. By contrast, the modern totem locates power in human beings: *we* classify the dinosaurs and identify ourselves with them; *we* bring the dangerous monsters back to life in order to subdue them. The McDonald's commercial perfectly illustrates this process: the resurrection of the monster followed by its transformation into a domestic pet that can be compelled to "play dead." The not-so-hidden message of this commercial might be summarized as follows: let's awaken and then subdue the totem animal of modern consumer desire (the *T. rex* as figure of rapacious, carnivorous appetite) with the totem *vegetable* of modernity, the french fry.[5] Since the vast majority of the world's potatoes wind up as french fries, this commercial is, in a very real sense, just telling it like it is.

What about the sexual and culinary "consummation" taboos that were thought to accompany the traditional totem, the prohibitions on eating the totem animal and having incestuous relations with a member of the same clan? I do not see any direct analogy with the mandate for exogamy in the folkways surrounding the dinosaur, but I do see a link with the fundamental issue of procreation that underlies the incest taboo. Anxieties about proper sexual roles and reproductive potency are connected with stories of dinosaur extinction and resurrection. Dinosaurs may have died out because they stopped having babies, or because they laid eggs that became increasingly vulnerable to nest robbers. Spielberg's *Jurassic Park* is not only about the bio-genetic cloning of dinosaurs, but also about the danger that humans will fail to reproduce. The relationship of Drs. Grant and Sattler, the male paleontologist and female paleobotanist, is shadowed by her anxiety over his dislike for children, and the story is largely about his learning how to care for children. One of the most interesting changes in the public image of the dinosaur since the 1960s has been its transformation from a solitary predator, the lone male hunter, into a "good mother" figure, guarding the nest and living in social groups. Spielberg's *The Lost World,* the sequel to *Jurassic Park,* is a veritable hymn in praise of dinosaur family values, portraying its *T. rex* couple as ferociously nurturing parents. The Field Museum dinosaur exhibition that opened in the spring of 1997 to coincide with the release of *The Lost World* was, not surprisingly, entitled "Dinosaur Families," building on the work of Montana paleontologist Jack Horner with the *Maiasauras* or "good mother lizard." Horner was the paleontological consultant to *Jurassic Park.*

The other meaning of dinosaur "consummation," having to do with the totem meal, reappears in the form of symbolic inversion. If the traditional totem animal was not to be killed, or was to be killed and eaten only under special ritual conditions, the dinosaur is an animal that cannot be killed (being already dead), but must be brought back to life so that it can be consumed as public spectacle. More generally, the dinosaur itself is generally portrayed as a massive eating machine. It provides a spectacle of rapacious consumption that becomes more fascinating the closer the meal comes to including one of our own species. I will have more to say about this in connection with the festive meals surrounding the debuts of dinosaur exhibitions (see chapter 18, "The Victorian Dinosaur," and chapter 36, "Carnosaurs and Consumption").

Perhaps the most subtle contrast between the modern and traditional totems lies in the question of their status, their authority and legitimacy as social symbols. We might be tempted to say that the traditional totem is religious and magical, an object of superstitious reverence and animistic thinking, while the modern totem enjoys the authority and prestige of science. But the contrast between science and religion is undermined by the tendency of science to play the role of a modern, secular religion, popularly misconceived as the final arbiter of truth and reality in all matters. This sort of "scientism" or scientific ideology needs to be distinguished, from the actual practice of science, which tends to be skeptical, provisional, and modest about the extent and durability of its claims. Traditional totems, similarly, are probably not as dogmatically religious or magical in their authority as early anthropologists thought. The notion of a radical distinction between the "savage" and "modern" mind is precisely what totemism tends to undermine. Traditional totem animals and plants may, in fact, have as much to do with ethnozoology and ethnobotany, traditional bodies of natural lore based in accumulated observations and experiments passed on over many generations, as with any magical or religious symbolism. As the rain forests disappear from our planet, we are learning too late that their human inhabitants possess a fund of "folk biology" that consists not of "superstition," but of refined and precise understandings of numerous exotic plants and animals, including their medicinal and poisonous properties.

The crucial point here is that ethnoscience and magic, just like modern science and that

12.2

Why do we want to bring dinosaurs back to life and, further, to imagine them devouring us? Traditional totem animals were the object of ritual sacrifices and spectacular feasts. The modern totem is brought back to life by means of a spectacle in which human sacrifice plays a central role. What is consumed in the dinosaur sacrifice is the spectacle of consumption itself. We love to watch them eat . . . us.

William Hayes in *Collier's Weekly*
"Adds a little life to the old place, don't you think?"

modern form of magical thinking known as "scientism," are woven together in the everyday life of human beings. There is no question that an essential part of the taboo (in the sense of aura or magic) of the dinosaur resides in its status as a scientific object, or more specifically, in its role as a monument to "Big Science," and even more aptly to what might be called "pure scientism."[6] The dinosaur exemplifies pure science because it is useless and impractical, and yet it provides a highly visible speculative object in which areas of uncertainty and controversy are very broad. "The" dinosaur is so speculative, in fact, that (as we have seen) it may never have existed as a natural kind or a coherent scientific concept, but only as a name that survives because of its popular appeal. The attractiveness of the modern dinosaur totem is, like that of the traditional totem animal, marked by ambivalence. The dinosaur is monument and toy; monstrous and silly; pure, disinterested science, and vulgar, fraudulent commercialism.[7] The taboos (in the sense of prohibitions) surrounding the dinosaur tend to manifest themselves, then, as efforts to deny or overcome this ambivalence by declaring the dinosaur to be a purely scientific object, a serious and real object untainted by magic, money, or "cultural" interest. Stephen Jay Gould's fear that the authentic dinosaur will be destroyed by the "deluge" of commerce and vulgar publicity is an expression of this taboo. The truth is that the dinosaur is never really separable from its popular and cultural status; the flood of publicity that seems to threaten its existence is the very thing that keeps it alive.

There is one conspicuous problem with the concept of totemism that needs to be faced at this point. Most anthropologists regard totemism as itself an obsolete notion, a relic of an earlier, Eurocentric, imperial phase of anthropology, when a radical division between the "savage" and the "civilized" mind was a basic assumption of all field research. Freud's absorption of totemism into the psychoanalytic paradigm simply extended this boundary to include children and neurotics among the "savages" who continue to hold the sort of animistic, superstitious beliefs on which totemism relies. In the early 1960s, however, Claude Lévi-Strauss declared that totemism was an illusion. It had been inflated, he argued, into an umbrella term for "primitive religion." Lévi-Strauss also pointed out that the totem had long been recognized as an incoherent scientific concept. As early as 1899, E. B. Tylor had noted that it had "been exaggerated out of proportion to its real theological magnitude."[8]

I trust that the parallels between the dinosaur and the totem are clear. Both are "scientific" concepts of dubious utility that have been inflated into master terms. Both involve a kind of back-projection into the "pre-history" of animal life and the human species, the one into the deep time of paleontology and geology, the other into the dreamtime of anthropology. Both were developed during the same imperial epoch of the sciences of nature and culture. Both involved the absorption of a diverse mass of evidence into a general concept of dubious coherence. Lévi-Strauss opened his critique of totemism with the following remark: "Totemism is like hysteria, in that once we are persuaded to doubt that it is possible arbitrarily to isolate certain phenomena and to group them together as diagnostic signs of an illness, or of an objective institution, the symptoms themselves vanish or appear refractory to any unifying interpretation."[9]

We might well ask, then, what is the point in using an obsolete concept from anthropology (the totem) to explain a possibly obsolete concept in paleontology (the dinosaur)? Can we use a dinosaur to catch a dinosaur? Or is this more like killing two birds with one stone? These questions are only made more vexing by the curious "afterlife" of both concepts. The dinosaur insists on living on as the marquee attraction of paleontology. Totemism continues to rear its head despite its authoritative dismissal by Lévi-Strauss. In fact, Lévi-Strauss himself rescued the concept by raising it to a higher level, linking it to an instinct for classification, an intellectual and ideological mapping of nature onto culture. There is a kind of uncanny parallel between the history of the dinosaurial and totemic concepts. Both enjoy an early flowering in the second half of the nineteenth century as key images and ideas in the development of paleontology and anthropology, respectively. Both fall into scientific disrepute and obsolescence in a middle period, the first half of the twentieth century, and enjoy a renewal in the sixties that has continued to the present day. The "dinosaur renaissance" inaugurated by John Ostrom and Robert Bakker is paralleled by a rebirth of totemism. As the anthropologist Roy Willis notes, "though officially pronounced dead nearly 30 years ago, totemism obstinately refuses to 'lie down.'"[10] It survives in social science and anthropology, now as a way of breaking down (rather than securing) the opposition between the "savage" and "civilized" mind and of reopening questions about the ecological and biological dimensions of modern culture and society. Similarly, the dinosaur, which had also been "pronounced dead" as a concept as well as a living thing, has been reborn in a new form. It is no longer an automatic synonym for failure and obsolescence, but has been refashioned as an evolutionary "success story," a 170-million-year saga of ruling reptiles that makes the prospects of human and mammalian world dominance look rather puny by comparison. We are almost tempted to say that the concepts of the totem and the dinosaur were made for each other, and that the dinosaur may well be not just a modernized version of the "savage" totem, but the first and last real totem in human history.

The relation between the dinosaur and the totem, finally, is not merely a matter of strikingly similar functions, or even of similar and parallel histories. The two concepts, and the real objects associated with them, constantly appear together in the concrete space of natural history exhibitions. Dinosaurs and totem poles are the marquee attractions of the two disciplinary "wings" of the natural history museum, the cultural and the biological. The McDonald's commercial stages their encounter quite explicitly: the dinosaur passes in review before the silent witness figures of the Indian totem poles; the shadow of the modern dinosaur skeleton passes over the faces of the traditional animal ancestors. Which object is more magical and superstitious, we must ask ourselves: the silent totem poles glaring out of the darkness, or the ghastly monster brought back to life by the miracle of digital animation?

What difference does it make to see the dinosaur as the totem animal of modernity? The crucial shift is in the one feature that the dinosaur does not share with traditional totems, and that is precisely the consciousness of its function as a totem.[11] The disavowal of the "savage" or "mythical" character of the dinosaur is what is crucial to its workings as the *modern* totem. Many people who might be willing to grant that the dinosaur functions as a cultural symbol would still hold out for a distinctively modern and scientific (that is, nonsymbolic, nonimaginary, and purely "real") role for the terrible lizards. My claim, however, is that this holdout position is no longer tenable once one sees that the dinosaur is a totem, not just a symbol. In other words, scientific interest in the dinosaur is not to be seen as a separate enclave, protected from contamination by "cultural" issues (values, myths, superstitions, false—and true—beliefs). Science is also a cultural practice, a ritual activity with traditions, customs, and taboos. The realization that this is so should not prevent science from producing the kind of knowledge it is equipped to produce, nor should it prevent nonscientists from trusting the validity and usefulness of that knowledge.

The dinosaur, however, may be another matter. Insofar as the successful functioning of the dinosaur as totem animal (and as scientific object) depends upon the *disavowal* of its mythical status, the dinosaur might not survive exposure as a cult object. When a magical object depends upon mystification and disavowal, its exposure to the light of reason may transform it or cause it to disappear. Could it be possible that the current worldwide epidemic of dinomania is making its cult status undeniable? Could *Jurassic Park* actually be the last hurrah of the terrible lizards, a premonition that they could disappear a second time?

My prediction is that second extinction of the dinosaur will be a slow, gradual process, but one in which the final decade of the twentieth century will be seen as decisive. A similar fate befell the dragon at the end of the sixteenth century. Spenser's *Faerie Queene* was the "apex of medieval dragon lore," providing the richest narrative and iconographic representation yet known.[12] *Jurassic Park* (both the novel and the film) may be the greatest dinosaur story ever told, but that doesn't mean it will have any worthy successors. It may have the effect of killing off the genre (except for parodies, sequels, and spin-offs) for a long time. (Crichton's own sequel is remarkably lame, even stooping to the theft of the title of an earlier dinosaur classic, Arthur Conan Doyle's *The Lost World;* Spielberg's sequel is a pale imitation of a pale imitation.) With the death of Spenser's dragon at the hands of the Redcrosse Knight (Saint George), as Jonathan Evans points out, "the dragon itself passes from English literature—or at least goes dormant. On the Continent, dragons remained active only as subspecies of serpents in encyclopedias and works of natural history."[13]

13.1

The dragon is the cultural ancestor of the dinosaur. It might be described as the "ruling reptile" of premodern social systems, associated with kings and emperors, with buried treasure (cp. fossil fuels), and with the fall of dynasties. If the dragon is the object of a knightly quest in which it is killed in order to save the community, the dinosaur is the object of a heroic paleontological quest in which the monster is brought back to life and displayed as a trophy of modern political and economic systems. St. George kills the dragon by thrusting his lance into its mouth; the museum guard pacifies the dinosaur by thrusting a Mcdonald's french fry into its mouth.

(St. George and the Dragon, nineteenth-century melkite icon, attributed to Palestinian painter Mikhaïl Mhanna al-Qudsi.)

13

The way of Dragons

Like the dinosaur's second extinction, the dragon's was an overdetermined event. Dragons may have been killed off by Enlightenment rationalism and skepticism, by the circulation of printed images and texts among a community of scientific researchers. Perhaps dinosaurs will be rendered boring by popular overexposure and irrelevant as a scientific class by "cladistics," a highly technical, nominalistic system of biological classification, one that has no truck with the hierarchies of Linnaean and evolutionary taxonomy, much less the vernacular classifications of folk taxonomy. Perhaps, like the dragon, the dinosaur narrative will have nowhere to go. Calvino's prediction will come true, and the memory of the dinosaur will fade. It will be a thing, like the totem, to think *with* rather than *of,* submerged in the folds of thought. There will simply be nothing more to be said about the dinosaur, and it will pass "out of literature and into the secondary realm of literary allusion—which is to say, that of metaphor, simile, poetic decoration."[1]

Dinosaurs have already reached this phase in their ubiquity as figures of speech. Evans notes that "overuse" of the dragon "may have turned exaggeration into melodrama—perhaps anticipating the comical tone later exploited by writers of children's literature." The same thing could certainly be said of the dinosaur. Like the dragon, the dinosaur may limp along in a scientific limbo, remaining an object of research only because of inertia and the reverence for tradition within the scientific community. As late as 1755, Samuel Johnson's *Dictionary* expressed a "lingering belief in the dragon as a subspecies of reptiles" by cautiously declaring that they are "perhaps imaginary." Now the reptiles themselves are gone as well, according to the latest thinking in animal taxonomy. The dinosaur may linger on in a similar way, slowly dying out from overexposure, while "dinosaurology" recedes into a residual formation of paleontology.

The dragon's period of dormancy lasted 300 years. It was resurrected as "folklore" in the second half of the nineteenth century—most notably in Tennyson's *Idylls of the King* (1859)—in precisely the same decade when the dinosaur was born as a public image, an "antediluvian monster" and a scientific reality.[2] There is no way of predicting when the dinosaur's revival will occur. Perhaps it will have to wait for alien visitors long after the human species has vanished. Fred Jameson observes somewhere that it is now easier to imagine the death of the human species than the end of capitalism. That may be why it is so hard to imagine the fading away of the dinosaur. If the human race is lucky enough to endure, on the other hand, the dinosaur may become part of the folklore of modernity, one of the symbols by which postmodern culture gains access to its own past and its own political unconscious.

In this rearview mirror, dinosaurs will look as if they were doing many of the same things for us that dragons did for medieval culture. Dragons were the guardians of buried treasure; dinosaurs are associated with that quintessential modern form of buried treasure, fossil fuels. It is no accident that the *Brontosaurus* becomes the logo of the Sinclair Oil Company or that the *Stegosaurus* is made of money. More generally, the dinosaur is a recurrent metaphor for the cycle of innovation and obsolescence that is central to the logic of both modern science and technology and modern capitalism. Dragons were the objects of heroic quest-romances, ritual tests of manhood culminating in fruitful marriage. Dinosaurs are the objects of a distinctly modern form of the "big game hunt" that proves the virility of the dinosaurologist and the triumph of science over death. Dragons were "prodigies" associated with catastrophe and historical crisis (the death of kings, the coming of plagues). Dinosaurs are invariably greeted as "big news," as revelations that mark a new era of scientific understanding. (The American Museum of Natural History advertised the 1995 opening of its new dinosaur hall with the words "The Dinosaurs Return. A New Era Begins.") The changing images of dinosaurs are invariably associated with collective anxieties about threats to human survival (war, deluge, ecological destruction, decadence, racial contamination).

Several differences between dragons and dinosaurs should be noted, however. Although dragons were important symbolic animals, they did not serve as a comprehensive totem animal of medieval culture.[3] They were important members of the bestiary of mythical and fabulous creatures, along with the unicorn, the griffin, the chimera, and the phoenix, but they did not comprise an entire bestiary of world-dominant creatures. The Chinese dragon, the sacred animal of the emperor, actually may have been more like the dinosaur, first, in its association with empire, and second, in its appearance as a kind of hybrid, composite bestiary, an animal that contains all the animal types within itself.[4] But neither the European nor the Chinese dragon seems to have been so widely and "democratically" available, as it were, to popular identifications. In contrast to dragons, we have to say that "Dinos R Us." The dragon, especially in Western culture, is associated with evil that must be defeated and killed. Saint George is supposed to track it down and kill it, with God's help. The dinosaurologist is supposed to track down the dinosaur and bring it back to life with the power of science, so that it may be consumed in rituals of public display.

A contemporary film that blurs the boundary between dragon and dinosaur is Rob Cohen's *Dragonheart* (Universal Studios, 1990). The dragon, Draco, claims to be the last of his kind. He points out to his nemesis, a dragon-hunting knight (played by Dennis Quaid), that if he is killed, they will both be out of business. Knight and dragon, therefore, agree to form a partnership. They will roam the countryside, staging dramatic haystack burnings, virgin sacrifices, and other draconian theatrics for the gullible villagers, who will pay handsomely for the knight's "protection" from the dangerous monster. Draco will pretend to be killed, the knight will collect the reward, and they will move on to the next town. The romantic feudal narrative is, in short, transposed into the key signature of the Barnumesque hoax and the modern busi-

13.2
Dragons. From *Historiae naturalis* (Amsterdam, 1657–65) by Johannes Jonstonus. Like the dinosaur, the dragon is a "modified" reptile, endowed with wings or legs. Contemporary paleontology argues that birds are descendants of dinosaurs. From the standpoint of cultural history, it seems clear that the composite image of a reptilian bird or "plumed serpent" is far older than the dinosaur.

89

ness proposition. The ironic treatment of the monster (played with world-weary urbanity by Sean Connery), his sense of impending extinction, and his eagerness to head off obsolescence with a shrewd manipulation of publicity all suggest that the figure of the dragon is now being assimilated with that of the dinosaur.

No matter how exact that assimilation becomes, however, a fundamental difference has to be maintained in order to preserve the illusion of the dinosaur's modern, scientific status. *Dungeons & Dragons* is a popular kids' game filled with medieval dragon lore. Its catalogues of weapons and armor and intricate rules and strategies rival the Byzantine complexity of dinosaur taxonomy. But no responsible first-grade teacher is going to let *Dungeons & Dragons* become part of the curriculum (more's the pity). It is regarded as an exercise in fantasy and role-playing. Dinosaurs, on the other hand, are thought to be science, real knowledge—no matter how much fantasy the child invests in them. The child expects and receives praise for mastering paleontological jargon and impresses adults by setting them straight about the latest dinosaur discoveries. Although dragons were part of premodern natural history, and some have argued that they may have been based in observations of dinosaur fossil remains, the major "source of Western dragons," according to Evans, "seems to lie in mythology, not science or history." They are monsters, often "composites of several animals and sometimes are many-headed" (33).

As we have seen, however, there is a sense in which dinosaurs are also "composites of several animals," and their linkage with dragons and other reptilian monsters at the level of visual representation is manifest. The distinctions between science and magic, the modern and the savage mind, are a very fragile basis for distinctions between the dragon and the dinosaur. If we moderns also have totems, then we are not qualitatively different in our "mentalities" from savages or premodern peoples.[5] We have more complicated tools and more powerful technologies, but we basically think in the same way (which is what makes us such a danger to ourselves and others). The recognition of our own modern forms of "savagery" might foster a little more humility toward our premodern kinfolk, and allow us to recognize the continuity and resemblance between dragons and dinosaurs. It would then be possible to explore the concrete history that connects them—an "evolution of the image" of the erect ruling reptile—and not just compile a miscellaneous collection of examples sorted into binary oppositions such as "science versus myth" and "modern versus traditional."

Such a history would, of course, have to be encyclopedic and global, and there is no question of providing it here. What I have offered so far is a sampling of tales, traces, and theories of the dinosaur. My aim has been simply to awaken the suspicion that dinosaur facts are never entirely separate from fiction, that real fossil bones are inevitable occasions for imaginative projection and speculation, and that the true history of the dinosaur as a cultural concept is stranger than any fantasy we might invent. I've suggested, further, that the whole phenomenon of the dinosaur requires an explanation that comes not just from natural science or common sense, but from cultural science—the historical and psychological study of images, representations, and narratives and the ritual practices that go with them. I've suggested that the dinosaur can best be understood as the totem animal of modern culture, a creature that unites modern science with mass culture, empirical knowledge with collective fantasy, rational methods with ritual practices. What I have not explained so far is the historical process that allowed a relatively obscure scientific discovery in Victorian England to grow into a globaly

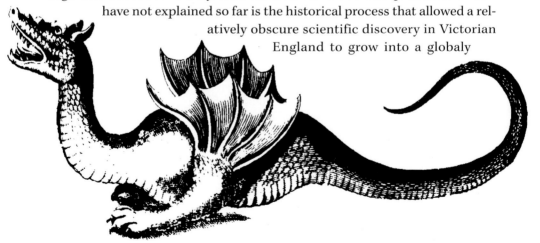

popular cultural icon. In one sense, our fascination with the dinosaur seems to have been fully formed from "the beginning," whether we find that beginning in mythical dragons and biblical leviathans or in mid-Victorian culture. But history does not happen all at once. It proceeds in fits and starts, by slow transformations, and by contrasts that may be evident only in the rearview mirror. It is this history to which we must now turn our attention.

HISTORIES

Mr. Waterhouse Hawkins requests the honor of Mr Joseph Prestwich's company at dinner in the model of the Iguanodon at the Crystal Palace on Saturday evening December the thirty first at five oclock —1853.

an answer will oblige

Invitation Card
Designed and Drawn for the occasion by
B. Waterhouse Hawkins

DRY BONES

ONE OF THE MOST STRIKING continuities in the history of dinosaur images is the notion of resurrection—the idea that the images are not merely reconstructions or restorations, but that they bring the dead back to life. The central modern myth of scientific resurrection, *Frankenstein,* is itself resurrected in the story of *Jurassic Park,* in which the new technologies of genetic engineering, cloning, and computer science are mobilized to create a new kind of "animation" of the dead. But the idea of resurrecting the dinosaur does not originate with *Jurassic Park.* It is central to the public display of the dinosaur from the first, and it depends, not just on modern technology, but on a deep reservoir of religious associations. In chapter 37 of the Book of Ezekiel, for instance, the prophet is led by God into the "valley of dry bones" and instructed to "say unto them, O ye dry bones, hear the word of the Lord." As Ezekiel speaks,

> **Our immortal naturalist has reconstructed worlds from blanched bones. He picks up a piece of gypsum and says to us 'See!' Suddenly stone turns into animals, the dead come to life, and another world unrolls before our eyes.**
>
> —BALZAC, ON CUVIER (quoted in John Noble Wilford, *The Riddle of the Dinosaur*)

there was a noise, and behold a shaking, and the bones came together, bone to his bone. And when I beheld, lo, the sinews and the flesh came up upon them, and the skin covered them above: but there was no breath in them. . . . So I prophesied as he commanded me, and the breath came into them, and they lived, and stood up upon their feet, an exceeding great army. (37: 7–8, 10)

14.1

Ticket of invitation to Waterhouse Hawkins's dinner party. (1854. Library, The Academy of Natural Sciences of Philadelphia.)

The first public "revivifying" of the dinosaur, for the 1854 Crystal Palace exhibition, built on precisely these associations. In this case, it was not a collaboration of God and his prophet, but of a scientist (Richard Owen) and his artist (Benjamin Waterhouse Hawkins)—though it is only a little less clear who was playing the role of God.[1] All that the public knows of the dinosaur, noted Hawkins, is the "bones" and the "names" that have been given to them: "it is only their names, and not the things themselves, with which we are acquainted . . . only dry bones or oddly shaped stones to the majority who see them." Without the leisure to fill in these skeletal remains with careful study, the public is unable to gratify its "natural sympathies . . . with life" and "to realize that life-like interest which becomes almost essential for the successful continuance of any pursuit." Hawkins proposes nothing less, therefore, than

> the revivifying of the ancient world—to call up from the abyss of time and from the depths of the earth, those vast forms and gigantic beasts which the Almighty Creator designed to inhabit and precede us in possession of this part of the earth called Great Britain.[2]

Unlike the ancient prophet, who calls the bones to life with words and breath, Hawkins resurrects them with images, a program of "Visual Education as Applied to Geology." Hawkins's new technology (one of the earliest uses of

THE DINNER IN THE MOULD OF THE IGUANODON

reinforced concrete, combining brick, cement, and iron supports) transforms death into life by translating the words of the scientist into the images of the artist, dry bones and skeletons into life-size and lifelike sculptures.

On New Years' Eve, 1853, Hawkins held a dinner party for Owen and other paleontologists in the belly of his half-finished *Iguanodon* model. The party was enlivened by a song that plays upon the resurrection theme:

> A thousand ages underground,
> His skeleton had lain,
> But now his body's big and round
> And there's life in him again!
>
> His bones like Adam's wrapped in clay
> His ribs of iron stout,
> Where is the brute alive today
> That dares to turn him out.
>
> Beneath his hide he's got inside
> The souls of living men,
> Who dare our Saurian now deride
> With life in him again?
>
> Chorus:
> The jolly old beast
> Is not deceased
> There's life in him again!

Hawkins's dinosaur is not just brought back to life, he is *pregnant* with the souls of "living men." (The out-of-control pregnancies of *Jurassic Park*'s dinosaurs have much more menacing implications.)

When Hawkins's finished sculptures were finally installed on an island in a suburban London water-meadow, where they remain today, the resurrection of the dry bones was to be completed by having them regularly bathed in a daily cycle of artificial tides. Unfortunately, this part of the display never worked out. Hawkins knew, of course, that he was not "really" bringing the dinosaurs back to life, just as Spielberg knows that biogenetic engineers can't really use extinct DNA to clone new dinosaurs.

14.2

Dinner party in the belly of the first dinosaur, New Year's Eve, 1853. The sculptor Benjamin Waterhouse Hawkins and the paleontologist Richard Owen, along with other dignitaries, celebrate the near-completion of the *Iguanodon*. The *London Illustrated News* and *Punch* did not miss the bizarre connotations of this scene. They saw it as a collective "Jonah" image, noting that, if the *Iguanodon* were alive today, these gentlemen would have been the meal in the belly of the *Iguanodon* rather than enjoying their meal there. They also saw the *Iguanodon* as a pregnant beast, its belly filled with the new men of the modern age. (*Illustrated London News*, 7 January 1854. Library, The Academy of Natural Sciences of Philadelphia.)

In both cases, it is the "imagineers" (Hawkins and Spielberg) who create the visual illusion of life. For Hawkins, the revivification is metaphoric but actual in the mind of the beholder whose "sympathies with life" are activated. For Spielberg, the revivification is literal, but fictional: the illusion of actual resurrection— staged as the hatching of dinosaur embryos from their eggs—is presented in the film, whatever the viewers' sympathies might be.

While the resurrection of the dinosaur is a consistent theme from start to finish, then, the exact form of the resurrection—its technique, purpose, location, and meaning—is quite variable. It is clear, for instance, that Hawkins's dinosaurs are deeply rooted in "Great Britain," whose soil they "possessed" and in which they laid their bones long before the present human inhabitants existed. They possess, in retrospect, a kind of national identity: in precise totemic fashion (with "bones like Adam's"), they are aboriginal ancestor figures whose bones are being brought to life to celebrate British imperial glory at the first great world's fair of the modern era. Forty thousand people will turn out to see their debut, and Queen Victoria will grace them with her approval and blessing.

Spielberg's dinosaurs, by contrast, are located in an offshore island theme park, a kind of biological experimental station-cum-wildlife preserve that is placed in Costa Rican territory to avoid troublesome U.S. environmental regulations. Jurassic Park is a leisure-industry counterpart to the NAFTA-esque movement of U.S. manufacturing to Latin America, where labor is cheap and governments weak and corruptible. The "blessing" these dinosaurs require is not the sovereign's, but that of a team of professionals (a lawyer, two paleontologists, and a chaos theoretician) who are called in to certify that the park is ready for the public.

If the dinosaur as totem is a symbol of collective social identification, the Victorian dinosaurs declare the power of the nation-state as

> And when the man was let down, and touched the bones of Elisha, he revived, and stood upon his feet.
>
> —II KINGS 14:21

14.3
The dinosaur fits perfectly into the grotesque melange of ancient and modern, exotic and familiar objects that filled the Crystal Palace exhibition halls and exemplified Great Britain's status as a world-dominant power capable of colonizing the remote past as well as the remote places of the earth. (*Punch* 28 [3 February 1855], p. 50. Photo courtesy of the Newberry Library, Chicago.)

deeply rooted in natural antiquities buried in British soil. At the same time, the temporal and spatial "reach" of these creatures (back into geological "deep time" and overseas in the global distribution of this world-dominant animal group) makes them apt symbols of imperial sway. By contrast, the Jurassic Park dinosaurs are *not* rooted in any local or national "soil" and have no special identification with any nation-state. They are the product of "Ingen" (Intel plus genetics?), a multinational and multicultural corporation, and of an expert "team" that coordinates a Japanese genetic designer with a black systems analyst and a white South African game warden under the direction of a Yankee entrepreneur with a British accent.[3]

The Hawkins and Spielberg "resurrections" of the dinosaur share another common feature, and that is a certain ambivalence about the life that is being resurrected. There is more than a hint that the Victorian monsters would, if brought back to life, consume the avid consumers who come to view them (cp. figure 12.2). As the dry bones are assembled into a complete and living structure, they threaten to swallow up their creators. Hawkins's festive dinner party in the belly of the beast can be viewed as a scene of pregnancy, in which the new leviathan is "big" with the new men of a modern scientific age. But

THE EFFECTS OF A HEARTY DINNER AFTER VISITING THE ANTEDILUVIAN DEPARTMENT AT THE CRYSTAL PALACE.

it can also be seen as a Jonah image, in which the men have been swallowed up by the leviathan even as they celebrate its resurrection. *Punch* congratulated "the company on the era in which they live; for if it had been an earlier geological period, they might perhaps have occupied the Iguanodon's inside without having any dinner there."[4] The ritual meal on the flesh and bones of the totem animal takes a very strange twist indeed. This "consumer spectacle" is one in which the spectator witnesses his own consumption and incorporation by a creature that he has brought to life.

Spielberg's spectacle of resurrection and violent consumption, by contrast, bypasses the "dry bones" phase and the slow building up of an architectural framework to which clay or concrete "flesh" will be added by the sculptor. *Jurassic Park* conducts its reanimation at two levels, the genetic code and the digitalized image (see figure 35.1). The computer promises both to simulate real life in the biological laboratory with cloning and gene splicing, and to produce a vivid new cinematic illusion of life with electronic animation. The rather humorous ambivalence about the danger of the Victorian dinosaur has, in Spielberg's fantasy, given way to nightmarish anxieties about biological science, computer technology, commercial spectacle, and transnational corporate power run amok. The humor is still there (recall figure 11.5), but it is the thrill-ride humor of a scream turning to a laugh, a yawn, or nausea.

Between 1853 and 1993, the dinosaur has clearly come a long way, while maintaining its basic ritual form as the totem animal of modernity. The question is, how did it get from there to here? How has the image changed, and why? How have its changes been affected by specific changes in paleontological evidence and in larger biological paradigms (most notably Darwinism)? By changes in the technologies of representation, from sculpture to painting through cinema to robotics and digital animation? By changes in the financial basis of paleontology, and in the larger sphere of "modes of production" (the rise of modern banking and industrialism)? How are changes in the dinosaur image connected to the evolution of capitalism from small manufactory production to the multinational corporation? How do its changes reflect its relation to cultural elites, to nations, empires, governments, and religions? To changes in the technology of visual spectacle and display? To shifting fashions in paleontological science? To changes in the "structures of feeling" common to a culture, a period, a society undergoing the historical transformations we call modernity?

For those who like to have everything laid out in schematic form, you may stop off, if you wish, at the table below, which provides a historical tableau of the evolution of the dinosaur image. For those who prefer a more leisurely path, you may go on here to the very question of what it means to think of the dinosaur image (or any image for that matter) as undergoing an "evolutionary" series of transformations. Does it make sense to think of the history of an image as the evolution of a *visual* species? If so, what sort of forces of "cultural selection" have favored one sort of image over another? How are images born? How do they evolve and proliferate? Is it possible for an image to die out, to endure the cultural equivalent of extinction?

A SCHEMATIC HISTORY OF DINOSAUR IMAGES

	American Revolution to the Civil War	Gilded Age to the Depression	World War II to end of Cold War
Period	American Revolution to the Civil War	Gilded Age to the Depression	World War II to end of Cold War
Dino-type	Mammoth to Victorian dinosaur	Classic or modern dinosaur	Postmodernism; dinosaur renaissance
Paradigm	Structure	Energy	Information
Prototype	Archetype	Engine	Program
Extinction scenario	Catastrophe	Entropy	Chaos
Historical schema	Creationism	Revolution	Evolution
Exemplar	Ark, frame, building	Train, automobile	Cyborg
Energy source	Water and wind	Fossil fuels	Nuclear energy
Stage of capitalism	Manufactory production	Mechanical production	Biocybernetic production
Exhibition site	Peale's museum Crystal Palace	Peabody Museum, AMNH, Carnegie, Smithsonian	Shopping mall Theme park
Sponsors	Jefferson Queen Victoria	Peabody Morgan Carnegie Sinclair	McDonald's Ingen Corp. Universal Studios
Image makers	C. W. Peale W. Hawkins	Charles Knight R. Zallinger Winsor McCay Walt Disney	Gregory Paul John Gurche Steven Spielberg
Narrators	Jules Verne	Conan Doyle Edgar Rice Burroughs	Michael Crichton Italo Calvino
Narratives	*Journey to the Center of the Earth*	*Gertie the Dinosaur* *Lost World* *King Kong* *Fantasia*	*Flintstones* *Godzilla* *Jurassic Park*
Scientists	Cuvier Richard Owen T. H. Huxley	Cope and Marsh H. F. Osborn Barnum Brown R. C. Andrews	Robert Bakker Jack Horner Paul Sereno

ON THE EVOLUTION OF IMAGES

15

15.1

The new-model dinosaur since the 1960s has tended to be much lighter, quicker, more intelligent, and adaptable than its modern (1900–1960) predecessor. It is portrayed as a social animal, a warm-blooded, birdlike, pack hunter, not a cold-blooded, sluggish, solitary leviathan. Here we see *Iguanodon,* one of the principal dinosaurs of the Victorian era, under attack by *Deinonychus,* the sort of dinosaur that has been popularized in the figure of the *Velociraptor.* This is not only an image of the progress of dinosaur imaging, but a scene in which the new model is shown attacking the old. Would it be far-fetched to see this as an image of the relation between Microsoft and IBM (compare with figure 29.6)? Could this be an allegory of the replacement of corporate giantism by the new model of "downsized" business organization, stressing flexible accumulation, rapid deployment of task forces to problem areas, and teamwork? (Painting by John Gurche, *Deinonychus and Iguanodon,* © John Gurche.)

ART HISTORIANS (with the exception of Henri Focillon, mentioned earlier) do not generally think of images as "evolving" the way that species do in Darwinian theory. Images are made by artists. They are artificial objects, not organic creatures. If we want to know where they come from, much less what they mean, we need to look at the intentions of their makers, and not think of them in terms of fanciful analogies between the "reproduction of life" and the "reproduction of images" of life. As for dinosaur images, art historians don't think about them very much at all. Dinosaur images are not art: they are scientific illustration, or kitsch.

When historians of science look at dinosaur images, on the other hand, they are likely to come up with a model of "progressive evolution." That is, dinosaur images are seen as progressing from error to truth, from ignorance to understanding. Scientific images, including those of the dinosaur, evolve by steady, gradual improvement toward more and more accurate reflections of the actual thing they represent. This progress is enabled by the convergence of two kinds of innovation: on the one hand, more complete knowledge of comparative anatomy and the filling in of the fossil record provides a basis for more accurate descriptions and restorations; on the other, advances in imaging technology allow for more realistic, accurate, and vivid representations.

The only problem with this story of progressive evolution is that it doesn't fit the facts, either of the history of dinosaur images or of the history of images more generally. The history of scientific dinosaur images is generally divided into three periods (see the table above):

1. The "Victorian" or early modern era (1840–1900), a period of eclecticism inaugurated by Hawkins's "antediluvian monsters," in which dinosaurs are depicted in a variety of shapes reminiscent of reptiles, lizards, dragons, large mammals, birds, fishes, kangaroos, and amphibians.

2. The period of what Stephen Jay Gould calls "the modern consensus" (1900–1960), when dinosaurs take on their "classic" and still popular image as "swamp-bound monsters of sluggish disposition, plodding with somnolent strides . . . dimwitted and unresponsive to change" on a slow path to extinction.[1]

3. The period of the "dinosaur renaissance" since the 1960s, which has transformed the image of the dinosaur into that of a lively, intelligent, agile, birdlike, warm-blooded creature that works in groups to solve problems.[2]

If the *Iguanodon* was the marquee attraction of the Victorian period, the *T. rex* and *Brontosaurus* share the modern stage (with a supporting cast of triceratopses and stegosauruses). This period is usually associated with the paintings of Charles Knight, especially those that show dinosaurs as heavily armored leviathans poised for single combat, and with the huge Rudolph Zallinger mural, "The Age of Reptiles," at Yale's Peabody Museum, showing all the dinosaurs gathered in a single arcadian panorama. Our contemporary, "postmodern" dinosaur is exemplified by *Velociraptor*, who achieves stardom in Spielberg's rendering as a "clever girl," a fast-moving, team-playing problem solver who hunts in packs.[3]

One could describe this progression simply as a movement from the errors and ignorance of Victorian fantasy to the scientific accuracy and certainty of our own day. And there's no doubt that today's dinosaur images are based on much more fossil evidence and dramatically improved technologies for comparing anatomical data. But it should also be clear that the progression is far from "progressive" in some crucial ways. For one thing, most of the dinosaurologists who would subscribe to this general narrative (Robert Bakker, for instance) regard the modern era of the slow, stupid, reptilian figure as a *regression* in the evolution of the dinosaur image. Bakker sees this whole period as an oppressive orthodoxy that is now being overturned by his own "dinosaur heresies." He portrays his "dinosaur renaissance" as a *revival* of Victorian images, particularly those that (like T. H. Huxley's)[4] emphasize the birdlike characteristics.

In short, even the simplest story of "progress" in the evolution of the dinosaur image turns out to move not in a straightforwardly progressive fashion, but dialectically, taking a very long step back in order to move forward. And the story becomes even more complicated when one delves into the details. The boundaries of the "periods" can shift unpredictably, depending on what examples, or what level of history, one is discussing. The paintings of Charles Knight, for instance, were crucial in solidifying the modern consensus around the slow-moving leviathan. But some of Knight's paintings, as

we have already seen (in figure 9.1), portray much livelier, birdlike figures. The "modern consensus" about dinosaurs was more like a papering over of the deep contradictions in the taxonomic classification of the group. It divided them into two groups ("lizard hips" and "bird hips") with no common ancestor, and yet continued to pretend that "dinosaur" was the name of a natural group of animals. No wonder that the image of the modern dinosaur as obsolete and dull seemed to infect the science of paleontology itself during the thirties. It was a science that couldn't face the prospect that its central concept was incoherent, an arbitrary, artificial classification that failed to pick out a natural kind of animal. Dinosaurology was in danger of going the way of its object of research.

What do we learn from this history of dinosaur images? First, that if scientific images do "evolve" in any sense, it's highly unlikely that their development will simply be "progressive." (Not that this should surprise us: the evolution of life, in the Darwinian paradigm, is not necessarily progressive.[5] It may be "punctuated," as Stephen Jay Gould has argued, by moments of relatively rapid change, and it inevitably involves sequences of devolution, degeneration, and

15.2

The latest development in dinosaur imaging: seismic images of fossil structures can now be constructed digitally without any need for actual excavation of the bones. This technology promises a major advance in the accurate representation of fossil structures, but it may also threaten to render the old-style paleontological "dig" obsolete. Dr. Grant (Sam Neill), the paleontologist of *Jurassic Park*, hates computers, and fears that computer-cloned dinosaurs will make his whole profession—and his passion for digging—obsolete. (Film still, *Jurassic Park*.)

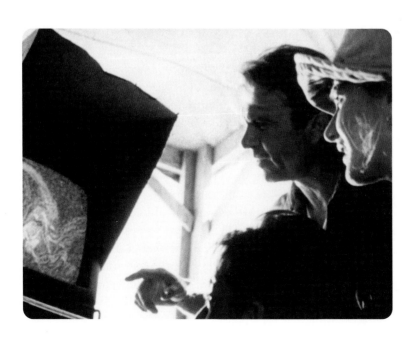

extinction.) This means that internal narratives of scientific progress will never be enough for the historian of scientific images. Scientists will always present their "latest findings," and their latest images, as the closest approximations to the truth, superseding all previous images and consigning them to the dustbin of history. "Truth," "novelty," "parsimony," and other shibboleths of this sort are forces of "cultural selection" in science's account of its own evolution. It is simply a built-in feature of the cultural formation we know as science, with all its attendant rituals, that "progress" is its most important product; progressivism is a rhetoric and an ideology that science cannot (and probably shouldn't try to) transcend. What we learn from the *history* of science, however, is that the claim of progress cannot be accepted at face value. The truth will always be provisional, temporary, and dependent on a more or less fragile consensus that is, in principle, always subject to challenge and therefore to change. This, in fact, is also part of the internal rhetoric of science when it is being frank about its claims, and not touting its latest results as "the truth" for popular belief.

Take the vast synthesis of the natural sciences known as "Darwinism," for instance. It is now widely believed that Darwin basically got it right about the meaning of life.[6] This still leaves a few questions unanswered, such as what we mean by "life" and what sort of rightness we are looking for. There are also debates about what Darwin actually said, or meant, and whether "Darwinism" is a coherent mode of thinking or a vast umbrella that covers a wide variety of notions, some very useful (natural selection), some rather silly or even dangerous (survival of the fittest). Some want to argue that Darwin got it right not only about biological life—the history of living things—but about social, cultural, and economic life as well. This is one of the great points of friction in contemporary intellectual life. Biological explanations of human behavior (tracing war to aggressive or predatory instincts, revolution to birth order, gender inequality to genetic coding, intelligence to racial stock) are notoriously easy, popular, and insidious. They reduce the complexities of human culture to patterns in animal behavior, and reinforce the status quo as "natural." This naturalizing of culture and society is what Marx called "ideology," and what I have been trying to render more specific under the rubric of "totemism," the systematic comparison of human beings to animals. When biology turns into the pseudoscience known as "sociobiology," it also becomes, as Marshall Sahlins has shown, a form of totemism.[7]

This doesn't mean, however, that biology and culture are utterly distinct, separate realms. If we learn anything from the dinosaur, it is that the flow of images, narratives, and concepts goes in both directions. The "life" of the dinosaur is at the intersection of nature and culture, biology and anthropology, the study of genes and of what have been called "memes," those cultural formations (like images themselves) that are *remembered* and passed on in human history.[8] While I think we should be skeptical about sociobiology and its (unacknowledged) totemism, then, I think we should be intensely interested in the intricate transactions between nature and culture, and the dis-

ciplines that attempt to explain them. One simple way of describing the position to be avoided here is "reductionism." Whenever culture is reduced to a mere projection, shadow, or mirror of nature—or vice versa—totemism is rearing its head. Unlike Marx, I do not think that totemism can be avoided or dispelled by modern criticism and rationality. My sense is that it has to be "worked through" (to quote Freud's phrase), lived out within a critical and historical struggle for understanding. Totemism is not merely a symptom that can be "cured" or relieved with a bit of self-consciousness. For one thing, "getting over" totemism would require a radically different relation between the human species and the natural environment; it would mean, among other things, a global revolution in ecological consciousness that now seems utterly utopian. For another thing, totemism is one of those crucial links between our supposedly modern, enlightened, and civilized mentality and those primitive, savage modes of thought we (mistakenly) suppose ourselves to have outgrown. For both these reasons, the totem, and especially our modern totem, the dinosaur, has "a life of its own," both as a scientific concept and as a cultural icon.

But how do we study the life of a cultural icon that is also a scientific object and the assembled relics of an extinct group of animals? What method is appropriate? To rely on Darwinism alone would clearly be a kind of reductionism. We need a synthesis of Darwin and those other two great early modern thinkers (now, alas, popularly dismissed as dinosaurs), Marx and Freud. We need Marx to understand the relation of dinosaurs to politics and economics, to the development of capitalism as a world system. We need Freud to grasp the psychological components of dinosaur fascination, its roots in unconscious processes of fantasy, identification, and desire. We also clearly need to adapt all three of our Victorian dinosaurs to the job at hand. All three have been associated at various moments with intellectual tyranny and reductionism. But they are still, like totemism and dinosaurs themselves, good to think *with*, especially if we can avoid thinking too much *of* them, turning them into idols or fetishes.

The very concept of an "evolution of images" is an ideal place to try out such a synthesis of Marx, Freud, and Darwin. Images are, as we have seen, a kind of artificial species. The dinosaur image is the intersection of cultural and natural determinants, a crossroads of scientific knowledge, social interests, and psychological desires. The dinosaur, as we shall see, has itself "evolved" from its original function as a counterexample to Darwinism into its current role as a kind of monument to the reign of Darwinism. Unlike most images, the dinosaur has an origin and development that are open to investigation. We know when it was invented, and we can describe how it changed.

These changes, however, clearly do not reflect a model of progressive evolution, but rather a dialectical, punctuated model of controversy, debate, and paradigm shift. The dinosaur, as we learned in chapter 8, is never seen "as such." It is always governed by the rule of what Ludwig Wittgenstein called "seeing as": the visual image is riddled with metaphor, with the representation of the unknown and the invisible in terms of the known and the familiar. The Victorians saw dinosaurs as terrible lizards, as reptilian hippos and rhinos, as scaly mammals, as kangaroos, as leathery, batlike birds, or just as all-purpose monsters and hybrids reminiscent of medieval dragons (see figure 10.1). The moderns settled on a view of them as giant erect reptiles. Now the postmoderns are attempting to forge a consensus around seeing them as birds. But this is occurring in a time when the relation of the unknown to the known, the invisible to the visible, has changed. The dinosaur is no longer an exotic, unfamiliar novelty; it is now the most publicized animal image on the planet. It hardly comes as a surprise, therefore, that the direction of "seeing as" is reversing field, and some paleontologists are beginning to urge us to see birds *as dinosaurs!* At this point, however, dinosaurology becomes so successful that it threatens to glut the market, to kill the romance and mystery of its object, and to disperse it into a dead metaphor, a framework for seeing almost anything "as" a dinosaur.[9] When Bakker concludes *The Dinosaur Heresies* by urging us to say, when we see Canadian geese flying north, "The dinosaurs are migrating, it must be spring!" we know that the cart is pulling the horse.

The internalist, progressivist history of scientific images depends upon a notion of visual transparency that ignores the inevitable role of metaphor in visual imaging. Paleontologist Dale Russell puts it this way: "Artists are the eyes of paleontologists, and paintings are the windows through which nonspecialists can see the dinosaurian world."[10] This clearly cannot be right. Artists, no matter how obedient, are not simply "eyes," nor are paleontologists simply "brains" waiting to be wired up to a cooperative retina. (If you want to think of the art-science collaboration in terms of body parts, a better comparison would be to think of the scientist as the eye and the artist as the hand. Their collaborative relation would then be more like "eye-hand coordination.") But the important point is that both scientists and artists are human beings, participants in cultures that impinge on their "pure" scientific pursuits, guaranteeing that their work will never be pure or pristinely objective. And even if their images were "windows through which nonspecialists can see the dinosaurian world" (which they clearly are not), those nonspecialists would also be coming to those windows not with pure, innocent eyes, but with preconceptions, fantasies, and prejudices much like those shared by the scientists and artists. There is no getting around "seeing as" to simple seeing as such. The innocent eye, as E. H. Gombrich showed long ago, is blind.

All this might be put in the form of a much less controversial claim: that the history of dinosaur images (like that of any other scientific representation, especially one put into mass circulation) is the product of a larger history than the sequence of events internal to science. From the standpoint of an iconologist, who looks at the history of images across media and across the boundaries of art and science, their history is more like the history of everything else in the period from 1840 to 2000: filled with crises, conflicts,

reversals, and multiple levels of determination. The wonderful histories of paleontology by Adrian Desmond, Martin Rudwick, Peter Bowler, Robert West Howard, Edwin Colbert, and others have made clear what a weird and intricate relation bone and fossil science has with social, political, and cultural issues. While the evolution of dinosaur images might seem incredibly brief compared with the history of dinosaurs themselves (150 years as contrasted with 170 million), their iconological history is probably just as complex and filled with incident. After all, not a whole lot happened in the average century or millennium of the long "Age of Reptiles." It is what Lévi-Strauss characterizes as a "cold" historical period, in contrast to the "hot" era of modernity. It has the temporality of a "frozen zone." Even a catastrophic (much less a gradual) extinction probably took many thousands of years to occur.

By contrast, the century and a half since dinosaurs first appeared in public has been filled with momentous transformations in the human condition and the physical condition of the earth. In that time, empires have risen and fallen, major revolutions and radical social experiments have occurred, new technologies, scientific paradigms, and habitats have been created, and the global ecosystem has itself begun to be modified by human activity. Most notably, the rate of extinction of plant and animal species has accelerated rapidly,[11] and a new, distinctly modern phenomenon has emerged in the mass extermination of human beings. The technologies of mass destruction, and the willingness to industrialize genocide and mass death, have reached unprecedented levels.

The history of the dinosaur image cannot be understood without connecting it to these larger issues. The following chapters, therefore, will revisit the Victorian, modern, and postmodern dinosaur images—the three stages of evolution—sketching out the relations of these images to larger cultural, social, and political forces. As a prelude to this history, however, it is important to reconstruct some of the "prehistory" of the dinosaur image—the era just before the invention of the dinosaur concept, when the emergent science of paleontology was building a public space in which dinosaurs could appear. Before something new can appear on the stage of history, that stage has to be built.

THOMAS JEFFERSON, PALEONTOLOGIST

> The President had spread the bones out in a large unused and unfurnished room in the White House in which he maintained other personal collections. This room, which served as what may be considered to have been the first paleontological laboratory in the country, had previously been used by Abigail Adams as a laundry drying room. It remained unused except for storage after Jefferson's tenure until the Jackson administration, and it is now the elegant East Room of the White House.
>
> —SYLVIO BEDINI, *Thomas Jefferson and American Vertebrate Paleontology*

ALTHOUGH THE DINOSAUR is an international (in the nineteenth century, a "transatlantic") phenomenon, it has a special relationship with the United States. After the founding of paleontology by Cuvier in France and the birth of dinosaurology with Owen in England, the action moves to America, whose western wilderness becomes the site of a "bone rush" alongside the various "gold rushes," and whose eastern metropolises become the sites of major new museums in which dinosaurs are featured attractions. The American Museum in New York, the Carnegie Museum in Pittsburgh, the National Museum in Washington, DC, and the Field Museum in Chicago are among the major institutions that emerge at the end of the nineteenth century and come to dominate paleontology in the modern era. Given the abundance of American bone resources, this development may seem simply "natural," but there is more to the story than that. The American obsession with bones, especially with *big* fossil bones left by gigantic creatures, has a history going back to the founding fathers, and is woven inextricably into an emergent sense of national destiny from the beginning.[1]

16.1 (Page 110)

The first museums in the United States were devoted to natural history. Lacking the cultural antiquities and ancient civilizations of Europe, the new nation emphasized the richness and antiquity of its "natural constitution," the flora and fauna that could be seen in North America as living specimens and as fossil remains. Here Charles Willson Peale prepares to unveil his reconstruction of the American *incognitum,* **or mastodon (whose legs and ribs can be glimpsed beyond the curtain). The jaw- and thigh-bones are visible in the lower right corner.** (Oil painting on canvas by Charles Willson Peale, *The Artist in His Museum,* 1822. 103¾ by 79⅞ inches. Courtesy of the Pennsylvania Academy of the Fine Arts, Philadelphia. Gift of Mrs. Sarah Harrison [The Joseph Harrison, Jr. Collection].)

If every nation has to invent an origin and an antiquity for itself, the United States sought its ancient origins in nature. Unlike Europe, with its relics of ancient civilizations, the young American nation had only two "aboriginal" resources: its native peoples, already on the endangered species list, dying off from diseases, dispossession, and the violence of white settlers; and its flora and fauna, many of them unknown in Europe, available in an abundance and variety unknown in the Old World. In the period of the American Revolution, institutions dedicated to natural history were established in Charleston and Philadelphia with the aim of gathering and cataloguing the entire range of North American biological diversity.[2] This was partly a practical project, given the nation's largely agricultural economic base. But it also had an ideological purpose: to demonstrate to the world (and to its own inhabitants) that North America had a rich and distinguished natural "constitution" that would be the basis for a great national destiny.

The principal defender of this natural constitution was, appropriately enough, one of the key framers of the written constitution, Thomas Jefferson. In his *Notes on the State of Virginia* (1781), written at a time when the Revolution was in deep trouble (Benedict Arnold had just inva-ded Virginia and forced Jefferson into retirement at his country retreat),[3] Jefferson defended the new nation against a less imme-diate threat: the "imputation of impotence in the conception and nourishment of animal life on a large scale."[4] At a moment when his own embryonic nation was in danger of being still-born, Jefferson mustered evidence from natu-ral history sufficient "to have stifled, in its birth, the opinion of a writer [the great French natural historian Buffon] that nature is less active, less energetic on one side of the globe than she is on the other," and that the cold, moist climate of North America was inimical to the fertility and potency of living things (47). As proof of his opinion, Buffon claimed that animals in the New World were smaller than those in Europe, that

animals brought to the New World had "degenerated" because of the climate, and that the New World had fewer varieties of animals than Europe.

Jefferson had many answers to these slanders on America's natural constitution (he once hosted a dinner party in Paris for Buffon at which American six-footers—including himself—were featured), but by far the most important was the abundant supply of what he called "the great northern bones" of the New World. Noting that "the tusks and skeletons" found in the mountains west of the Missouri were "much larger than those of the elephant, and the grinders many times greater than those of the hippopotamus, and essentially different in form" (44), Jefferson argued that "the largest of all terrestrial beings" (47) had flourished in North America. The bones of the "American *incognitum*," named the mammoth or mastodon, "bespeak an animal of six times the volume of the elephant, as Mons. de Buffon has admitted" (45). "Nature," he argued,

> seems to have drawn a belt of separation between these two tremendous animals . . . to have assigned to the elephant the regions South of these confines, and those North to the mammoth, founding the constitution of the one in her extreme of heat, and that of the other in the extreme of cold. (46)

Jefferson's sense of the word "constitution" here is based in a whole cluster of commonplaces in natural philosophy. The "constitution" of an animal is rather like what biologists today call its genotype, the program or pattern carried in the genetic code that gives each species its specific form, shape, size, and structural organization—what Jefferson called their "elaborative organs." Jefferson held a relatively conservative antievolutionist position on the question of the natural constitution of animal species. Just as he had written in the Declaration of Independence that "all men" were "endowed by their Creator with certain inalienable rights," he contended that "every race of animals seems to have received from their Maker certain laws of extension at the time of their formation." Climate and diet may have some effect on the actual individual specimen, but the archetypal structure and size of the animal is laid down by the great framer of the natural constitution: "all the manna of heaven," declared Jefferson, "would never raise the mouse to the bulk of the mammoth" (47). The mammoth was constituted to fit in its proper ecological niche or habitat: "the Frozen zone" to the far north "may be the Achme of their vigour, as that of the Torrid is of the elephant."

Jefferson resisted the idea that the American mammoth might be an extinct species that had flourished during a different climatological era. His chief evidence for its continued existence came, ironically enough, from the Indians whose impending extinction he was documenting in his *Notes.* Jefferson reports the speech of a Delaware chieftain who

> informed him that it was a tradition handed down from their fathers, "That in ancient times a herd of these tremendous animals came to the Big-bone licks, and began an universal destruction of the bear, deer, elks, buffaloes, and other animals, which had been created for the use of the Indians." (43)

"The Great Man above" intervenes and kills the giant animals with lightning bolts—all but "the big bull" who flees "over the Ohio, over the Wabash, the Illinois, and finally over the great lakes, where he is living at this day."

Jefferson is in a position rather like the "New Ones" of Calvino's story of the last dinosaur. He is in a transition space between traditional knowledge, oral tales of monsters from "ancient times," and the new Enlightenment science of vertebrate paleontology, of which he will become the American patron. His argument shuttles between myth and legalistic reasoning against "negative evidence": the fact that the northern territories remained to be mapped and explored, Jefferson argued, made it possible that the mammoth would eventually return or be discovered living in some remote northern region. This "lost world" argument would become the basis of paleontological fictions about dinosaurs in the novels of Jules Verne, Arthur Conan Doyle, and Edgar Rice Burroughs. For Jefferson, however, the yet-to-be explored northern territories provided a skeptical hedge against unfounded speculation and a refuge for the perfect stability of natural constitutions.

16.2

"I would propose, therefore, that you should come a few days before Congress rises, so as to satisfy that article of your curiosity. The bones are spread in a large room, where you can work at your leisure. . . . It is a precious collection, consisting of upwards of three hundred bones . . ." Letter from Thomas Jefferson to Dr. Caspar Wistar, 20 March 1808. There is no surviving image of Jefferson's bone collection in the East Room of the White House; this installation by Allan McCollum of bone castings from Dinosaur National Monument will have to do as a substitute. See chapter 37 for further discussion. (Allan McCollum, *Lost Objects*, Carnegie Museum of Art, Philadelphia, PA, 1991.)

frames, skeletons, constitutions

For thirty years following the American Revolution, Jefferson's public career as Secretary of State, Vice President, and President of the United States was accompanied by a continued passion for paleontology.[1] Some commentators have regarded Jefferson's interest in natural history as a mere leisure occupation to relieve the pressures of public office.[2] But Jefferson was not given to idle pursuits, and it is clear that his avid search for "big bones" was deeply connected with his sense of the natural constitution of the American nation. When Jefferson urged Congress to authorize the Lewis and Clark expedition of 1803 (which he helped personally to finance), he urged the explorers to investigate Big Bone Lick in Missouri and to send specimens of large-animal fossils back to Washington. He set aside what is now the East Room of the White House as a "bone room" for the study of these relics, and he missed no opportunity to send shipments of big bones off to France. He presented a complete moose skeleton to Buffon in 1787, and the remains of a mammoth went to the National Institute in Paris in 1808 with a cover letter that opened with the following remark:

> Washington, July 14, 1808: To Monsieur de la Cepede. If my recollection does not deceive me, the collection of the remains of the animal incognitum of the Ohio (sometimes called the mammoth) possessed by the Cabinet of Natural History at Paris, is not very copious.[3]

One can almost imagine Jefferson relishing the enjoyment of bestowing a rare and valuable gift

> A constitution is not a thing in name only, but in fact. It has not an ideal, but a real existence; and wherever it cannot be produced in visible form, there is none.
>
> —THOMAS PAINE, *The Rights of Man* (1791–92)

on a nation that, for all its vast cultural riches, was "not very copious" in its natural treasures, not well endowed with big bones, and (for all its eminent scientific authorities) sadly mistaken about the "impotence" of America's natural constitution. Is the sending of the letter on Bastille Day just a coincidence?

If Jefferson had learned anything from the famous debates between Edmund Burke and Thomas Paine on the nature of a modern constitution, it was that it is not enough just to "have" a constitution: it must be made visible and public. For Paine and Burke, this debate came down to the choice between a visible *written* constitution, on the model of the French "Declaration of the Rights of Man," and the English model of an *invisible,* unwritten constitution based in oral tradition, custom, and common law.[4]

Jefferson's obsession with big bones was not confined to learned correspondence with paleontologists or the bone room of the White House. Equally important to him was the public display of the American mammoth, a way of making the natural constitution of North America as publicly visible as its political constitution, while emphasizing America's ties with the scientific and political revolutions going on in France. Shortly after Jefferson's inauguration as the "Mammoth President" in 1801, Charles Willson Peale excavated the skeletons of three mastodons from a marsh in southeastern New York. Peale's mammoth became the premier attraction at his natural history museum in Philadelphia, which Jefferson supported. Peale hoped to create the first truly national and public museum in America, a place where the mammoth would serve as "a monument, not only of some stupendous creation, and some wonderful revolution in nature," but also to the private labors of Peale himself, who was a veteran of the Revolution and a self-made man

> **The Constitution of the United States— May "its ribs be as ribs of brass, and its back-bone as molten iron."**
>
> —*The Port-Folio* (1802)

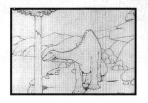

exemplary of Jeffersonian Republicanism.[5] The mammoth became, in short, the first symbolic "political animal" of the United States, an emblem of Jefferson's vision of an ever-expanding continental empire of small farmers and artisans. Against this vision was ranged the ideology of Alexander Hamilton and the Federalists, who opposed Jefferson's French-oriented and deistic natural theology with an English model based in urbanization, commerce, and a strong central government.

Jefferson's aim, like that of every American politician since, was to create the illusion that his party was above politics, and that his vision of a natural constitution would, like the paper constitution, provide a frame within which all parties could cooperate. In his inaugural address in 1801, he stressed the theme of national unity: "We are all republicans; we are all federalists," he declared, urging tolerance for all dissent, even to those who would destroy the basic framework of the U.S. Constitution: "If there be any among us who wish to dissolve this union, or to change its republican form, let them stand undisturbed, as monuments of the safety with which error of opinion may be tolerated where reason is left free to combat it" (33).

Needless to say, this sort of rhetorical sleight of hand was no more successful in Jefferson's time than it is in ours. And the most vulnerable point of Jefferson's "natural constitution" was in its visible, monumental, and public image—the giant skeleton of the mammoth. William Cullen Bryant (a precocious 13-year-old at the time) showered ridicule on Jefferson's obsession with natural history as a distraction from the duties of his office:

> Go wretch, resign the presidential chair,
> Disclose thy secret measures foul or fair
> Go, search, with curious eye, for horned frogs,
> Mongst the wastes of Louisianan bogs;
> Or where Ohio rolls his turbid stream
> Dig for huge bones, thy glory and thy theme.[6]

17.1

Cornelius Tiebout, engraved portrait of Thomas Jefferson as a man of science, 1801. Jefferson's interest in paleontology earned him the title of the "Mammoth President."

Paleontology, then as now, was anything but a neutral science. It was associated with French atheism and materialism, with the memories of a recent re-volution that had led to a Reign of Terror, with the impiety of a "curious eye" that pries into nature. The great American bones had long ago been identified by Cotton Mather "as the remains of Nephilum, the half-human/half-divine giants destroyed by God in the biblical flood."[7] Fancy French theories about vast stretches of geological time seemed as threatening to traditional cultural (that is, Christian) values then as deconstruction does today. In short, the bones that Jefferson hoped to erect in a framework emblematic of national consensus became bones of contention. The national monument was a target of ridicule from the beginning, and Peale's museum became a penny arcade, passing into the hands of P. T. Barnum.[8]

It is crucial to keep in mind this mockery and disavowal of the first national animal when we try to assess the status and significance of its totemic descendant, the dinosaur, in its later American incarnations. For one thing, it may help us to keep a sense of proportion about the importance of such monuments in relation to other objects of national pride, from the grand parks and landscapes of America to the classical architecture of Washington, DC, to the skyscrapers of New York and Chicago. America's big bones and monster skeletons are important, but just *how* important? Are they monumental allegories of the natural American constitution, or just a silly kind of national kitsch? How can we get their seriousness into a stable relation with their silliness?[9]

The three-way metaphoric equation of a nation with a giant body and an architectural framework was a well-established trope in political and religious discourse. The comparison of the human body to a temple, and the comparison of the church to both the body of Christ and to the assembled congregation, had made this triple play a commonplace. Hobbes's *Leviathan* had made explicit the association of the biblical sea monster with the idea of a commonwealth: "For by Art is created that great Leviathan called a Common-wealth, or State . . . which is but an Artificiall Man . . . in which the Soveraignty is an Artificiall Soul."[10] When Theodor Adorno later declares that dinosaur discoveries, "like the repulsive humoristic craze for the Loch Ness Monster and the King Kong film, are collective projections of the monstrous total State,"[11] he is tapping into this same metaphor, giving it an apocalyptic turn reinforced by fresh memories of fascism and the Holocaust. Adorno certainly was aware of the defense of Hobbes's Leviathan by the Nazi political theorist Carl Schmitt, who traced the dragon's fading from its medieval function as a legendary creature and Germanic tribal emblem into its use by Hobbes as a metaphor for the modern absolutist and totalitarian state. Schmitt's account of the Leviathan as "the unity of the political commonwealth in the image of a powerful monster that combined god, man, animal, and machine" has an uncanny similarity to the figure of the dinosaur.[12] The difference is that the dinosaur, despite its cultural function as an emblem of states and nations, is rarely acknowledged to be playing this role. And despite

its *terribilita,* the dinosaur tends to be presented as tamed, domesticated, under control. Schmitt laments the "eviscerating" of Hobbes's Leviathan: "What could have been a grand signal of restoration of the vital energy and political unity . . . became a grotesque horror picture." Leviathan is placed "like other saurian[s] and mastodons, under protection in a preserve," and is displayed "as a museum curiosity in a zoo" (81). Adorno, like Stephen Spielberg, envisions the possibility of the monster breaking out of the museum. Perhaps this is why *Schindler's List* and *Jurassic Park* seem to correspond at so many levels.

Jefferson was certainly no Hobbesian. He anticipated Adorno's wariness about the "monstrous total State," and thought that a judicious framing of the different "organs" of government in a constitutional balance of powers would prevent his American mammoth from behaving like an absolutist leviathan.[13] He also believed that, however unalterable the natural constitution might be, artificial, legislative constitutions could (and should) be changed with every generation. A weak central government and a decentralized body politic, with autonomy for individual states and for the individual small farmer or artisan, was fundamental to the Jeffersonian vision. This vision depended crucially on the openness and emptiness of the western frontier as a space for imperial expansion. This would not be the British style of empire, with its occupying armies and world-encircling navy, but a "soft," gradual, natural empire of civilizing progress. In a very real sense, the existence of an unknown frontier, of a yet-to-be-explored territory where the mastodon might still be living, was a condition of Jefferson's expansionist policies.

But Jefferson never seems to have forgotten that he was dealing in metaphors. He certainly understood that his big bones would play a relatively small part in the fortunes of the nation.

His sly teasing of the French natural historians as he sent them a crate of mammoth bones suggests a certain urbane and cosmopolitan detachment about the whole matter. On retirement from the presidency, he turned away from natural history and busied himself with the framing of a different kind of constitution: the institutional structure of the nation's first public university, the University of Virginia, which he designed down to its precise architectural details. The bones he had gathered so carefully in the White House were dispersed to various collections, never to be reassembled.

If Jefferson's public life had been dedicated to the framing of a national constitution based in natural theology, his retirement was devoted to leaving in place a framework for reproducing his legacy in future generations of national leaders—the wealthy sons of Virginia. Jefferson's structure of "huge bones" turned out to be a kind of transitional object[14]—an obsession bordering on fetishism for a time, but something he was willing to let go. If the mammoth served as a monument to the "republican form" of government, it was a monument Jefferson was willing to see dismantled or defaced, if only to incorporate even the vandals into its structure. He could call the U.S. Constitution "the ark of our safety, and grand palladium of our peace and happiness,"[15] but warn with equal force against those who "look at constitutions with sanctimonious reverence, and deem them like the ark of the covenant, too sacred to be touched" (199). This is something we should bear in mind as we trace the ambivalence provoked by the dinosaur, its double status as an object of monumental awe and trivializing mockery, and the constant revision and contention that has surrounded it.

What does the American mastodon finally "mean"? The deep truth was glimpsed by the Delaware chieftain who saw it as a reminder of a time of terrible violence, when game was scarce and extinction faced the tribe and the animals it depended upon. What the Indian orator did not see (at least in Jefferson's recital of his words) was that the traditional tale was a projection of a possible—indeed, an inevitable—future. In a very precise sense, the arrival of white men in America meant the return of the mastodon, not just in their "exhumation" of its bones from the ground, but in their effect on the environment—killing the game, taking the land, and dispossessing the Indians. The coming of the mastodon was, like that of the medieval dragon, the omen of a plague of death and destruction from the Indian point of view.

Jefferson, as Secretary of State in 1781, could see this plague coming as he wrote his *Notes on the State of Virginia*. (Actually, it had already come, in the form of diseases brought from the Old World throughout the seventeenth and eighteenth centuries.)[16] He urged respect for the Indian nations, and argued against aggressive encroachment on their lands. They would, he thought, be absorbed soon enough by the inevitable progress of civilization.[17] By the time Jefferson was president, however, the issue of what is politely called "removal" had become unavoidable. The ideology of the "Mammoth presidency" guaranteed as much, for its vision of a coast-to-coast continental empire of small farmers and independent artisans was death to the Indian way of life, especially the Indian understanding of land as a collective possession. Jefferson

designed policies to lure the Indians into debts that they would have to pay off by giving up their land.[18] He took measures to discourage them from hunting and encourage them to go into trade, agriculture, and manufacture—in short, to give up their traditional economic system, their national identity, their customary laws and governmental structures, and above all, their land.

Jefferson thus built the structure of policies, legal devices, and ideological facades that made Andrew Jackson possible. Jackson, "land speculator, merchant, slave trader, and the most aggressive enemy of the Indians in early American history,"[19] put the iron fist into the Jeffersonian vision when he began the systematic genocide of the American Indian. The Jefferson who could not believe that God's natural constitution would ever allow a species to be extinguished wound up as the creator of a political and legal constitution designed to wipe out the native peoples of North America.

17.2
The bones of *Megalonyx jeffersoni.*

123

THE VICTORIAN DINOSAUR

IN NATURAL HISTORY the dinosaur precedes the mastodon. In cultural history it is the other way around. The image of the mammoth, and its function as a monument to American national and imperial destiny, was not lost on the British. Peale's mammoth, housed in Independence Hall in Philadelphia, was a model for the way in which science and art, commerce and politics could be brought together to form a potent symbol of a nation's natural constitution. If America had a mastodon that could be scientifically certified as a native, indigenous, aboriginal species (Jefferson saw the importance of distinguishing it from the Asian mammoth and the African elephant), then the glory of Britain could be secured, as the title of Richard Owen's report suggested, by a display of "British Fossil Reptiles."[1]

Owen, who wanted to be known as "our English Cuvier," was also quite conscious of a threat on the other flank. French materialism and atheism, and especially the Lamarckian hypothesis of "the transmutation of species," a "march of development occasioning a progressive ascent in the organic scale" (196), had to be vigorously opposed on both political and theological grounds. Owen designed the dinosaur explicitly as a refutation of progressive evolution, treating the terrible lizards as evidence of an "archetypal" theory of creation: "specific characters," he argued, are "impressed upon" each species "at their creation, and have been neither derived from improvement of a lower, nor lost by progressive development into a higher type" (202). If progressive evolution *were* true, Owen argued, it should be visible in the history

18.1

In contrast to the mastodon reconstruction of Peale (see figure 16.1), the Hawkins models were "total fabrications": that is, they did not contain a single bone or fossil trace of the original animals but were constructed entirely out of modern materials—brick, cement, and iron reinforcement. (Benjamin Waterhouse Hawkins, *Iguanodon* sculpture at Crystal Palace Park, London. Photo © Steve McCarthy, 1994.)

of fossil reptiles because "reptiles form the class which is least fixed in its characters, and is most transitional in its range of modifications" (197). If this sinuous, slippery, shape-shifting animal didn't evolve, surely none of them did. For Owen, dinosaurs exemplified a "height of reptilian achievement" compared with which modern reptiles could only be seen as degraded, simpler specimens.[2]

Although Owen was too cagey ever to say it out loud, it seems clear that he believed in a theory of continuous or "staggered" creation, in which God introduced successive species at different eras of natural history, and then wiped them out or allowed them to degenerate and die of "natural" causes.[3] Since the fossil evidence did not support the notion that dinosaurs had been wiped out by floods, Owen speculated that the cause of their demise was air pollution—more precisely, a change from a high level of car-

bon dioxide compatible with reptilian metabolism to a high oxygen level more suitable for warm-blooded mammals. This may have been a persuasive notion in the smog-choked air of Victorian London, but it made it difficult to explain why so many other reptiles had survived. Unlike Jefferson, Owen was fully persuaded by Cuvier's doctrine of catastrophic extinction, but like Jefferson, he understood that the possession and explanation of big bones was a matter of national honor. Owen's dinosaurs, as Adrian Desmond points out, "were created less by God than by human ingenuity. . . . He *needed* a race of super-reptiles, so he created one."[4]

The influence of the American mastodon on the British dinosaur may not be merely a matter of cultural translation. There is a persistent tradition in the history of paleontology that Charles Willson Peale, the excavator of the mastodon, was a close friend of the father of Waterhouse Hawkins, the designer of the Crystal Palace dinosaurs. Hawkins's famous dinner party in the belly of the *Iguanodon* model may have been staged as a reenactment of the mastodon dinner at which his father was present. The reconstruction of the mastodon was celebrated on Christmas Eve, 1801; the restoration of the dinosaur, on New Year's Eve, 1853. Like Peale, Waterhouse Hawkins came from that class of inventors and "self-made men" who were providing the technological innovations (steam engines, cotton gins, iron bridges) on which modernity depends.[5] Hawkins's father may have been the inventor of a "portable grand piano" that provided the music for Peale's celebration.[6] This transatlantic father-son genealogy—even if it turns out to be a fable—may help us to measure the cultural evolution of the giant bone monument over a half century, as it migrates from America to Britain and ultimately back to America.

The most obvious and visible contrast is in the material character of the monuments themselves. The American mastodon was what paleontologists call a "reconstruction," an assemblage of actual bones into a total skeletal form supported by a scaffold, with the missing bones supplied by sculpted wooden parts. The dinosaur was what is called a "restoration," a sculptural representation of the living animal, complete with skin, hair, and soft tissues.[7] These two constructions are rather like the two stages in Ezekiel's story of the dry bones, the moment when the dry bones miraculously "came together, bone to his bone" (chapter 37, verse 7) and the moment when "the sinews and flesh came up upon them, and the skin covered them above" (verse 8). (Movie dinosaurs take us to verse 10, when "the breath came into them, and they lived.") The difference between the American and British monuments is the distinction between a real, natural skeleton and an artificial, fabricated surface, between what Jefferson and Paine would have called a "visible constitution" or "frame" and a frame that is hidden from sight, supporting the illusion of a natural surface.

It is one of the most remarkable features in the evolution of the dinosaur image that its public life begins not with a skeletal reconstruction, but with an artificial restoration, indeed, a *total fabrication,* of the living appearance. In the evolutionary history of this animal image, the surface precedes the

skeletal structure, and the popular illusion precedes the scientific display—at least as far as public consumption is concerned. I do not mean to suggest that Owen and other paleontologists began from these iron, brick, and cement restorations. Owen was a brilliant anatomist, and his verbal descriptions of dinosaur skeletons (based on remarkably sparse fossil evidence) are compellingly precise. But they could convey nothing of the appearance of dinosaurs to the general public.[8] Owen's words were, as Hawkins suggested, just "dry bones," "only . . . names, and not the things themselves."[9]

The "things themselves" were sculpted buildings of brick and cement, iron ribs and legs, that contained not a single material fragment of the things they represented. Even Owen had only fragmentary evidence to work with, projecting his verbal reconstructions mainly from skull bones. By contrast, Peale excavated and reconstructed two nearly complete skeletons of the mastodon, filling in the missing parts of each by using the pattern of its companion, and sculpting wood and papier-mâché "fill-ins" for missing bones. Peale's role in the production of the mastodon is much more comprehensive than Hawkins's part in the dinosaur. Peale digs up the bones, assembles the skeleton, hires a sculptor to help with the missing parts, and displays the results in a museum of which he is the founder and proprietor. In that museum, he hangs a monumental painting of himself raising a curtain to reveal his collection and the mastodon. The whole cycle of production and display is calculated to represent Peale's "mammoth" labors as a self-made man, a heroic exemplar of the new Jeffersonian republic. While Waterhouse Hawkins is also a self-made man of many skills, he does not have the same status as an independent entrepreneur and jack-of-all-trades in an artisanal economy. (Laura Rigal calls this early nineteenth-century economic phase "manufactory production," the stage of small entrepreneurial capital that precedes industrialism.)[10] Hawkins is in the service of a great scientist (Owen) to whom he must submit his judgment, and in the service of a great corporation (the Crystal Palace Company) that will cut off his funding before he can complete what would have been his crowning achievement: a life-size, lifelike restoration of the American mammoth.

The setting and reception of mastodon and dinosaur also stand in sharp relief to each other. The mammoth is the feature attraction of a privately owned "public" museum that, like the traditional collector's cabinet, attracts those who want to contemplate and study the wonders of nature. (Peale's own painting [see figure 16.1] shows only a few visitors—a woman gesturing in amazement at the giant skeleton, and a man absorbed in examining a bird specimen.) Hawkins's dinosaurs are located in a suburban theme park outside London, one of the "outdoor" attractions in one of the greatest mass spectacles of the nineteenth century. Forty thousand people attended the opening ceremony on 10 June 1854, and the Crystal Palace averaged 2 million visitors a year until the end of the century. Hawkins's dinosaurs immediately generated a brood of secondary "tie-ins" in the form of miniature replicas, toys, and educational pamphlets that ensured their circulation among children throughout the empire.[11] Hawkins predicted that his system of "visual education" would present these creatures "to the people; and not only the people in the restricted sense of the word, but to the million, including the well-informed and those above the average in education and acquirements" (89).

If the mastodon was the product of individual industry in the service of a breakaway settler colony aiming to invent a past for itself, the dinosaur was the monstrous monument of the world's largest empire at the peak of its glory and self-confidence. The great age when reptiles ruled the earth was a fitting epitome of the naturalness of the historic mission of the British empire in the modern age. Hobbes's Leviathan became a global concern while Britannia ruled the waves.

COMING TO AMERICA

"WESTWARD THE COURSE of empire takes its way," wrote Bishop Berkeley over two hundred years ago in his treatise *On the Prospect of Planting the Arts and Sciences in America*. The dinosaur image was naturally destined to migrate to America, and ultimately to the rest of the world. (It was already, in the nineteenth century, migrating from France to Germany and to Eastern Europe, where Louis Dollo's reproductions of the Belgian *Iguanodon* led the way.) Today the "modernization" of backward African countries is measured in part by their willingness to sustain up-to-date scientific dinosaur excavations and give up traditional superstitions about the great bones.[1] Everywhere that the modern world goes, it finds the dinosaur already there waiting for it. Places that don't have dinosaurs by nature (like Southern California) produce them by art. The La Brea tar pits may boast their authentic mastodons, but they must also offer life-size robotic dinosaur models to gratify popular demand.

The migration of dinosaurology to America is sometimes seen as a natural inevitability, given the brute fact of the abundance of easily accessible bones in the New World and the long-standing interest in natural history as a national pursuit. North America's "bone fields," like its reserves of minerals and precious metals, were

> There is apparently much truth in the belief that the wonderful progress of the United States, as well as the character of the people, are the results of natural selection; for the more energetic, restless, and courageous men from all parts of Europe have emigrated during the last ten or twelve generations to that great country.
>
> —DARWIN, *The Descent of Man* (1871)

a natural resource awaiting exploitation in the midst of what chroniclers never tire of calling a "virgin wilderness," a phrase that erases the presence of native populations. From a scientific point of view, the abundance of fossils and the vast number of complete skeletons promised an access to ancient times unheard of in the fragmentary and deeply buried fossil record of Europe.[2] Actually, the survival of the North American bone reserves was not merely a "natural fact," but a result of a rather consistent set of Native American cultural attitudes toward them. The Delaware Indians who reported their

Wherever the European has trod, death seems to pursue the aboriginal.

—DARWIN, *Voyage of the Beagle* (1839)

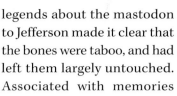

legends about the mastodon to Jefferson made it clear that the bones were taboo, and had left them largely untouched. Associated with memories (and perhaps premonitions) of famine and war, the bones were relics of God's justice and mercy—his destruction of the enemies of the Indians and his protection of them from extermination.

There were similar legends about large animal bones among the Plains Indians. The big bones found in the bluffs of Nebraska and Dakota were thought by the Sioux to be the remains of the Unktehi, subterranean and sub-aquatic giants and reptilian monsters who were big enough to eat men, and whose appearance would make one go crazy or blind.[3] The Unktehi were sometimes described as huge oxen, or as giant rattlesnakes with legs, and their destroyers were the sky gods, especially the Thunderbird. Despite their archaic, ancient pedigree, the Unktehi were often depicted with modern metaphors: "Its back-bone is like a cross-cut saw, being flat and notched like a cog wheel" (441); its "den" is "constructed of iron." One legendary sighting even makes the water monster sound like a strangely familiar spectacle on the Missouri in the 1870s: "Long ago . . . the people saw a strange thing in the Missouri River. At night there was some red object, shining like fire, making the water roar as it passed upstream. (441)." Given the catastrophic results for Indians of the arrival of the iron horse and the paddle-wheel steamboat in their country, it is hard to see their perception of these monsters as Unktehi as a mistake.

One of the still unsolved puzzles of the bone rush is the curious tolerance shown by the Indians for bone hunters.

19.1
After the Civil War, the dinosaur came to America at the invitation of the New York City Board of Commissioners of Central Park. If not for the opposition of Boss Tweed, this scene of ancient American life might still be there. (New York City Parks Photo Archive.)

19.2

Unlike Hawkins's reinforced concrete reconstructions of ancient life at the Crystal Palace, his *Hadrosaurus* was a skeletal construction based on the most complete fossil remains known in his time. His *Hadrosaurus* was reconstructed for the 1876 centenary of the Declaration of Independence and was recently elevated to the status of the "Official New Jersey State Dinosaur." (Victor Petryakov and Rais Muharamov, New York City Parks Photo Archive.)

19.3

The preeminent American dinosaur is not a sprawling quadruped like those Hawkins constructed for the Crystal Palace, but an erect biped, most notably the *Hadrosaurus,* whose skeletal reconstruction is shown here standing in the background of Hawkins's studio, while a sphinxlike restoration of the same animal reclines in the foreground. (New York City Parks Photo Archive.)

Dinosaur bones were not, like the relics in Indian burial mounds, sacred traces of the ancestors that it would be impious to disturb, but relics of enemies whose death had made Indian life possible. O. C. Marsh, the leader of the Yale paleontological expeditions after the Civil War, was actually able to befriend Chief Red Cloud when the Indians decided that the bone hunters (unlike the miners and ranchers) were not attempting to take possession of their land. In return, Marsh helped to publicize the reduction of the Sioux to abject poverty as a result of corruption in the Bureau of Indian Affairs.[4] Marsh's chief rival in the bone rush from 1864 to 1889, Edward Drinker Cope, managed to charm the Crow Indians into tolerating his excavations during the very summer (1876) when Custer and the Seventh Cavalry were being wiped out 150 miles to the south of his dig (229). Cope's theatrical flaunting of his false teeth reportedly led to his being named "Magic Tooth" among the Crow. One senses in these stories a toleration for the manifestly crazy white men who would want to risk their lives for worthless and probably dangerous relics. The bones of "enormous serpents" found in the Black Hills, for instance,

were thought to be certain death to the finder.[5] The testimony of frontiers-man James H. Cook about paleontologists is that "they were usually spoken of as bone- or bug-hunting idiots."[6] In any case, the Indians were in no position to challenge the paleontologists, who were working with the permission and protection of the U.S. government (and often a company of cavalry). The Indians were probably too concerned with their own extinction to worry about a few crazy white men robbing the bones of dead monsters.

If the dinosaur was at the leading edge of the advancement of empire, then, it played a role rather different from those self-evidently valuable objects of imperial expansion—fertile land and mineral resources. In the transit from England to America, it encountered both straightforward resistance and complex forms of ambivalence and transformation. Jefferson may have established the institutional space in which big American bones could find a home, but the contention about those bones had not ended with the Mammoth Presidency. Peale's attempt at a national museum of natural history was in ruins, his mastodon destroyed by fire, his museum in the hands of P. T. Barnum. Waterhouse Hawkins came to America at the invitation of New York City's Central Park Commission in 1868 with the goal of establishing a Jurassic Park near the Sixty-third Street entrance, adjacent to the present location of the American Museum of Natural History. His hopes for repeating his Crystal Palace triumph were dashed, however, when thugs hired by Boss Tweed and the Tammany Hall ring broke into his studio and destroyed his dinosaurs with sledgehammers. Adrian Desmond speculates that the motive (aside from the usual power struggles of big city politics) may have been "religious prejudice": Tweed referred to Hawkins's dinosaurs as "specimens of animals *alleged* to be of the pre-Adamite period."[7] "Antediluvian monsters," victims of Noah's Flood, were one thing. At least they could be reconciled with the Bible. But pre-Adamite monsters, even the specially created divine "archetypes" of Richard Owen, were enough to produce a coalition of Catholic and Protestant reaction, countered only by Quakers, Unitarians, and some quiet support from Episcopalians.[8]

Although dinosaur research and the bone rush became a mania in post–Civil War America, dinosaur publicity (with the exception of the Cope-Marsh "bone wars") lagged behind. Dinosaurial fame in America seems to begin not with the bones, but with the bone hunters. Marsh was probably the most famous scientist in the United States in the late nineteenth century. Waterhouse Hawkins, despite some successes (most notably the construction of a short-lived plaster *Hadrosaurus* for the centennial of the Declaration of Independence in Washington), never managed to adapt his reconstructions to the conditions of American mass culture. He returned to England shortly after completing his *Hadrosaurus* and died in obscurity in a cottage near the Crystal Palace.

The American public had plenty of other spectacles to distract them in this era. P. T. Barnum had once considered hiring Hawkins to make some replicas of the Crystal Palace dinosaurs for his American Museum, but he decided

that it was a "European phenomenon"[9] and confined himself to pious hoaxes such as
the "Cardiff Giant," a ten-foot
fake "fossil corpse" that had
been "excavated" (after a discreet burial) in
upstate New York. The Bible did say that there
were "giants in the earth" before the Flood, and
Milton had depicted the serpent as walking
erect before God condemned him to crawl on
his belly for tempting Adam and Eve. (We have
already noted the uncanny resemblance between the erect reptilian tempter and Hawkins's
Hadrosaurus: see figures 6.3–6.5 above.) But the
American public after the Civil War was simply
not ready for the dinosaur. Perhaps the surplus
of public attractions was compounded, para-
doxically, by a surplus of dry bones. The wealth
of authentic and complete skeletal reconstructions being assembled in Philadelphia, New
Haven, and later New York were not accompanied by the kind of widely circulated sculptural
or pictorial "restorations" necessary to create a
public image of the dinosaur for America. That
had to await the formation of a modern image
of the dinosaur, one that would break decisively
with the Victorian archetype and epitomize the
New World Order at the end of the nineteenth
century.

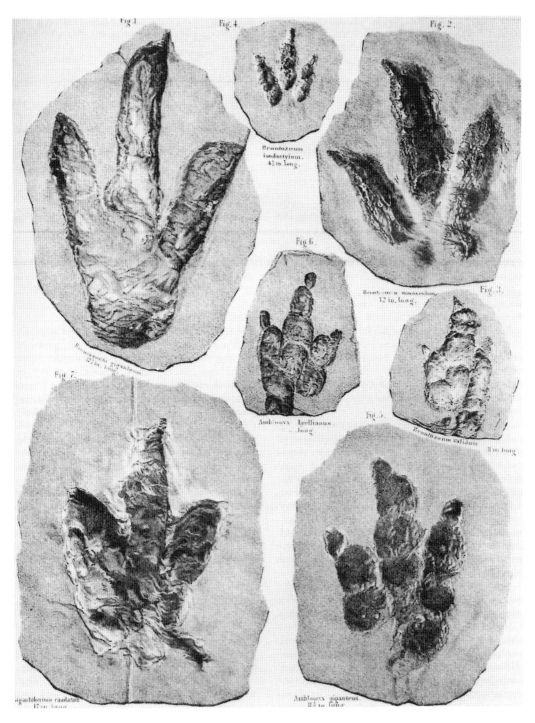

20.1

Edward Hitchcock's "stony bird tracks" from the Connecticut Valley. (Engraving from *Ichnology of New England: A Report on the Sandstone of the Connecticut Valley, Especially Its Fossil Footmarks* [Publication of State of Massachusetts, 1858.])

BONES FOR DARWIN'S BULLDOG

Thus the scepter passed from France, and North America became the chief seat of the world's learning in the science of ancient life.

—HENRY FAIRFIELD OSBORN

IF THE FIRST AMERICAN dinosaur was a popular bust, it was a professional blockbuster in England. T. H. Huxley, the first great Darwinist after Darwin himself, saw immediately that the new American bones made the Owens-Hawkins models obsolete. That also meant, of course, that creationism was obsolete, and that evolution would take its place as the modern paradigm.

Huxley wasted no time in "remodeling" the dinosaur and appropriating it for an evolutionist narrative. The key move in this remodeling was the shifting of dinosaurs from the class of reptiles to the class of birds—a gesture that has been repeated (with much fanfare) by Robert Bakker in contemporary dinosaurology. But Huxley's avian hypothesis didn't succeed in wiping out the reptilian model in paleontology, any more than the victory of Darwinism wiped out creationism in popular culture. Instead, it left dinosaurology with a "great schism" that remains with it to the present day. This schism survives in the compromise that Edwin Colbert has called "dinosaurian duality."[1] In 1887 the canonical division was laid down by the British paleontologist Harry Seeley:

> the Dinosauria has no existence as a natural group of animals, but includes two distinct types of animal structure with technical characters in common, which show their descent from a common ancestry rather than their close affinity. These two orders of animals may be conveniently named the Ornithischia and the Saurischia. (102)

"Bird hips" and "lizard hips" became the anatomical skeleton key, not so much for "decoding" or unlocking the dinosaur, but for giving it an equivocal, ambiguous identity. While dinosaurian duality might seem like a disadvantage from the standpoint of popular taxonomy, the sort of animal classifications that laypeople like you and I employ, it actually had the advantage of producing something absolutely novel in the animal kingdom, a new group of vertebrates on the same level as the mammals, reptiles, birds, amphibians, and fishes, and not reducible to any of them. In this sense, the dinosaur was (and is) a definitively *modern* animal, at once a discovery and a creation

of modern science, both a "natural kind" and an artificial construction. Its irreducibility to any previously known group, its status as a novel public spectacle, and its hybrid character as both "bird/reptile" and "artificial/natural" made it the epitome of a modernized natural history. Like so many other discoveries/ inventions of modern science, it had the ability to conjure up a visible public spectacle from a previously invisible world. It didn't merely explain what people could see, but produced a new appearance, a monstrous apparition, in the world.

A not-so-incidental side effect of dinosaurian duality is its ability to befuddle the amateur. If you look up the term *saurian,* you will find that it means "lizard" or "reptile" (thus dinosaurs are "terrible lizards"). And yet you will also be admonished by the dinosaurologist that dinosaurs are not reptiles, and are quite distinct from lizards. If you persist and go to the heart of dinosaurian duality, the division between ornithischian and saurischian, you will be informed that it is the saurischians ("lizard hips") that evolved into birds, while the ornithischians ("bird hips") went the way of the dodo and the passenger pigeon. The mastery of these paradoxes provides an aura of technical complexity that unites the dinophile and the dinosaurologist.

20.2
Casts of dinosaur footprints by Allan McCollum. The three-toed footprints of dinosaurs found in Connecticut encouraged T. H. Huxley in his belief that the dinosaurs are related to birds. (Allan McCollum, *Natural Copies from the Coal Mines of Central Utah,* John Weber Gallery, New York, 1995.)

21.1

Charles Knight's depiction of *Tyrannosaurus rex* and *Triceratops* is arguably the most famous single dinosaur image ever made. It captures perfectly the "dinosaur duality" that characterizes this animal subgroup, its distribution between two distinct groups, the Ornithischians, or "bird hips" (*Triceratops*), and the Saurischians, or "lizard hips" (*T. rex*). Do these very different animals have a common ancestor? Whatever scientists decide about this, popular culture has already fused them into one thing—"the" dinosaur— an image of nature as a scene of combat between predator and prey, carnivore and herbivore, biped and quadruped. (Oil painting by Charles Knight, 1900. Field Museum of Natural History, #CK91, Chicago.)

schizosaur

THE PAINTINGS OF Charles Knight established the canonical version of the dinosaur for at least half a century. Knight began by making small sculptural models under the direction of Cope, then went to work for Henry Fairfield Osborn, who served as president of the American Museum of Natural History from 1908 to 1933. Knight's pictorial restorations, along with the gigantic skeletal reconstructions of the Dinosaur Hall, made the American Museum the premier location for the public display of the modern dinosaur. Knight's images then circulated in museum publications, teaching aids for public schools, innumerable children's books, and on the covers of *Scientific American*.[1]

Knight's images can best be seen as compromise formations that stitch together the dualities of the dinosaur image. Although he is often blamed by contemporary dinosaurologists for fixing the stereotype of slow, stupid, clumsy giants headed for extinction, it would be more accurate to say that he works both sides of every border he encounters.[2] His dinosaurs may drag their tails on the ground, but they stand erect on their hind legs. They may have reptilian coloration, but they have the limbs of giant quadrupeds and bipeds. They may be thought of as "cold-blooded" by the paleontologists, but that is their problem—blood temperature is outside the province of the visual artist.

It seems unfair for dinosaurologists to complain about the misleading "popular conception" of the dinosaur fostered by Knight's images. In the first place, if they are serious sci-

One
of the best
"recreators" of this
"dinosaurism" is
Charles R. Knight. In
many ways he excels the
Pop artists, but he comes
closest to Claes Oldenburg, at
least in terms of scale. Knight's
art is never seen in museums
outside of the Museum of
Natural History, because it
doesn't fit in with the contrived
"art-histories" of Modernism or
the Renaissance. . . . Knight can
be seen as a combination
Edouard Manet and Eric
Temple Bell (the professor
of Mathematics who
wrote for *Wonder
Stories Magazine*).

—ROBERT SMITHSON

entists, this image won't impede their research. In the second place, Knight has been given a bum rap. He worked from the instructions provided to produce a convincing image of an incoherent, hybrid creature that straddles two different zoological groups, the reptiles and the birds. His "schizosaur" dominated popular imagination from 1900 to 1960, and rightly so. When we think of "the" dinosaur, we should probably not imagine any single figure, but rather the confrontation of two figures, the bipedal carnivore and the armored quadrupedal herbivore—saurischian versus ornithischian—that is presented by Knight's most famous painting, his rendering of *Tyrannosaurus rex* and *Triceratops* for the Field Museum in Chicago.

Knight was equally adept at providing subtle compromises in the cultural connotations of his dinosaurs. His scene of *T. rex* and *Triceratops* poised for single combat was a perfect visual conclusion to the nineteenth-century cult of the big game hunt.[3] It appeared at the moment when the big game was beginning to vanish, and the hunt itself was in danger of becoming a vanishing ritual of Anglo-Saxon manhood. Teddy Roosevelt's African safari in 1908 may have begun as an emulation of the classic killing sprees of the nineteenth century, but Roosevelt realized it was too late for that kind of thing, and moved to convert it into a research expedition to obtain specimens for the Smithsonian. The dinosaur is thus portrayed by Knight as the biggest and most dangerous "game" of all time, an animal to be brought back as a trophy and mounted alongside the elephants, rhinos, and great apes in the American Museum of Natural History.

But the dinosaur could play its role as "big game" only in an imaginary and compromised form. The only people who ever have to face the "restored" and lifelike image of the dinosaur are the painter and his public. What kind of courage does it take, after all, to dig up the bones of dead animals? Some kind, evidently, given the way the aura of the dinosaur seems to rub off on the "hunters" who bring back big bones. Chief Red Cloud evidently found something to respect in the quest of Professor Marsh for the bones of the Unktehi, and dinosaur hunters continue to have a knack for romanticizing their profession. Roy Chapman Andrews, one of the chief bone hunters for the American Museum in the modern period, became the prototype for Indiana Jones of Spielberg fame.[4] My colleague Paul Sereno at the University of Chicago has become the media heir to the "Indy" role, serving (in his own rueful words) as "the virile dino-boy of the moment" (see figure 27.3).

The greatest bone hunter of the modern era (between the world wars) was the virile "father of the dinosaurs," Barnum Brown, whose name suggests that the aura around the dino-hunter may be derived not so much from the magic of the bones as from the mystique of mass publicity and the pseudoscientific hoax. That is why it feels so appropriate that Knight's paintings are located on a border very like the one between Clement Greenberg's "avant-garde and kitsch": they unite the scrupulous rendering of an absolutely modern novelty with the recycling of familiar clichés and outmoded pictorial styles. I say this not to put them down as trivial works of art, but to specify their precise cultural location, a location that is not quite captured by terms like "scientific illustration" or "popularization."

The ambiguity of Knight's images becomes even more pronounced when one reads them as cultural allegories, symbols of the historical forces that surrounded their production and consumption. Knight's scenes of single combat between heavily armored leviathans are the paleontological equivalent of that other war of giants, the struggles among the "robber barons" in late-nineteenth-century America. This period, so often portrayed as the era of "social Darwinism," economic "survival of the fittest," ruthless competition, and the formation of giant corporate entities headed by gigantic individuals, is aptly summarized by the Darwinian icon of giant reptiles in a fight to the death. The archaic, dragonlike character of the dinosaur combines with its scientific novelty to capture perfectly the paradoxical synthesis of feudalism and modernism in America during this period. The new wealth of American financiers and industrialists after the Civil War produced an instant aristocracy, complete with Gothic castles and manor houses and a wealth of second-rate European art and furniture to fill them up. Knight's *T. rex* and *Triceratops* look like monstrous reptilian knights in armor poised for the joust. And the link between these "barons of bone" and the robber barons was not just a distant analogy. Most of the dinosaur research after the Civil War was financed by the American industrialists and bankers who were carving out the new feudal order in the United States. J. P. Morgan, Andrew Carnegie, George Peabody, and other pillars of the new American aristocracy were providing the money that made it possible to bring the bones out of the ground and Knight's images into the world.[5]

These feudal overtones of Knight's dinosaurs must be seen, at the same time, as woven through with undertones of modern technology.[6] If we see *T. rex*, for instance, as a knight in armor or a robber baron, we must also see him as an armored vehicle, one of those clumsy tanks lumbering across the trenches of a World War I landscape. "Seeing as" is too weak a term here, however. It is as much a matter of proximity as of similitude, a "seeing with" or "seeing together." The dinosaur makes its appearance along with all the other modern monsters, coming into public consciousness in the same period, and as a product of the same forces, that produced the tank, the locomotive, the steamboat, and the skyscraper. The cutting open of the Western landscape by the railroads was spilling dinosaur bones out of their primeval graves. The railroads were bringing back carloads of bones to New York, Philadelphia, and New Haven, and railroad money was helping to finance the bone rush and the new museums.[7] Leo Marx describes the late-nineteenth-century American landscape as the moment of the "machine in the garden," when that new animal, the "iron horse," bursts into a pastoral, agrarian scene.[8] Henry David Thoreau saw that the horse was perhaps not the adequate image:

> I hear the iron horse make the hills echo with his snort like thunder, shaking the earth with his feet, and breathing fire and smoke from his nostrils, (what kind of winged horse or fiery dragon they will put into the new Mythology I don't know,) it seems as if the earth had got a race now worthy to inhabit it.[9]

The Sioux may have mistaken the steamboat for one of their water monsters, and we can understand why Thoreau looks back to the dragon for an image adequate to the locomotive. What they did not see was that the central figure of the new mythology would be a modern dragon, a "thunder horse" resurrected from the soil beneath their feet and reconstructed in museums all over the eastern United States.

21.2
Gertie the dinosaur playing with a train. The dinosaur is routinely paired up with—and compared to—modern vehicles (locomotives, steamboats, tanks, trucks, automobiles). This linkage is reinforced by the common association of dinosaurs and machines with fossil fuels and the gigantic storehouse of buried energy that is unleashed by modern technologies.
(Film still, *Gertie on Vacation* [Winsor McCay, 1918].)

22

Dinosaurs Moralized

CHARLES KNIGHT'S DINOSAURS are really schizosaurs, uniting scientific novelty and kitsch familiarity, feudalism and modern technology, the most dangerous and the safest game, the agility of modern birds and the clumsiness of lumbering leviathans. The schizosaur is the perfect totem animal of modernity because, like the traditional totem, it is a shape-shifting, transitional figure that can seem to mean almost anything one minute and almost nothing the next.[1] There is always a moral lesson to be attached to the dinosaur, some homily about giantism, violence, or extinction. They died because they got too big, and couldn't move, migrate, or adapt. They died because they became too highly specialized; or because they *did* migrate and transmitted diseases to one another. (Specialization and migration are Osborn's hypotheses about extinction; I will return to their application in racial theory.) They died because they were so violent that they killed each other off (a popular Cold War scenario). Or they weren't violent *enough:* they became decadent and degenerate, lost their virility and competitiveness and fighting spirit (this is the Roosevelt line). They were killed by a natural catastrophe. They died because God wiped them out (this Victorian view continues to survive in contemporary tabloids). Or (my favorite) they were abducted by aliens, and have been returning in the form of reptilian bipeds in flying saucers.

These "morals" are not esoteric: they are the commonplaces (some admittedly more common than others) that allow the dinosaur to circulate as a universal symbol and focus of argument. They are usually seen not as "readings" or "interpretations" of the dinosaur as a cultural symbol, but as a set of self-evident facts that the dinosaur just happens to illustrate. In this sense, the dinosaur is a peculiar kind of transparent cultural symbol, in that its meaning is always taken to lie outside or beyond culture. It is not "we" who give meaning to the dinosaur; its authority comes from the earth, from nature, from the objective, impersonal laws of Darwinian necessity, from science. The suspicion that Darwinian necessity is, as Marx and Engels suggested, a projection of bourgeois capitalist values onto nature can always be met with the response that those values are themselves dictated by nature, and have now been rediscovered by the "modern synthesis" of sociobiology.

The most important morals to be drawn from natural history at the dawn of the twentieth century were, as Donna Haraway has demonstrated,[2] those that sustained the supremacy of the classes, races, and genders that supported it—the new Anglo-Saxon warrior brotherhood of American aristocrats. Nature was designed to promote the "survival of the fittest"—to produce a natural hierarchy dominated by an aristocracy whose right to rule was guaranteed, not by heredity or genealogy, but by the laws of the free market and unrestrained competition. The dinosaur exemplifies an archaic, natural "ruling class" of animals. It simultaneously justifies the rule of the few over the many—the predator over the herbivore—and admonishes the ruling class with an image of its potential fate. Like the monument to Ozymandias, it invites the mighty to look on and despair—or prepare ("if this could happen to them . . . "). It also invites the multitude to look on and be thankful that they live in an age when the laws of nature (and the instincts of the big predators) are moderated by civilized societies, enlightened altruism, and benevolent patriarchy—especially the sort that provides free public museums like the American Museum of Natural History. One American Museum curator described the probable response to a mounting of an *Allosaurus* devouring an *Apatosaurus* in precisely these Hobbesian/Darwinian terms: the exhibit "gives to the imaginative observer a most vivid picture of a characteristic scene of that bygone age, millions of years ago, when reptiles were the lords of creation, when 'Nature red in tooth and claw' had lost none of her primitive savagery."[3]

Pale-ontology, or It's Not Easy Being Green

Contemporary, postmodern dinosaurs are multicolored, striped, spotted, and festooned with gay plumage, as befits an age of multiculturalism and sexual multiplicity. The modern (1900–1960) dinosaur was a uniform, monotonous gray-green color that served to unite perfectly the savage, organic, reptilian skin and the modern armored military vehicle. The lean, mean fighting machine had to be green because war is a return to the state of nature, and camouflage is a natural adaptation.

As Kermit E. Frog's plaintive song reminds us, however, "it's not easy being green." Skin color is the easiest cue for racial stereotyping and those forms of "natural" classification that confuse the visible differences among human beings with species differences. Among the more dubious legacies of Darwinism were theories of "cultural evolution" and practices of "physical anthropology." The former portrayed the history of humanity as a progression from savage, primitive "natural man" (invariably represented by nonwhite peoples) to "civilized man" (invariably portrayed as white). The latter put these racial classifications on a firm anatomical basis with skull measurements and estimates of brain capacity.

> **There is a racial soul as well as a racial mind, a racial system of morals, a racial anatomy.**
>
> —HENRY FAIRFIELD OSBORN

So where does this leave greenness? Is it a symbol of the "colored" racial other, the savage, primitive denizen of the green world? Or is it an emblem of the white man's burden, the color of the military camouflage required for the

147

Great White Hunter to blend in with the jungle and thus to dominate it?[1] The answer by now should be evident: gray-green is both black and white, both "colored" and no color at all. It designates both sides of the "color line," the "veil" between the races that W. E. B. Du Bois was announcing in 1903 as *the* problem of the twentieth century. The dinosaur can symbolize the dominant "master race" that commands a global empire, the vanished, savage races that lost out in the Darwinian struggle, or an invading horde of aliens who threaten white supremacy.

The links between dinosaurs and racial theory cannot have been lost on Henry Fairfield Osborn, the most powerful figure at the American Museum in the modern period. Osborn's racial views have been amply documented in Ronald Rainger's excellent study, *An Agenda for Antiquity*. A member of the anti-immigration Galton Society and a strong believer in human eugenics and racial purity, Osborn thought that "the massive influx of Asian and southern and eastern European immigrants" in the modern era "threatened the existence of the Nordic race that had founded this country."[2] He supported the program of "racial hygiene" developed by Hitler and Mussolini in the 1930s, and wrote a laudatory preface to one of the most notorious racist creeds of the early twentieth century, Madison Grant's *The Passing of the Great Race* (1916). Grant argued the familiar racist paradox of miscegenation: that intermarriage between the races would produce a degeneration in the superior breed, not an improvement of the inferior "stock." As long as the contact between races is kept at the level of competition for wealth, territory, and resources, he claimed, the superior courage, intellect, and strength of the white races will predominate. But intimate sexual contact and social "intercourse" will lead to the decline of the superior breed.

Osborn's answers to the riddle of dinosaur extinction begin to make sense in this context. Dinosaurs died out, in Osborn's view, because

23.1

Mark Hallett's *Australian Dinosaurs* illustrates the tendency of contemporary dinosaur restorations to move away from the gray-green reptilian coloration of the "modern" dinosaur (1900–1950) and to portray the dinosaur in all the colors of the rainbow. (© 1981 Mark Hallett Illustrations.)

they migrated, spreading diseases to one another. Osborn mounted "public health" exhibitions at the American Museum that made the anti-immigration message explicit. Osborn's other explanation for dinosaurial demise was "specialization," a term that links modern technical innovation with biological diversification, the process by which sexual reproduction produces a continuous proliferation and differentiation of phenotypes, adding new variations to the gene pool. Osborn was a romantic, reactionary antimodernist who hated the proliferation of technologies and specialized division of labor. In his own work, he was an interdisciplinary aristocrat who ranged with the confidence of a virtuosic amateur over vertebrate paleontology and dabbled in anthropology and social theory, exploiting the work of the specialists under him at the American Museum. Osborn could see the dinosaur as an object lesson in the need for a racially pure elite and an avoidance of narrow specialization. It was one thing, as Josiah Strong had argued in *Our Country*, to improve the racial stock by interbreeding the various Aryan types from Northern Europe; but world dominance and colonization carried with it the danger of "contamination," both genetic and bacterial. The dinosaur, as Mary Douglas might put it, is in this context a colossal monster that straddles the border between contamination and purity.[3] Is greenness a sign of sickness or health, youthful venery or corruption and decay? Either way, it's not easy being green.

Perhaps Osborn's most important contribution to the myth of the modern dinosaur was his linkage of it to questions of male potency. The connection between big bones and virility had already been established by the Jeffersonian mastodon. Big bones were also trophies of the masculine ritual of the big game hunt, and the phallic overtones of "bones" need no belaboring by me (but see appendix A, *"Scrotum humanum,"* below). Osborn's initiatives led to the reconstruction of the first complete *Tyrannosaurus rex* at the American Museum in

1910–11,[4] providing a macho figurehead for the entire dinosaur clan and a sensational spectacle of animal violence unprecedented in natural history display.

So important has the dinosaur become to the public image of the American Museum that in 1991 it moved into the central sanctum of the Roosevelt Atrium, the grand entrance hall that had been kept empty (except for temporary exhibitions) to honor the centrality of the Roosevelt ideology to the museum. In front of the entrance to the museum is an equestrian statue of Roosevelt as the "White Father" protecting the "savage" races—Indians and Africans—whose artifacts are conspicuously displayed in the anthropological sections. Roosevelt's attitude toward the Indians is well known ("I don't wish to take the Western attitude, that the only good Indian is a dead Indian, but the fact is that it is true of nine out of ten of them").[5] Inside the grand entrance hall now stands the "world's largest free-standing reconstruction" of a dinosaur skeleton, a *Barosaurus*

23.2
Paleontology, along with other "historical sciences" (archaeology, anthropology, and geology), has historically been an "imperial discipline." Expeditions to Africa, China, and South America (and to the American West in the nineteenth century) were accompanied by the conquest and colonization of aboriginal peoples all over the globe.

Leonard Dove, in *Collier's Weekly*
"We had seven hundred natives excavating the ruins, but you'll never guess who found it."

lentus rearing up on its hind legs (see figure 26.2). This erect reptilian giant is surrounded by walls engraved with the words of Theodore Roosevelt and decorated with murals celebrating his imperial achievements. The words of Roosevelt express the cult of masculine struggle and virility common to the inner circle around Osborn at the American Museum, and they make explicit the "lesson" that is being subliminally aimed at the multitudes of school-children who visit the museum every day. Osborn, one supposes, would have approved of the installation of this giant figure as the first animal one encounters in the museum—except for one detail that jars the masculinist decorum of the space: the *Barosaurus lentus* is shown as a protective mother rearing up to defend its baby, whose skeleton takes cover at its feet.[6]

For Osborn, the lessons of natural history, especially in the museum's "outreach" programs to the public schools, were part of a struggle to roll back the tides of modern decadence, specialization, racial mixing, and effeminacy. "We have," noted Osborn in one of his many pronouncements on modernity, "taken away from our boys and girls the stern element of the struggle with the forces of Nature; we have, as a final step in the emasculation, substituted the woman for the man teacher."[7] Osborn might not have appreciated the irony in the fact that the multitudes of first-graders who make the ritual visit to the American Museum every year are generally in the care of female teachers. Or that they are paying little attention to the words of Roosevelt or the images of imperial glory, but are busy cavorting about under the ribcage of the matriarchal *Barosaurus,* playing out games and fantasies undreamt of in Osborn's *naturphilosophie.*

Dinosaurs have a tendency to escape the kind of ideological programming that would stabilize their meaning. You can moralize and monumentalize them all you like, but someone will always come along who reads them in a different way, and shatters the monument you have erected (see figure 29.3). If the modern dinosaur was a monument to manliness, racial purity, and the naturalness of big capital, it was also a fragile skeleton that could easily be sent crumbling into a heap of dry bones. The difficult question is whether the demolition of the dinosaur, the shattering of any specific message or status it might have, is really a transgression, or just another part of the dinosaurial ritual, like *T. rex* playing dead for a french fry.

POTLATCH AND PURITY

At that time Chief Wiah had built an enormous house, generally referred to as Monster House, which was more than sixty feet wide and had nine large totem poles. When Chief Edenshaw came to Masset in the 1870s, he brought with him a totem pole that belonged to his ancestors. He carried this pole into Monster House. First he danced before it; then he had it burned.

—American Museum of Natural History: 125 Years of Expedition and Discovery

THE DINOSAUR WAS FROM THE FIRST a pure, free, no-strings-attached gift to the American public, typically from a wealthy individual. In the first part of the twentieth century, the monumental reconstructions of bones and the painted or sculpted restorations in U.S. natural history museums were generally financed by private philanthropy, rarely by public revenues. There is a purely practical explanation for this fact: vertebrate paleontology was not widely regarded as a high priority for public investment in the United States in the late nineteenth century. Most research and educational institutions were turning their attention to experimental biology of the sort that could lead to practical results in the breeding of animals and plants. (The story of *Jurassic Park* unites experimental and evolutionary biology in its fantasy of cloning extinct species from DNA traces.) In 1900, however, actual living things and real wealth came first, extinct creatures and theoretical speculation a distant second. Giant skeletons and "birds with teeth" might be important in debates among the Darwinians, but it was easy for elected officials, sensitive to religious and practical objections, to find other priorities. If it were not for the generosity of J. P. Morgan, George Peabody, Marshall Field, and Andrew Carnegie, the great halls filled with

24.1
The Field Museum's John McCarter (from left) and Peter Crane meet with art
dealer Richard Gray beside the skull of the "*T. rex* named Sue," purchased
by the Field for the record sum of 8.8 million dollars in the fall of 1997.
Mr. Gray's experience with high-stakes art auctions made him the ideal
representative at the Sotheby's auction. The "war-chest" to purchase Sue
included a gift by the McDonald's Corporation (which has a restaurant in the
basement of the Field Museum) in exchange for the rights to reproduce
Sue's image in certain selected venues. (AP/Wide World Photos, 1997.)

monster skeletons in New York, New Haven, Chicago, and Pittsburgh would not exist.

Other than being grateful for these wondrous gifts, what are we to make of them? The anthropologist Marcel Mauss notes that in traditional cultures, rituals of gift-giving are essential to social solidarity.[1] The gift in these societies is never "free" or "pure," but is always given with the expectation of some return, and the failure to reciprocate (or the refusal to accept) a gift is an insult that can lead to war. Rituals of exchange, called "potlatch" (meaning "to feed" or "consume") among the Indians of America's Pacific Northwest, are central to the social order. *The Encyclopedia of Religion* summarizes their function as follows:

> Potlatches maintain social equilibrium, consolidate chiefly power over commoners, provide for the orderly transfer of wealth and power, provide a measure of group identity and solidarity, redistribute surplus wealth, level economic imbalances, provide outlets for competition without recourse to violence, and provide an occasion for aesthetic expression and dramatic entertainment.[2]

The potlatch at Chief Wiah's "Monster House" is an extreme example of this practice that involves the destruction of a valuable object (the burning of a totem pole) as a gift to the gods—a gift that is understood as reciprocation for gifts that the gods have already given to a wealthy and powerful chief. The most grievous sin is meanness and miserliness, making an idol of wealth. Great gifts from the gods become a guilty burden if they are not reciprocated with some dramatic sacrifice of a valuable object—perhaps a totem or idol—in a public spectacle.

> **Man must have an idol—the amassing of wealth is one of the worst species of idolatry—no idol more debasing than the worship of money . . . therefore should I be careful to choose that life which will be the most elevating in its character. To continue much longer overwhelmed by business cares and with most of my thoughts wholly upon the way to make more money in the shortest time, must degrade me beyond hope of permanent recovery.**
>
> —ANDREW CARNEGIE, *Diary* (1868)

Modern rituals of gift-giving and philanthropy are generally contrasted with these archaic or "primitive" practices—what our uncomprehending racist vernacular calls "Indian giving." The modern gift is supposed to be pure and "free." Of course, we know that gifts are never free, that they confer obligations and imply reciprocity, but a crucial part of modernity—especially its economic mythologies—is the fiction that some part of exchange lies outside financial interest, outside reciprocity and the expectation of rewards. The idea of the pure gift is a systematic disavowal of the everyday reality we all know, perhaps to compensate for the actual contamination of everyday modern life by the cash nexus.[3]

The dinosaur emerged as an ideal object of philanthropic giving at the end of the nineteenth century for many reasons. First, it was an exemplar of what Roosevelt called "science . . . followed purely for the sake of science." Roosevelt had made it a principle that this sort of pure research had to be supported, partly because it might pay off "in the long run," and partly because it seemed like a kind of moral corrective to the prevailing utilitarian and pragmatic character of American culture.[4] Second, the dinosaur was a highly visible gift. Like Chief Edenshaw's totem pole, it was both monumental and monstrous, a surefire popular attraction. Third, this monstrous image came with associations of modernity and novelty (as a contribution to scientific progress and the filling in of the evolutionary record) as well as an aura of unimaginable antiquity. Fourth, the American dinosaur had inherited the role pioneered by Jefferson's mastodon and could thus serve as an emblem of national pride. America's big bones were a demonstration of its "natural constitution," its virility, potency, and dominance in the Darwinian struggle among nations.

Above all, the dinosaur is an object that seems to lie outside both use value and exchange value. It is a kind of pure surplus or excess, what Thorstein Veblen called "conspicuous consumption" and "sumptuary display."[5] It is no accident that dinosaurs proliferate when there is an excess of capital to be expended, and tend to go out of style when times are hard. Unlike fossil fuels or valuable minerals, they do not have the obvious material and visual properties associated with value. They are, after all, merely old bones brought back to life by the miracle of modern science. They are the sacred animals of modernity, totems for the expenditure and purification of excess capital. Unlike valuable works of art, they are supposed to reside outside the realm of artifice, and to exemplify the deepest secrets of nature. And yet for the dinosaurologist or the dinomaniac, they also participate fully in the aura surrounding the traditional work of art, producing a synthesis of aesthetic, religious, and scientific wonder. Robert Bakker describes his experience of unearthing a bone with his chisel: "This bone is a holy relic for me, as beautiful in its roughly hewn outline as Michelangelo's bound slaves struggling to free themselves from the enveloping surface" (31).

DIPLODOCUS carneGII

ANDREW CARNEGIE'S DINOSAUR *Diplodocus carnegii*, perfectly fulfilled all the functions of colossal philanthropy. As the story goes, Carnegie's first inspiration for his gift came in November 1898, when he read about a new dinosaur discovery in the New York papers and saw a pictorial "restoration" of the reported beast looking in the eleventh-story window of the New York Life Building. Carnegie immediately sent off a check for $10,000 to the director of his newly founded Carnegie Institute with a note instructing him to "buy this for Pittsburgh."[1] Although the newspaper report turned out to be a hoax, Carnegie's money launched an aggressive program of big bone acquisition and lured some key bone hunters away from the American Museum. The *Diplodocus* was not long in arriving. "Dippy," as it was popularly named (the capacity for diminutive ridicule dogging the leviathan as always), rapidly became a gift that kept on giving. Replicas were sent as gifts to the crowned heads of Europe with the same theatrical magnanimity that had characterized the gift of the Jeffersonian mastodon. Carnegie could simultaneously present his gift as a symbol of national pride, as a conspicuous display of American wealth, bigness, and modernity, and as a personal display of his own power as one of the chief baronial figures in the new feudal order of the Gilded Age.

A crucial feature of the gift rituals analyzed by Mauss is the identification of the gift with the giver. Ideally, one doesn't give away a mere object, but something of oneself. Carnegie's

When It Walked the Earth Trembled Under Its Weight of 120,000 Pounds.

When It Ate It Filled a Stomach Large Enough to Hold Three Elephants.

When It Was Angry Its Terrible Roar Could Be Heard Ten Miles.

When It Stood Up Its Height Was Equal to Eleven Stories of a Sky-Scraper.

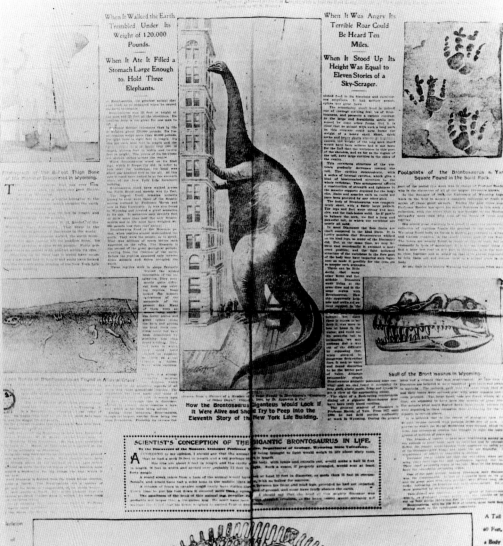

How the Brontosaurus Giganteus Would Look If It Were Alive and Should Try to Peep Into the Eleventh Story of the New York Life Building.

Footprints of the Brontosaurus a Yard Square Found in the Solid Rock

Skull of the Brontosaurus in Wyoming.

SCIENTIST'S CONCEPTION OF THE GIGANTIC BRONTOSAURUS IN LIFE.

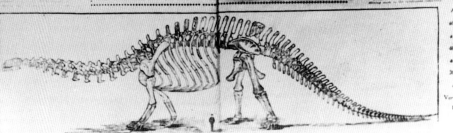

A Tail 40 Feet, a Body 60 Feet, a Neck 30 Feet, and a Very Small Head

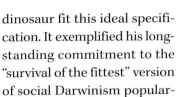

dinosaur fit this ideal specification. It exemplified his long-standing commitment to the "survival of the fittest" version of social Darwinism popularized by his friend and intellectual adviser, Herbert Spencer. It also manifested the "bigger is better" philosophy of industrial integration that Carnegie pioneered in the steel industry, an association that was probably triggered by the juxtaposition of the dinosaur and the skyscraper. As if to confirm these identifications, the *Diplodocus* carries Carnegie's name: it is not only a gift given by him, but a Carnegie itself.

Unlike Chief Edenshaw, Carnegie did not dance in front of his *Diplodocus* and set it on fire. He was not, after all, giving this present to the gods, but to the public. Carnegie's public reputation in the nineties was at an all-time low in the wake of the notorious 1892 Homestead Strike, during which his absence—he was in Europe, pursuing "high culture"—gave his manager, Henry Frick, a free hand to destroy the steelworkers' union with the aid of Pinkerton thugs.[2] For years Carnegie had been seeking ways to retire from the "survival of the fittest" world in which he was so dominant and pursue a career of polite learning and philanthropy. But Carnegie's philanthropy was always on his own terms. He did not believe in giving to established charities, preferring to create his own symbolic outlets (education, museums, and "world peace" were the primary recipients). *Diplodocus carnegii* was the perfect symbolic gift to this public: the "most colossal animal ever on earth" exemplified the magnitude of the donor. It stood for Roosevelt's "science for its own sake," and of course it was radically distinct from that other (decadent) form of cultural "purity" that was available at the turn of the century, "art for art's sake." Its status as an extinct creature, a figure of massive power that had died and been restored to "life," placed it in a narrative cycle of destruction and resurrection at least as

25.1
Dinosaurs invariably measure themselves against skyscrapers (see chapter 32). This is the dinosaur that, as legend has it, launched the Carnegie Museum of Natural History. When Andrew Carnegie saw this story (later revealed to be a hoax) on the front page of the *New York Journal*, he is reported to have said, "We have to have one of those for Pittsburgh." (Courtesy of Carnegie Museum of Natural History.)

25.2
(Detail of 25.1.)

impressive as Chief Edenshaw's immolation of the totem pole, with its figures of ancestral animals. And when the dance was over, "Dippy" would still be there.

If every gift demands something in return, what did Carnegie expect in return for his *Diplodocus?* The simplest answer is: absolutely nothing. Any return gift by the public would have spoiled the whole effect. One of the key features of potlatch is its competitive character, the establishment of social hierarchy and chiefly status by an overwhelming generosity that puts the recipient in an abject position of indebtedness. Mauss notes that in some aboriginal cultures, failure to reciprocate a gift puts the recipient in a position of slavery toward the donor. Carnegie didn't expect anything quite this dramatic (the shattered unions in his mills had left his workforce in a sufficiently abject condition of servitude). But he did clearly hope for gratitude, wonderment, and admiration. Perhaps a by-product of this gratitude would be public acceptance of the Carnegian philosophy as right and natural for America, and forgiveness of his shameful conduct during the Homestead Strike.

Outsize gifts always make the recipient feel uncomfortable and ambivalent: "it's too much," is the ritual protest. It seems safe to assume that the public was, as always, ambivalent about Carnegie's gift of big bones. *Diplodocus carnegii* no doubt served, and still serves, for the recitation of pieties about its beneficial effect on the public and as a stimulus for the unpredictable play of children's fantasies. As it happened, Dippy turned out to be something of a "transitional object" for Carnegie himself. In 1917, two years before his death, he decided to stop funding paleontological research, and the museum's scientific involvement with dinosaurology went into a long decline.

25.3

The *Diploducus carnegii,* the monumental figurehead of
Andrew Carnegie's philanthropic efforts in natural history.
This reconstruction was recast in numerous copies that
were presented as gifts to the peoples of Germany,
England, France, and Mexico, where they still stand in
museums of natural history. (Photo of *Diploducus carnegii*
as it appeared in the Berlin Museum in 1908, courtesy of the
Carnegie Museum of Natural History.)

26.1–26.2

The images that introduce the 125th anniversary volume celebrating the American Museum of Natural History exemplify the two major public attractions that have been central to the museum's popular image: Native American sculptural artifacts (especially masks and totem poles) and dinosaur restorations. (Nootka wooden mask used in Wolf Dance, a ceremony during which a wolf spirit abducts novices; found among the Quileute. [H: 89cm W: 51cm. Catalog 3 16/5976. Transparency #3852(3); photograph by Stephen S. Meyers, 1988.] **Below:** *Barosaurus lentus,* **in the Roosevelt Memorial Rotunda.** [Transparency #4692(A), courtesy Department of Library Services, American Museum of Natural History, AMNH Photo Studio, 1992.]**)**

TOTEMS AND BONES

How FAR-FETCHED IS the analogy between modern philanthropy and traditional potlatch, between the "gift" of the dinosaur and of the totem pole? What are the limits of this comparison? Is it just an application of anthropological theory to the wrong domain, an attempt to reduce science to culture (and thus to politics, social issues, and economics)? The thing that makes it more than just a clever analogy is the actual convergence of these two objects, and their respective disciplines, in the "Monster House" of the natural history museum.

In New York's American Museum, the giant skeletons erected with Morgan money to display Henry Fairfield Osborn's racial agenda were only a short walk away from the display of totem poles and masks being brought in from the Pacific Northwest by the anthropologist Franz Boas. As the pioneer of cultural anthropology and liberal notions of cultural relativism, Boas was a bitter enemy of the racism inherent in evolutionary and physical anthropology, with its "progressive" movement from inferior (colored) to superior (Anglo-Saxon) races and its faith in cranial measurements as a key to racial classification.[1] Boas was a firm advocate of the rights of Native Americans, an ardent opponent of American participation in World War I, and a Jew. Osborn and his circle (including Madison Grant and other politically and racially "sound" members of the Galton Society)[2] attempted a takeover of the American Anthropological Association in 1919. They succeeded in censuring Boas, stripping him of his

> **Osborn was to vertebrate paleontology what Boas was to anthropology.**
>
> —DOUGLAS PRESTON,
> *Dinosaurs in the Attic*

membership in the Association's governing council, and threatening him with expulsion from the Association.

In the first quarter of the twentieth century, the premier public attractions at the American Museum of Natural History were the magnificent totems of the Northwest Coast Indians and the dinosaurs, with the great apes (as Donna Haraway has argued) not far behind. These attractions were quite consciously devised to bring in the public, and the priorities are clear in the pictorial layout of the museum's 125th anniversary retrospective volume.[3] The frontispiece is a Nootka mask collected in Washington in 1898. It is followed by a series of landscapes in which the museum's fieldwork has been conducted. The next object shown is the *Barosaurus* in the Roosevelt Atrium, on the page facing the "Message from the President" of the museum. Here are the two professional totems of the American Museum—one traditional, the other modern; one belonging to cultural anthropology, the other to vertebrate paleontology. United in the space of the museum, they illustrate what Marcel Mauss calls a "total system" of economic exchange, social relations, and cultural symbolism.

What would it mean to cross the border between "science" (or nature) and "culture" that separates these two objects? It would clearly suggest, as Bruno Latour has put it, that "we have never been modern." Our rational, scientific object, the dinosaur, is in its way an even more deeply superstitious thing than the Indian totem with which it is so often contrasted, if only because our superstitions about it are so consistently disavowed. But this point does not need special arguments from me. The McDonald's television commercial (see chapter 11 above), with its *T. rex* running past the totem poles in search of french fries, makes it clear that the distinction between science and culture is already being transgressed in the most ordinary, familiar kinds of places. While the Indian totem poles stand silently in the shadows, the animated *T. rex* skeleton gallops through the Monster House looking for food, only to be instructed to play dead. Something very strange is going on here that is undreamt of in the science of paleontology. (Perhaps it would be better to say it is *only* dreamt of in the science of paleontology—it is a dream that bursts into the open whenever the romanticism and fetishism of this profession rears its head.) The "real" dinosaur may remain securely buried in the earth or mounted in the museum, but its image has escaped into every dimension of cultural space, evolving into new species, colonizing new habitats.

Indiana Jones and Barnum Bones

By the onset of World War II, the dinosaur had firmly established itself as a familiar figure in the American cultural landscape. The Jeffersonian dream of a great national museum of natural history had come true several times over, and in distinct ways, in New York, Chicago, Pittsburgh, and Washington, DC. The 1826 bequest of an eccentric English benefactor, James Smithson, a "gift horse" whose mouth Congress examined for almost a decade, had grown into the magnificent community of museums we call the Smithsonian Institution. The American Museum in New York had gone well beyond the boundaries of U.S. "national nature," sending expeditions to Africa and Asia in search of fossils and fetishes, paleontological bones and anthropological totems. The heroic nationalist era of a continental western wilder-

27.1

Dinosaur paleontologists are generally presented as "Indiana Jones" figures—frontiersmen, big-game hunters, adventurers. Jack Horner, the Montana paleontologist, is the model for Dr. Grant (Sam Neill) in *Jurassic Park*. (© Copyrighted Chicago Tribune Company. All rights reserved. Used with permission.)

27.2

Barnum Brown, chief bone-hunter for the American Museum of Natural History and renowned ladies' man, ready to depart on the 1934 Sinclair Expedition.

(From *A Great Name in Oil: Sinclair through Fifty Years,* © 1966, Sinclair Oil Corp.)

ness penetrated by the railroad gave way to an imperial quest into far-off deserts and jungles opening up to the range-roving off-road vehicle. (The Dodge automobile company was a major sponsor of Osborn's Gobi Desert expedition.) The era of crazy, magical bone hunters like Cope and Marsh gave way to the frankly imperialistic image of Roy Chapman Andrews, a "famous explorer, dinosaur hunter, exemplifier of Anglo-Saxon virtues, crack shot, fighter of Mongolian brigands, the man who created the metaphor of 'Outer Mongolia,'"[1] and one of several prototypes for Spielberg's Indiana Jones.

As a result of the expeditions of Andrews and Barnum Brown, the American Museum assembled the largest collection of dinosaur bones in the world in the period between 1900 and 1930. Brown, who found the first *T. rex* in 1902, was so prolific he became known as "Mr. Bones" and "the father of the dinosaurs" by the popular press. These names were reinforced by his reputation as a ladies' man and his habit of referring to the skeletons in the American museum as his "children" (81). Brown also lived up to the reputation of his namesake, P. T. Barnum, as a master of publicity. His arrival at a bone quarry was treated as a major event, and the

debuts of his "offspring" in the American Museum established the pattern of treating new dinosaur discoveries as front-page items in American newspapers.

Brown's discovery of a giant "dinosaur graveyard" in the Bighorn Mountains in 1934 led him to speculate that the dinosaurs had gathered together seeking water in a drying lake bed, only to be wiped out by a drought, a scene that became fixed in the popular imagination by Walt Disney's *Fantasia* (1940). Disney's dinosaurs turn into oil, the principal fossil fuel of the automotive age. Brown, meanwhile, turned to the Sinclair Oil Company for financial support for his expeditions, and Sinclair returned the favor by building its entire corporate image around the figure of *Brontosaurus*. Harry Sinclair's philosophy of corporate giantism (now generally regarded as an obsolete business strategy) was aptly represented by "Bronty," and the grades of premium and regular gasoline were advertised (falsely) as linked to a paleontological "aging" process. Brown pro-

27.3

Paul Sereno, University of Chicago paleontologist, has been called "the Indiana Jones of paleontology." Here the news photographer presents him as a kind of combination of shaman and lion tamer, his head framed by the jaws of a dinosaur, his hands conjuring the beast back to life. (© Copyrighted Chicago Tribune Company. All rights reserved. Used with permission.)

27.4–27.5
A billboard advertising Sinclair gasoline and a barge full of dinosaur models on their way to the 1963 World's Fair. The Sinclair Corporation chose the dinosaur as its logo for its easy recognizability and its associations with giantism and great age. Sinclair promoted its higher-priced "premium" gasoline as if its quality depended on the aging process, a kind of crossing of gasoline and whiskey advertising strategies. The *Brontosaurus* expressed Harry Sinclair's philosophy of corporate giantism. The company's aim was to control the entire process of exploration, drilling, shipping, and retailing, from the wellhead to the pump. This strategy has itself become something of a dinosaur in the age of corporate downsizing. (From *A Great Name in Oil: Sinclair through Fifty Years*, © 1966, Sinclair Oil Corp.)

vided the company logo, which still appears on many gas stations in the western United States despite the demise of the Sinclair Corporation, and designed dinosaur stamps and booklets that were given to motorists as gifts with every tank of gas.

Brown became, in short, a key figure in the three-way relationship of big capital, mass culture, and big bones in the modern era. He and Andrews carried out Henry Fairfield Osborn's program of making the dinosaur the marquee attraction in the modern natural history museum and disseminating it beyond the museum as a staple of popular culture.[2] They also personified the Anglo-Saxon male potency that had been central to the American bone cult since Jefferson's mastodon.

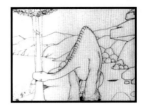

28

WORLDS WELL LOST

FOR EVERY DINO BOOM there is a bust. By the thirties, America was deep in the Depression, and war was looming. Paleontology was in the doldrums, research at a standstill, and the dinosaur image began dispersing itself throughout popular culture, in monster movies, cartoon strips like *Alley Oop,* and the kitsch attractions of Sinclair Oil. Dinosaurology, as Gregory Paul notes, seemed itself to be an endangered species of scientific activity, surrounded by a "circus air" that drove away serious paleontologists (see chapter 4). The fortunes of dino-science seem to flourish in inverse relation to dinomania: when the scientific side is depressed, the popular image seems to become even more inflated and prolific. As the real dinosaur fades, the imaginary one comes to life in "lost worlds" where it encounters human beings face to face.

"Lost world" fictions typically reinforce the neo-Darwinist, Osbornian mythology of Anglo-Saxon superiority. Conan Doyle's *The Lost World* (1912), for instance, tells the story of a young Irish journalist, seeking an adventure to win the love a young woman, who joins a Brazilian expedition composed of an aristocratic big game hunter and two quarrelsome zoologists. Deep in the jungle, the expedition finds a plateau where time has been suspended and evolution stopped, where all the "links" in the chain of vertebrate being, from dinosaurs to ape-men to Indians to Anglo-Saxons, reside in not-so-peaceful coexistence. In between hair-raising battles with the dinosaurs, the expedition forms an alliance with the Indians against the ape-men, conducting a war of extermination in which all

28.1
Film still from *King Kong* (RKO
1933, Ernest B. Schoedsack and
Merian C. Cooper). King Kong is
transformed from a monstrous
"other" to a heroic ally during
his fight to the death with *T. rex*.

the adult ape-males are driven off a cliff and the
women and children are consigned to slavery.
The only relief from racist dogma is the figure
of "Challenger," the combative paleontologist,
whose physique reveals him clearly to be closer to the ape-men than to *Homo sapiens* in every
respect except cranial size. With the mission to
discover the dinosaur and the missing link completed, the Irish journalist returns home to find
that his lady fair has married a solicitor, so he
resigns himself happily to a life of adventure
among men.

The circus atmosphere surrounding the
dinosaur was enhanced by its emergence as a
staple of cinematic animation, from the Barney-
esque cuteness of Gertie to the implacable reptilian monsters of the filmic *Lost World* (1925)
and *King Kong* (1933). The dream of visual
"restoration" of dry bones into living, moving
animals comes true in these films. These
dinosaurs are fully released from science (while
retaining their pseudoscientific legitimacy) into
the realm of mass mythology and imagination,
becoming in effect a whole new vernacular class
of animals on a par with mammals. The jerky,
robotic movements of these new leviathans do

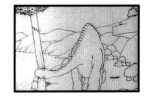

not, curiously enough, detract from their realism, but fit perfectly with their role as embodiments of machine technologies. (Spielberg's dinosaurs, by contrast, with their smooth digitalized animation and robotic servo-motors, exemplify the age of biocybernetic reproduction, in which computer information and genetic engineering converge—for more on this, see chapter 35 below.)

Why is there never a dry eye in the house when the mighty King Kong is gunned down by airplanes and falls to his death from the Empire State Building? Answer: the dinosaurs. Kong's battle with *T. rex* initiates the audience's shift in sympathy from modern white men to the giant ape. The movie's narrative proceeds, in fact, through a series of encounters with increasingly menacing "others," the first of these being "the white woman" (Fay Wray) herself. The heroic first mate who rescues her from King Kong confesses early on that he is afraid of her, and she is generally regarded as a danger to the expedition (though a necessary one, given the need for some "love interest" in the adventure film they are making). The next "other" is the tribe of black people on Kong's island, who dress up as apes, worship Kong as a god, and sacrifice virgins to him. In the face of a common enemy—Kong himself—these racial divisions collapse, and black joins Anglo-Saxon in the battle against the ape. When Kong saves Fay Wray from the dinosaurs, however, we finally see him as closer to us than to them.

Far from being the alien or outsider to humanity, Kong becomes its massive, tragic personification. As ape, he is the spirit of mimesis ("monkey see, monkey do") itself; as giant, he embodies collectivity—not that of the modern masses with their mediated spectacles, but a traditional, premodern form of mass spectacle, the ritual sacrifice with the tribal totem animal at its center. "In his own world he was a god," notes the master of ceremonies at Kong's debut, but in New York City he's just another "attraction" for the gullible masses. Kong's humiliation, his reduction from god to modern spectacle, and his refusal to submit give him tragic stature. Unlike the dinosaur, who consistently measures up to (or towers over) the modern skyscraper, Kong is killed by his fall from the skyscraper. As an animated figure, he is endowed with *anima,* a soul and a loving heart. He is the vanquished guardian that stands between us and the Age of Reptiles, both the generation of vipers that precedes the mammals and the one that is emerging in new forms of modernity. By the end of *King Kong,* the producers of modern mass spectacle—the reporters with their flash cameras, the hysterical radio commentators, the Barnumesque hucksters—are morally indistinguishable from the reptiles that Kong battles on his home turf. After Kong's arrival in New York City, every one of his heroic trials on his home island is replayed in a modernized form: the shattering of the natives' palisade is repeated in his breaking of the chains that tether him to the stage; the battle with the *T. rex* is echoed in his destruction of the elevated train; his fight with the pterodactyl is reenacted in his losing battle with the airplanes. Kong is transformed from the god to whom a

28.2–28.3

In Kong's fight with the pterodactyl (top), he success-
fully defends Fay Wray from the dragonish flying reptiles. He is no match, however, for the machine guns of
the modern pterodactyl, the airplane (bottom). Unlike
the dinosaur, he cannot measure up to that modern
monstrosity known as the skyscraper and falls to his
death from the Empire State Building.

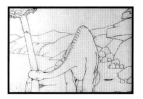

sacrifice is offered into the sacrificial animal itself.

If the dinosaur displaced the mastodon as the nineteenth-century figurehead of the modern evolutionary life sciences, in the twentieth century it triumphs over the ape. It is only a step from *King Kong* to "Fossil Fuels," the McDonald's commercial that stages its skeletal *T. rex* as a Kong-like leviathan, breaking its chains and going on the rampage before falling over and playing dead. (The contemporary remake of *King Kong* shifts the goal of the expedition from movie-making to fossil fuel in the form of oil.) If Kong dies for our sins like a proper tragic hero, the McDonald's *T. rex* plays dead for our amusement like a domestic pet. The modern totem animal is capable of standing tall as a fearsome leviathan one moment and crawling on its belly like a carnival reptile the next. Calvino's "last dinosaur" is on the runway, ready to take his final bow.

28.4

This cartoon by Danny Shanahan recognizes that, no matter how different their ultimate fates, the dinosaur and the great ape belong together in the big city.

(Danny Shanahan © 1997, from The New Yorker Collection. All rights reserved.)

"Let's face it—the city's in our blood."

173

29.1–29.2
Cary Grant as "Dr. Huxley,"
paleontologist, also known as
"Mr. Bones" in Howard Hawkes's
1938 classic, *Bringing Up Baby*
(above). Dr. Huxley is trying to
figure out where to put his bone,
but he will not succeed until he
has "gone gay" (right) and overcome his bone fixation. Katharine
Hepburn shows him that it is
"just an old bone" and that there
are more interesting things in
the world (herself, for instance).

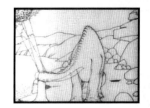

29

BRINGING DOWN BABY

I can't give you anything but love, baby.

THE SETTING: the Stuyvesant Museum of Natural History. The time: the 1930s. The situation: A white-coated paleontologist named David Huxley (played by Cary Grant) sits high atop the scaffold surrounding a *Brontosaurus* skeleton in the pose of Rodin's *The Thinker,* holding a bone in his hand. Dr. Huxley is trying to figure out where to put his bone. Yesterday he tried to put it in the tail, but it didn't fit. He may also be worrying about the financial state of his museum, and the appointment he has later that day with "Mr. Peabody" to raise a million dollars. While he is thinking, a telegram arrives, informing him that the "intercostal clavicle," the last bone needed to complete the *Brontosaurus,* has been dug up and is arriving tomorrow. Thoughts of tomorrow's celebration remind him, naturally, that he's going to be married tomorrow to his research assistant, Alice, and so he gives her a hug and a kiss. She repulses him, and tells him that the arrival of the new bone means that they will have to postpone their honeymoon indefinitely so that nothing will interfere with his work.

> ALICE: Our marriage must entail no domestic entanglements of any kind.
> DAVID: You mean, you mean . . .
> ALICE: I mean, of any kind, David.
> DAVID: Oh, well, Alice, I was sort of hoping . . . well, you mean, you mean children and all that sort of thing . . .
> ALICE: Exactly. [*David mutters to himself.*] This . . . [*making a large sweeping gesture with her left arm*] . . . will be our child.
> DAVID: Huh? [*He looks above and behind him at the brontosaurus . . .*]

The opening of Howard Hawks's classic 1938 comedy, *Bringing Up Baby,* plays upon the double entendre that has been endemic to the subject of "bones" at least since Thomas Jefferson, and probably all the way back to Ezekiel's dry bones erecting themselves as living warriors. Once this cat has been let out of the bag, there is no containing it. Dr. Huxley has tried unsuccessfully to fit his bone into the tail, and he has been told that his marriage will "entail" no entanglements. He has been told that the only babies he's going to make, much less "bring up," are his dinosaur skeletons. Later, his new bone will be stolen and buried in a garden by a dog belonging to a madcap heiress (played by Katharine Hepburn). This woman subjects him to a whole series of embarrassments, including the stealing of his golf ball and his car, the crushing of his top hat, and the stealing of his clothes (so that he is forced to wear one of her negligees). The movie will end with Katharine Hepburn returning his lost bone to him, while shattering the *Brontosaurus* skeleton on which he has been laboring for four years.

It seems safe to say that the masculinity of the big bone cult is under some stress in this movie. Times are hard, and a devoted paleontologist has to put up with a lot for the sake of raising money. The madcap heiress is worth a million dollars (she has influence with a potential donor to the museum), and besides, she looks like a million bucks (not that he would notice). Cary Grant plays the paleontologist directly against the type of the big game hunter, as an absent-minded, mild-mannered professor, befuddled and easily led by women. As he is led through a whirlwind of crazy girlish games by Hepburn, he finds that he has "gone gay," been renamed "Mr. Bones, the Big Game Hunter" while wearing a frilly negligee, and trapped a dangerous leopard only to faint in the arms of his lady.

The brilliance of Cary Grant's performance in *Baby* consists mainly in his physical literalizing of the "bone metaphor" that frames the entire film. Grant plays the role of "stiff" or "straight man," a figure of mechanical rigidity who needs to be awakened to life by Hepburn's vivacity and playfulness. At the verbal level, his stiffness is expressed by inarticulateness, his contributions to the dialogue mainly consisting of expressions like "well . . . " and "but . . . " and "oh, well . . . ." Like the bones that are his obsession, like the skeleton he cannot complete, his sentences tend to be fragmentary, and when he does complete a sentence, it is generally to say the wrong thing ("I've gone gay"). At the level of emotional-physical affect, Grant's Dr. Huxley maintains a stiff sense of propriety, a firm intention to go ahead with his transparently bad marriage, and a rigid posture of anxiety that resists Hepburn's liveliness and gaiety throughout. He does not relax his paralyzed resistance to his female seducer until the final scene, when she shatters the skeleton of his *Brontosaurus* and forces him to rescue her.

The scene of this rescue, in which the collapsing framework of bones leaves only a bare scaffold with two acrobats clinging to it, closes the narrative. The film opens with its visual space literally framed by the nearly completed skeleton and closes with the collapse of that skeleton. "It's either me or those old bones, take your pick," the movie seems to say, speaking with the

voice of the woman. We can say that this is also the voice of animal desire. Hepburn has her own totem animals, her live leopard ("Baby") and her lapdog ("George"). Against these weapons, Huxley's stiff, dead bones don't have a chance. A sophomoric joke about lapdogs, bones, and pussies hovers over the whole screwball scenario, but it need never be articulated. The wondrous thing about the double entendre of bones is that it can be disavowed, ignored, or misunderstood at any time. Sometimes, as Freud noted, a cigar is just a cigar. And sometimes a bone is, as Hepburn remarks at one point, "just an old bone."

When bones are erected in a total framework, however, they become something more. The dinosaur skeleton has, by this time, become an unacknowledged image of the U.S. Constitution. Its cultural ancestry in the Jeffersonian mastodon, its association with a specifically North American antiquity and nature, and its status as a symbol of big capital and manhood in modern America have given it an aura and prestige that are unavoidable—but not unimpeachable. Like Jefferson's mastodon, the dinosaur is a bit silly. It is vulnerable to a shattering blow that will reduce it to fragments.

But what can this shattering of the dinosaur skeleton mean? Is *Bringing Up Baby* proposing a Jeffersonian revolution that would destroy the old Constitution and require the building of a new one? In a certain sense, the answer is yes, and the revolution is perfectly obvious. It is the Nineteenth Amendment, which, by giving women the vote, doesn't merely add a new clause to the old framework, like inserting a new bone into an old skeleton. The new clause makes all the old ones read in a different way. Words like "happiness," "pursuit," "all men," "endowed," and "created equal" change their meaning when women are part of the picture. Katharine Hepburn's character is, as Stanley Cavell has pointed out, one of the daughters of the suffrage movement; she takes a certain emancipation and revolution in women's expectations for granted.[1] "We the people" are now gendered: "All men—and women—are created equal." Everything has to be rearranged in order for the basic right to the "pursuit of happiness"—understood to mean the pursuit of love or money—to be possible.

Cavell argues that *Bringing Up Baby* belongs to a genre of films that he calls the "comedy of re-marriage," which redefines the relations between the sexes in the United States during the Depression. He suggests further that the basic American right to the pursuit of happiness is being reconfigured in these films, that they mark a moment when women have become different and men are learning how to become different. *Bringing Up Baby* strikes me as the film in this genre that presents this argument most comprehensively as something like a "constitutional issue," with its framing of the whole narrative inside the fate of a dinosaur skeleton. Certainly the dinosaurian image of capitalism is already under severe stress in the 1930s: the cycles of boom and bust that punctuated the Gilded Age and the first thirty years of the twentieth century have hit a new nadir. If "Mr. Peabody," Dr. Huxley's potential donor, is meant to remind us of the nineteenth-century banker who financed the Peabody

29.3
The collapse of the dinosaur into a chaotic jumble of bones is as important to the American dinosaur narrative as its resurrection to life. If the giant skeleton is a symbol of America's "natural consti-tution," then the constitutional right to the "pursuit of happiness" seems to require the periodic deconstruction of the whole framework. Thomas Jefferson would have approved of Gary Larson's destructive geek.

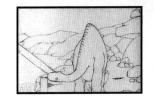

Museum of Natural History, it soon becomes clear that he has no money to give. If the dinosaur reminds anyone of the robber barons and the Wall Street tycoons at this point, they will not be surprised to see it collapsing. Happiness (love, money) is no longer facilitated by this framework. On the contrary, it is the major obstacle to the comic resolution. The *Brontosaurus* is literally what stands between the lovers; it has to be surmounted and shattered in order for them to get together.

I conclude, therefore, that *Baby* is not so much about re-marriage, and re-fashioning the Constitution, as it is about the prevention of the wrong kind of marriage, the wrong kind of happiness, and the shattering of an oppressive constitution, with perhaps not a clue as to what will replace it. Our happy couple has never been married, and we have no idea how it will work out. Their courtship has scarcely gone beyond the level of children's games, and Cavell is right to see them as occupying something like Freud's "latency period" of sexual development, after the Oedipus complex is resolved but before puberty and mature sexuality have arrived (roughly between the ages of six and twelve). If the dinosaur is an ancestral figure at the level of community or nation, it is the oedipal father in the private sphere. Children generally get obsessed with dinosaurs in kindergarten and first grade, and get over it as they move into the latency period. In that sense, *Bringing Up Baby* is about the slightly more mature girl bringing her boy along into latency, where games can be played that might lead to something more grown-up. In short, it is about outgrowing the dinosaur, about the end of that oedipal phase of history we have called "modernity."

I don't want to overstate the radicality of *Bringing Up Baby*. Although at some levels (the imaginary and symbolic) it is a subversive, even revolutionary film in the Jeffersonian sense, with its anarchist shattering of the constitutional skeleton, at another level (the Real) it is just a comedy about an absent-minded professor, a dizzy heiress, and some old bones. The Nineteenth Amendment gave women the vote, but not much more. Dr. Huxley will get his million dollars, and a girl who looks the part. We can expect that he will rebuild his dino-baby and make real babies who will be brought up in a house full of living animals. This sounds more like domestic life in the suburbs than the dawning of a new era.

Or maybe domestic life in the suburbs *is* the face of the new era that is dawning in American life. Stephen Spielberg seems to have sensed this possibility in his allusions to the ending of *Baby* in the climax of *Jurassic Park*. Like Hawks, Spielberg concludes with a spectacular scene of skeletal collapse. Instead of a pair of lovers being united over a heap of dry bones, however, we witness the formation of a whole domestic unit—the prototypical white, suburban, nuclear family (mom, dad, and two kids)—amid the collapsing skeletons in the atrium of Jurassic Park's visitor's center. These four people are not a real family (the kids are the grandchildren of John Hammond, Jurassic Park's founder), and the possibility that this couple might never have children

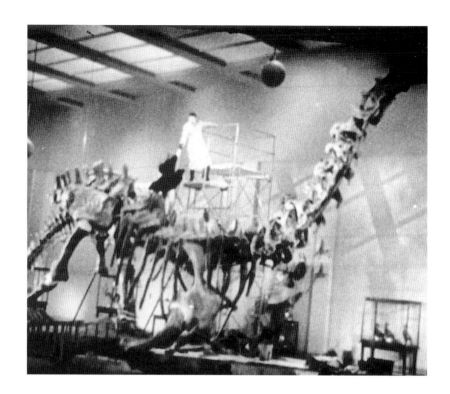

has been at issue throughout the story. Like Cary Grant's character, "Dr. Grant" (Sam Neill), the paleontologist, is too wrapped up in his work to be concerned with marriage or children, much to the annoyance of Ellie Sattler (Laura Dern), the paleobotanist, who is clearly ready to have some children. (This impression is conveyed by Spielberg's view of Laura Dern as an "earthy child-woman" who is happiest when reaching into mounds of dinosaur shit.) Dr. Grant's dislike of children is overcome as the story unfolds by his being compelled to rescue them repeatedly from dinosaurs. It's as if this paleontologist can get interested in children only when he can see them as members of an endangered species. Spielberg, similarly, understands that the endangered species symbolized by the old dinosaur at the end of the twentieth century is the nuclear family.

Jurassic Park shows us a world in which the chief threat to the pursuit of happiness is not an old framework of dry bones—the archaic oedipal structure of white male supremacy—but a new form of living dinosaur based in new technologies of "restoration" and new forms of capitalization. The old era of "Mr. Peabody," of the Morgans, Roosevelts, Fields, and Carnegies, is a distant memory in *Jurassic Park*. Now we have a multinational, multicultural corporation, financed with fast-moving venture capital, undertaking a high-risk, high-tech, environmentally dubious scheme. The program of "visual education" for the public—the awakening of scientific curiosity through the display of natural wonders—is still evoked as a piety, but it is overwhelmed more than ever by the "circus atmosphere" around dinosaurology, the frankness about Jurassic Park's status as a commercial venture rather than a public museum. Potlatch will be at a minimum in this Monster House. When John Hammond expresses his grandfatherly hope that children will be brought to the park free of charge, the park's lawyer returns him quickly to the bottom line. At the

29.4–29.5
Katharine Hepburn and Cary Grant are united over the collapsing skeleton of his *Brontosaurus* in the final scene of *Bringing Up Baby* (top). Spielberg replays this spectacle as a family reunion in the climax of *Jurassic Park*, bringing his broken nuclear family (the paleontological couple and the two kids they have "adopted") together over the collapsing skeleton of a *T. rex* (bottom).
(Film stills from *Bringing Up Baby* and *Jurassic Park*.)

first sight of the living dinosaurs, as the rest of party is gaping in wonder, the lawyer declares, "We're going to make a fortune!"

So it is not the dry bones of the old order that stand in the way of love and child-rearing in *Jurassic Park*. The threat comes from the *new* order, from the lively, warm-blooded, intelligent new-model dinosaurs, the velociraptors, who stand ready to devour the nuclear family and turn the suburban theme park back into a Hobbesian jungle. It's only appropriate, then, that the deus ex machina who arrives to rescue the family is that representative of the old order, the King of the Reptiles, *Tyrannosaurus rex*. It's almost like that moment in *King Kong* when the great ape rescues Fay Wray from the dinosaurs, except that *T. rex* is in no danger of being humanized and set up as a sacrificial animal, a dying god brought down by modern technology. The only "aura" surrounding *T. rex* is a kind of nostalgia for the good old days of "feudal" capitalism, when companies were identified with individual "giants" (like Spielberg himself) who were capable of great evil and great good. The raptors, by contrast, represent the new stage of postmodern capitalism, of "downsizing," flexibility, rapid strike forces, teamwork, adaptability, steep learning curves, and (not incidentally) gender confusion. From the opening scene of *Jurassic Park,* the raptors are presented as "clever girls" who are "figuring things out" and hatching plots (along with unauthorized eggs) to prepare for their eventual takeover. The male hysteria and anxiety about impotence that shadow *Baby* are on full display in *Jurassic Park*.

"*Today, gentlemen, we trade in the brute force of the T. Rex for the cunning of the raptor.*"

29.6
Central to the American right to the pursuit of happiness is the freedom to get rich any way one can. Styles of capital accumulation, like dinosaur fashions, go through historical shifts, and yesterday's business strategy can come to seem obsolete. (Drawing by Lorenz; © 1997. The New Yorker Magazine, Inc.)

miner's canary or trojan horse?

I CAN THINK OF (at least) two objections to these readings of *Bringing Up Baby* and *Jurassic Park* (and perhaps to everything that has preceded them): first, that they are excessive "readings into" what are, after all, nothing but Hollywood entertainments; second, that they simply use the films to talk about other things (the history of capitalism, of American ideology, of sexual anxiety) that might be better discussed directly. If the modern dinosaur, for instance, is simply a symbol of the robber barons, why not just discuss the robber barons? If the bone is a phallic symbol and the skeleton a symbol of the Constitution, why not just talk about male hysteria and constitutional history?

The first objection is usually met by defending the dignity and complexity of mass culture and arguing that it will sustain just as much high-powered interpretation as Shakespeare. The fact that Shakespeare's plays *were* in fact the mass culture of their day, that the division between elite and popular art is always being blurred by history, helps this argument considerably. The only problem with this defense is that in a certain sense, I don't really want to argue for the "complexity" of these works—not, at least, in the way one might argue for the moral complexity of a Henry James novel. I want to suggest, by contrast, that these works are actually simple, that they are vulgar, and that that is part of the secret of their mass appeal. Saying that they are simple and vulgar doesn't mean that they are stupid or worthless: on the contrary, as the Quakers remind us, 'tis a gift to be simple, and it takes real talent to be a master of the vulgar. It is part of the magic of the dinosaur image that it is so irredeemably vulgar, so inescapably familiar, and so simple. Big, fierce, extinct reptiles: that's all there is to it. The rest is what we make of it. If that involves some creativity on the part of bone hunters, artists, entrepreneurs, filmmakers, and spectators, then that creativity is what we are really studying when we "read into" the dinosaur image.

The second objection, that we should cut to the chase and talk about real history instead of these symbolic substitutes, is usually met by stressing the importance of culture as an autonomous sphere of human activity. Yet everything we have learned from and about dinosaurs suggests that "autonomy" is not quite what they exemplify. They work more like symptoms, eruptions on the surface of the body politic that indicate deeper, less visible pathologies. The question, "why do we need dinosaurs?" is something like the question, "what good is a fever?" They are warning signs, like the canaries that were taken down into nineteenth-century coal mines to test the atmosphere: if the canary dies, the miners will not be far behind. We might see the dinosaur as obeying the same logic, with a reverse twist: when the dinosaur comes to life, some group of human beings is on the endangered species list. This extraordinarily simple moral of the story was seen clearly by the Indians, who understood that the return of the American *incognitum* (the mammoth) or the Unktehi (the giant reptiles) would mean the destruction of their game, their lands, their very existence as peoples. This moral was also seen clearly by the first visitors to the Crystal Palace exhibition, who understood that if the creatures displayed there were to come back to life, we would not be having dinner in them; they would be dining on us. As the nuclear family escapes from the raptors in *Jurassic Park,* Dr. Grant tells the park director, "After careful reflection I've decided not to endorse your park."

The lameness and obviousness of Dr. Grant's remark, however, make it stick out like a sore thumb. This "moral conclusion" is so flagrantly "too little, too late" that the remark itself seems merely an annoying little pain, symptomatic of some much greater failure of moral and political imagination. Earlier in *Jurassic Park,* a more refined version of this moral reasoning is uttered by chaos theoretician Ian Malcolm, who objects to the shallowness of the whole concept of the park, and especially to the failure of its designers to recognize the monstrous implications of the technologies they are unleashing. This is the Frankenstein or "modern Prometheus" homily: we are like children playing with fire, or (even more ominously) moths drawn to the flame, in our attraction to the mass destruction symbolized by the dinosaur. Insofar as the dinosaur turns the spectacle of mass death into a massive public attraction, its function is less like that of a miner's canary than that of a Trojan horse. We compulsively ignore the warnings of the moralizers who understand that this monstrous animal is a harbinger and instrument of our destruction. Instead of leaving the monster alone, or presenting it as a gift to the gods by burning it in a potlatch ritual, we take it into our cities and treat it as a monument. (For an alternative response, see the discussion in chapter 40 of Utah's

Dinosaur National Monument, which leaves the partly exposed bones in the ground.)

Is the dinosaur more like a miner's canary, a warning of disaster, or a Trojan horse, an instrument to lure us into destruction? Or could it be some complex combination of the two, a monstrous image that invariably provokes the ritual recitation of moral lessons and admonitions, while subtly preparing us to accept the fate it is prophesying? *Bringing Up Baby* and *Jurassic Park* conjure with all these possibilities, which is why neither story is content to erect the giant skeletons for our wonder. Instead, both films insist on staging their destruction as the necessary prelude to possible futures: in the earlier film, the pursuit of happiness; in the later, survival (and the certainty of a sequel). Both films refuse, in short, to settle for a reading of the dinosaur either as "mere symptom" (to be "read" and bypassed in favor of deeper or more real issues) or as the pathology itself, the actual agency of disaster (to be destroyed as a simple, conclusive remedy to the evil they foreshadow). They provide, instead, a comprehensive representation of the ritual cycle of the dinosaur, both its birth/resurrection/restoration *and* its destruction. They treat the dinosaur, in short, as a totem animal—as a convergence of at least four distinct dimensions—sex, money, politics, and nature—in a single ensemble of symbolic objects.

The Lost World (1997), Spielberg's sequel to *Jurassic Park,* concludes with the dinosaur returned to its most fundamental totemic role: it becomes a taboo object, to be permanently quarantined and left alone. Whether this untouchability is a sign of its sublime, dangerous magic, or simply reflects a cagey marketing sense that the dinosaur is now becoming an exhausted consumer attraction, is really the only interesting question raised by *The Lost World.* In the opening scene, Spielberg segues from the face of a terrified little girl under attack by small scavenger dinosaurs to the bored yawn of Jeff Goldblum on a street corner in New York City.

The audience laughs in instant recognition of Spielberg's anticipation of their response: dinosaurs provoke yawns almost as readily as they incite screaming and terror.

When Theodor Adorno called the dinosaur a symbol of the "monstrous total State," he forgot to specify what state and what totality he had in mind. We assume he was thinking of fascism, but he was writing in and about America, and he could as easily have been talking about the Soviet Union or the emergent world system of late modern capitalism. The dinosaur isn't merely "read" or interpreted as sign, symptom, or allegory, and it isn't merely acted upon as if it were a living thing. It is treated as both a symptom and the pathology that it signifies, both as the sign of an event and the event itself. That is why it is best described as a "transitional object," not just in the sense of individual psychology and child development, but at the level of history and (possibly) the evolution of the human species.[1]

"The Dinosaurs Return. A New Era Begins," trumpet the ads for the opening of the new (1995) dinosaur hall at the American Museum of Natural History. What is this new era? What was the old one that was left behind? To answer these questions, we need to return to our narrative of the modern dinosaur, focusing on the consolidation of what Stephen Jay Gould called "the modern consensus." But this time we will see it, not in the form of the volatile, unstable "schizosaur" perfected by Charles Knight between 1900 and 1930, but in the stabilized utopian form it assumed during World War II.

THE AGE OF REPTILES

A work of art is immersed in the whirlpool of time; and it belongs to eternity. A work of art is specific, local, individual; and it is our brightest token of universality. A work of art rises proudly above any interpretation we may see fit to give it; and, although it serves to illustrate history, man and the world itself, it goes further than this: it creates man, creates the world and sets up within history an immutable order.

—HENRI FOCILLON, *The Life of Forms in Art* (1934)

IN 1940, A STUDENT in his final year at Yale's School of Fine Arts received a call from the Peabody Museum of Natural History, asking if he would be interested in a job. The museum's board had determined that its large dinosaur hall needed some sprucing up. There was no money available to hire a "star" artist like Charles Knight to decorate the hall, but a salary of $40 per week had become available when the museum's electrician went off to war in Europe. So Rudolph Zallinger was hired. He had never been in the Peabody Museum before. He had only the vaguest notion of what a dinosaur was, and had to take a crash course with the Peabody paleontologists. A calm, patient, perfectionist artist-illustrator of the "old school," Zallinger took his time with the job. When he finished five years later, World War II had come and gone, America was a new place, and the Peabody Museum had one of the largest mural frescoes in the world, a magnificent panorama entitled *The Age of Reptiles*, 110 feet long and 16 feet high.[1]

One's first impression of *The Age of Reptiles* is likely to be oblique and mediated. For one thing, its images have been reproduced in numerous children's books, in *Life* magazine's 1950 series on the history of life, and in 70 million postage stamps.

31.1

Among the world's largest authentic fresco wall
paintings, Rudolph Zallinger's *The Age of Reptiles* at
Yale's Peabody Museum synthesizes the understanding of dinosaurs in the modern period and envisions
a dinotopic refuge from World War II. Painted
between 1940 and 1945, Zallinger's mural displays
the 170-million-year evolution of ancient life as a
single, unified landscape panorama, a symmetrical
tableau of stately reptilian demigods in a peaceable
arcadian kingdom. (Copyright 1989, Peabody Museum
of Natural History, Yale University, New Haven, CT, USA.)

Like Charles Knight, Rudolph Zallinger is among the most famous unknown painters in the world, an artist whose images are instantly recognizable, as if we had already seen them, as if they had always existed, like the anonymous animal cave paintings of Lascaux. When you enter the Peabody

dinosaur hall, moreover, the mural is not the first thing you see. What stands before you are the giant dinosaur skeletons gathered by O. C. Marsh and reconstructed by his successors. The mural is up high and to your right, first glimpsed in your peripheral vision, then seen through the framework of the skeletons, looming above them like a vast dream or hallucination. (The poor

lighting augments the effect of the obstructed view, making the mural almost impossible to photograph. If you want to see the colors clearly and study the figures, you must look at the excellent photographic reproductions in the recent handbook on *The Age of Reptiles,* published by Harry Abrams in 1990.)

The program of the mural is simplicity itself. Its narrative unfolds from right to left (opposite to the normal direction of reading) as a chronological panorama comprehending 170 million years of geological time, from the Devonian to the Cretaceous, with the intermediate periods of the Carboniferous, Permian, Triassic, and Jurassic marked unobtrusively by foregrounded trees. As you take in the entire panorama, the sense of the image as a temporal procession is steadily overwhelmed by a synchronic, spatial apprehension of the entire painting as a single, unified image of mass gathering or assembly. This impression is reinforced by two formal features of the painting: first, its right-to-left arrangement "against the grain" of a textual reading sequence; and second, the fact that the larger, "later" figures on the left (the *T. rex* and *Brontosaurus*) face to our right, "backward" in time, as it were, while the "early," smaller figures on the right face left, that is, "forward" in time. One can see this effect by concentrating on the sequence of dominant figures, *Dimetrodon, Edaphosaurus, Plateosaurus,* and *Allosaurus,* which make the transition from the Permian to the Jurassic seem like a procession to the right.

At almost the exact center of the mural appears *Stegosaurus,* a highly symmetrical creature whose head and tail seem almost identical, and which in fact (or fantasy) was once thought to have a "second brain" in its tail. In short, despite the chronological program dictated by the scientific subtext, Zallinger obeyed the cardinal rule of artistic form and unified his image in a single, massive gestalt that can be seen in and as a single moment.

This effect is sustained by the materiality of the mural, its texture, surface, coloration, disposition of figures and space. Everything is delineated in the most precise detail; the atmosphere is transparent; the figures are arranged in "echelons," military formations in which each unit is staggered so that the full array of masses is made visible and put in perspective. All of this grows out of a quite amazing convergence between medieval painting techniques and modern subject matter, resulting in something very different from the romantic Gothicism of Charles Knight. Knight was essentially a nineteenth-century animal landscape painter, and his work is full of dash, movement, and atmosphere. His barons of bone are neo-Gothic, romantic leviathans, bursting with energy, rendered in oil and gouache. Zallinger is what Heinrich Wolfflin called a "linear" artist,

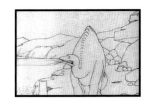

while Knight is "painterly." The Giotto of dinosaur illustration, Zallinger displays with pristine clarity the eternal forms of underlying reality, not passing, mutable appearances. Vincent Scully notes that his fresco owes both its technique and its conception to the fifteenth-century painter and theorist Cennino Cennini, whose *Libro dell'Arte*, the "bible" of the Yale School of Fine Arts from 1937 to 1950, stressed the ability of painting "to discover things not seen, hiding themselves under the shadow of natural objects."[2]

Zallinger's mastery of this idealist theory and technique of painting found its perfect theme in the problem of dinosaur restoration. The dinosaur is, strictly speaking, an invisible, conceptual, theoretical object, a speculative construction that has to be projected from fragments that bear little visual resemblance to the unity they betoken. A strange paradox confronts the dinosaur restorer: the more "realistic" or "illusionistic" or "convincing" the restoration, the more it betrays the truth of the image as a constructed, made thing. The more illusionistic the dinosaur image, the more fraudulent it seems. The technique of the fresco resolves this paradox by refusing to serve mere appearances, presenting instead the eternal archetypes, the way late medieval painters represented unseen divinities in visible forms.

Zallinger's composition utterly renounces, therefore, both "painterly" effects of light and shadow and theatrical devices of compositional arrangement. There are no "dramatic scenes" in *The Age of Reptiles*, no little vignettes or subplots. Each figure occupies its own space. Action, motion, and (most notably) violent confrontations are completely absent from the composition. If anything, the painting suggests a kind of stately, slow-motion procession or promenade. It portrays the imperceptible evolution of life-forms in a majestic tableau that itself had to unfold over a five-year period of slow, solitary manual labor. Henri Focillon, who was a visiting professor at the Yale School of Fine Arts during Zallinger's student days, could have recognized in it an unforeseen confirmation of his theory of the "life of forms in art": a synthesis of vision and technique, subject matter and style that is "immersed in the whirlpool of time" and yet "belongs to eternity."[3]

From a paleontological point of view, *The Age of Reptiles* summarizes in an encyclopedic panorama what Gould calls "the modern consensus" about dinosaurs. Many of its features are now seen as obsolete: there are mistakes in the vegetation, and its swamp-bound *Brontosaurus* has been restored to dry land. It shows no "high browsers" rearing up on their hind legs to graze on treetops. It contains none of the lively, birdlike figures that appear in some of Knight's paintings, and which now dominate dinosaur illustration so completely that the contemporary *T. rex* looks like a large and very dangerous plucked chicken. Zallinger's painting is often blamed for fixing the "classic" image of the dinosaur as slow-moving, swamp-bound, and doomed to extinction. Robert Bakker, for instance, regards *The Age of Reptiles* as the epitome of the "dinosaurian orthodoxy" that he has overturned with his own "dinosaur heresies." He traces the "Eureka!" moment of his own research to the experience of standing in the dinosaur hall at the Peabody Museum and saying to himself, "There's something very wrong with our dinosaurs."[4]

Zallinger, of course, is not to blame for the scientific mistakes in his painting. Perhaps more than any previous dinosaur restorer, he was merely a servant to scientific knowledge, taking his orders from the Yale paleontologists. (After his first visit to the Peabody, he came home and looked up dinosaurs in the encyclopedia.) What was clearly "right" about his composition is virtually everything else one can say about it. Zallinger used the right medium and displayed the right figures in the right way at the right place and time. He created a modern monument, both a classic image-repertoire and a total gestalt. Daniel Varney Thompson called it "the most important" achievement in fresco "since the fifteenth century."[5] It deserved the Pulitzer prize for painting that it received in 1949; it deserved to be put into global circulation by *Life* magazine and the U.S. Post Office.

Rudolph Zallinger lost his job at the Yale School of Fine Arts when Josef Albers took over in 1950 and purged the school of its illustrators and picto-

rialists in favor of pure geometrical abstraction on the Bauhaus model. Zallinger held no artist's rights to *The Age of Reptiles*. His $40 a week wages for the five years of work and the thought of serving his beloved Yale were enough for him.[6] Zallinger continued to work as a muralist and natural history illustrator until his death in 1994. He never produced any other work that came remotely close to his masterpiece, either in scale and ambition or in cultural impact.

What, then, is the meaning of *The Age of Reptiles?* More precisely, how are we to understand the minor miracle that this painting exists at all in the precise form and with the vast influence that it has? This work exemplifies, in my view, a very little understood phenomenon in Focillon's "life of forms," the moment when an image undergoes a decisive evolutionary transformation. Focillon says that "plastic forms are subjected to the principle of metamorphosis, by which they are perpetually renewed."[7] The image of the dinosaur was already in circulation when Zallinger accepted his commission, but Zallinger was almost completely innocent about

31.2

The contemporary or postmodern dinosaur. *T. rex* is no longer seen as a lumbering giant, analogous to a tank or locomotive, but is depicted as a large and extremely dangerous chicken. (Painting © Gregory S. Paul 1997.)

it. He had never seen the paintings of Charles Knight, and he had never been to the Peabody Museum. What Zallinger brought to the painting was a high level of competence in a theoretical and technical tradition of image making. What the paleontologists brought to it was "normal science," a fairly stable and (in the thirties and forties) relatively boring and stagnant body of knowledge. The Depression and World War II were, by all accounts, the "dark ages" of dinosaurology. But these elements (technical skill, a moribund field of knowledge) hardly seem to be sufficient components for the production of a monumental, classic, enduring image. Or perhaps we should say that they are *merely* favorable conditions for such an achievement. Something, it seems, is still missing from the account, some angle of vision from which the inevitability and rightness of Zallinger's painting can be understood.

Sometimes an artist works "in the grip" of an intuition that can be deciphered only in retrospect. It is unfashionable these days to talk about artistic inspiration as an explanatory notion, especially since it only seems to defer explanation. But perhaps we should pause over this possibility for a moment. William Blake (another idealist fresco painter and follower of Cennini) is one artist whose work seems, as it were, "dictated," not just by authorities or texts, but by a visual-technical convergence that makes the act of composition almost compulsive and involuntary, even as it is precise and incisively deliberate. The photographer Robert Frank, who produced a photographic essay in the 1950s called *The Americans,* seemed to work "in the grip" of an inspiration for an extended period, producing a body of images that has decisively influenced all photographic practice since. Frank gave up still photography after completing this work, as if he had been wrung out by being employed as the vehicle of an intuition, an instrument of an insight into his own medium and the condition of the American nation at a specific moment in history.

Zallinger was, I suspect, in the grip of dinosaurial form, a cultural image-repertoire that had, by the end of the 1930s, taken on a life of its own, independent of its scientific interest. What had not yet been provided for this image, what it "wanted" at this moment in its history, was a comprehensive world-picture—not just all the kinds, but all the *times* comprehended in a single image, showing a place (the world) and a period (the 170-million-year Age of Reptiles). In an age of what Heidegger called "world-pictures," this was the biggest, the most temporally and spatially comprehensive. Covering 170 million years and the entire range of global habitats, it dwarfs its main competitor in vertebrate paleontology, the Age of Mammals, and reduces our time, the time of *Homo sapiens,* to a mere moment.

The great intuition Zallinger had (and this was evident to him from his first sketch) was to see this picture of endless deep time as itself only a long moment, a kind of utopian *tableau vivant*, a reptilian Garden of Eden, completely devoid of violence or dramatic action of any kind. The only activity, in fact, is the scavenging *Allosaurus* chewing on a carcass. There is, at the same time, tremendous energy in the landscape and the giant figures, the former

in the warm, glowing pink cliffs, water, and atmosphere, the latter marked by the cold, serene menace in the reptilian faces. This is not so much a pacified utopia as a mobilized one, a scene of gathering, assembly, a passing in review (the "echelon" structure contributes to this impression). It's impossible to resist the notion that this is a picture of its own time as well, the historical moment of World War II in New Haven, Connecticut, with the battlewagons and the lend-lease armadas gathering on Long Island Sound and in Mystic Seaport.[8] The period from 1933 through 1945 was a time of gatherings—migrations, refugees, concentration camps, mass rallies, massive armies and navies. Disney's *Fantasia* (1940) had gathered the dinosaurs around a dry lake bed in accordance with a scenario provided by Barnum Brown. There was also the persistent tradition of the Victorian antediluvian monsters assembling to board the Ark, and in Europe, Capek's "War with the Newts" of mass society.

American tabloids still announce the discovery of remnants of Noah's "second Ark" in the Nevada desert. But Zallinger's gathering doesn't seem to prefigure imminent catastrophe. Extinction is not a prominent feature of his pictorial narrative. It elides the great mass dying

31.3

Another way of depicting the gathering of the dinosaurs is to link them with the story of Noah's Ark. Some creationists argue that the dinosaurs died out in the flood because they were too large for the Ark. Others speculate that there was a second ark for the ruling reptiles, but it went down in a storm. American tabloids report regularly on the "discovery" of the remains of Noah's second ark along with its dinosaurial cargo.

("Dinosaurs on Noah's Second Ark," *Sun*, 3 August 1993.)

at the end of the Permian period, for instance, into a gentle transition from the swamp to the dry land. Perhaps the distant volcanoes in the Cretaceous (or the anachronistic blooming magnolias in the foreground) signal a change in the atmosphere reminiscent of Richard Owen's "air pollution" scenario of extinction. But the only unambiguous sign that the end is at hand is so unobtrusive as to be nearly invisible. It is *Cimolestes,* the little mouselike mammal at the foot of the magnolias, the herald of the new mammalian world order that will succeed the Age of Reptiles. Thomas Jefferson thought that species were eternal, that nothing could change a mouse into a mammoth, but that is exactly the possibility that Zallinger evokes with his mouse, our diminutive ancestor. This is the last figure that Zallinger painted on the mural, before affixing his signature a few inches away. Gary Larson captures this moment in a cartoon showing dinosaurs laughing at a little furry mammal, while one of them is noticing the fall of the first snowflake.

31.4

Rudolph Zallinger's speculation about what killed the dinosaurs: perhaps a mouse (a fur-coated egg-robber that could survive harsh winters) or some magnolias (flowering plants that might have changed the percentage of oxygen in the atmosphere, to the detriment of the dinosaurs).

(Detail of figure 31.1.)

Zallinger's peaceable kingdom has to be seen, then, as a utopian refuge seen through rose-colored glasses, a kind of compensatory image of a world at peace conceived in the midst of a world at war. At the same time, it is an image of both war and peace as gathering and mobilization rather than actual conflict, showing a panorama of assembled forces, a prophetic vision of the coming Pax Americana after World War II. It marks the dawn of the Cold War era and what Philip Wylie called a "generation of vipers," the complacent era of the fifties. It heralds the period of *Life* magazine's panorama of life itself, and the globalization of American values in *The Family of Man.* Dinosaurs will move to the suburbs and into the curriculum of

American elementary education. They will appear in TV sitcoms, roadside attractions, national parks, children's books, toy stores, and the funny papers, becoming as familiar as the family dog and cat, and more familiar, perhaps, than farm animals, which will rapidly become exotic features of urban petting zoos. Again, Gary Larson comprehends the scene perfectly with his picture of a cow in a marsh with *Stegosaurus* in the background, the caption reading, "65 million years ago when cows ruled the earth." Zallinger's vision of dinosaurs as mighty demigods, eternal archetypes in a procession of slow time like the figures on Keats's Grecian urn, will give way to the domestication of the dinosaur, its humiliation as a figure of obsolescence and failure to adapt. "Slowness" will lose the stately, dignified aura that Zallinger gave it, turning into an image of stupidity and dullness that can be contrasted with the cult of progress, technical innovation, and scientific competition that will mark the fifties and sixties.

At the same time that the dinosaur serves as an image of backwardness, however, it (as always) plays an equally important role as a figure of novelty and sometimes runaway innovation. The image of the Ford Edsel as dinosaur works in this way, exemplifying an innovation that failed to catch on, a kind of evolutionary mutant or dead end in the survival-of-the-fittest world of rapidly changing automobile styles. The "arms race" finds its appropriate reptilian allegory in the spectacle of endless new developments in offensive and defensive weaponry. The most spectacular example of this metaphor is the phenomenon of the Japanese Godzilla, a new dinosaur that originates in the 1950s as a by-product of the American atomic bomb, a genetic mutation produced by radioactivity.

Every dinosaur quickly reveals itself as a transitional object, however, and Godzilla is no exception. He moves rapidly from being the

31.5
All automobiles (and, indeed, all technical innovations, most notably computers) are destined to become dinosaurs in one way or another: if the machine breaks down (as it inevitably does in an economy of planned obsolescence), it becomes part of the junk-heap of history; if it survives as a "classic" or "masterpiece," it becomes a nostalgic fossil trace, a relic of a "lost world." The Edsel began as a dinosaur in the first sense and now is a dinosaur in the second sense.

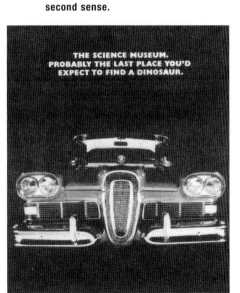

THE SCIENCE MUSEUM. PROBABLY THE LAST PLACE YOU'D EXPECT TO FIND A DINOSAUR.

scourge of Japan to being its defender against even worse threats, such as the Smog Monster. The totem animal of American modernity is adapted and remodeled at the moment when Japanese industries are beginning to adopt and transform a whole range of American technologies—automobiles, electronics, and (more recently) genetic engineering. It comes as no surprise that the resurrection of the latest-model dinosaur in *Jurassic Park* depends heavily on Japanese financial and technical input. The dinosaur always was an international phenomenon. Even in the Victorian moment of "British fossil reptiles," Richard Owen knew that he was uncovering the traces of a globally distributed group of animals. While important work in paleontology had been carried out in Europe since the nineteenth century, it was the United States that moved the dinosaur from its role as premier museum attraction to a key position in national and international popular culture. If Carnegie had treated the *Diplodocus* as a monster gift to foreign powers, after World War II the American dinosaur would become an export commodity to the world—a process that would reach its culmination in the unprecedented success of *Jurassic Park*.

31.6

Chrome bumper dinosaurs, by John Kearney. These dinosaurs, resurrected from the junkyards of West Chicago, were commissioned as public attractions to help "resurrect" an economically depressed neighborhood. Unfortunately, the businessman who commissioned them went bankrupt, and the dinosaurs were sold off to pay his debts. (Photo by Lynn Kearney.)

THE HUNDRED STORY BEAST

WALLACE STEVENS THOUGHT there were "Thirteen Ways of Looking at a Blackbird." There are at least that many stories of the dinosaur, and like the stories of a skyscraper or the stacked faces on a totem pole, they keep piling up. The earliest stories are on the bottom, like the lowest levels of an archaeological dig or the "low man on the totem pole." But even the earliest stories, the deepest in time, no matter how fantastic or disgraced, never seem to be completely lost or forgotten. Dragons and biblical beasts, the behemoth and the leviathan, underlie the modern stories of the dinosaur like the foundations of a building, and they continue to be available right alongside the "higher," more advanced stories. Creationist accounts of dinosaurs continue to flourish even now, and not just in the tabloids. At William Jennings Bryan College in Tennessee, the battle against Darwin continues. Feasibility studies of Noah's Ark are being published, and debates are being waged on the Internet about what *T. rex* could have eaten in the Garden of Eden, given the prohibition on death and violence. (Answer: Eden lasted only a few weeks, and it is a well-known fact that reptiles can go longer than that without food. The Fall of Man came along just in time to save the great carnivores from starvation.)[1]

Another "foundational" story of the dinosaur is offered by Carl Sagan in *The Dragons of Eden*. Sagan argues that "deep down," human beings themselves are actually dinosaurs, because the "most ancient part of the human brain" is the "reptilian or R-complex." Like every other organ in the body, the brain had to evolve

32.1

If the dinosaur is itself a kind of animate skyscraper, it is also the antagonist of the skyscraper, the giant crane with its wrecking ball that is tall enough to attack the city. Gary Larson reframes this familiar modern story as the scene of a kid entering an amusement park ride.

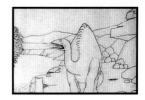

from simpler, more primitive structures to its present state of complexity. The central core of the human brain is reptilian; the intermediate layer is the "limbic system," which we share with other mammals, but not reptiles; and the outer, upper layer is the "neocortex," which we share with higher mammals such as dolphins and apes. Conclusion: "we should expect the R-complex in the human brain to be in some sense performing dinosaur functions still; and the limbic cortex to be thinking the thoughts of pumas and ground sloths."[2]

Sagan argues that much of what is irrational or "savage" in human behavior can be traced to the dinosaurian nature still at work in our reptilian brains. He notes that "it is striking how much of our actual behavior . . . can be described in reptilian terms. We speak commonly of a 'cold-blooded' killer. Machiavelli's advice to his Prince was 'knowingly to adopt the Beast.'" The R-complex "plays an important role in aggressive behavior, territoriality, ritual and the establishment of social hierarchies" (63). Sagan even suggests that the triune structure of the brain may correspond to Freud's tricameral models of the psyche, id/ego/superego or (even more precisely) unconscious/preconscious/conscious. Language and higher-order reasoning are functions of the neocortex, then, while irrational, instinctive, and compulsive or ritualistic behavior is traceable to our deep dinosaurian nature.

How much more plausible is Sagan's story of the dinosaur than the creationists' feasibility studies of Noah's Ark? Sagan sounds more plausible because he appeals to what has become a powerful modern consensus built on Darwinian evolutionary biology. The creation-

32.2

Although Creationist accounts of the dinosaurs are now generally discounted by mainstream educators and scientists, they still survive among the rather large minority of Christian fundamentalists in the United States. What is the correct educational policy with regard to these discredited stories? Should creationism be taught as an alternative to evolution? Should the beliefs of Native Americans about prehistoric monsters be part of the curriculum? Should we censor children's fantasies about dinosaurs? What does it mean to "teach evolution" to first-graders? (Cartoon by Marc Zingarelli, "God's Country," in *Mother Jones*.)

ists, by contrast, build their story on a "literal" reading of the Bible (I put "literal" in quotation marks because there is no evidence that the creationists actually read the Bible in its original language). So while Sagan engages with the modern, scientific paradigm, the creationists steadfastly oppose it, and (in their more ambitious moments) actually hope to overturn it. Their efforts to politicize the debate by arguing that evolution and creationism should be taught in public schools as "rival theories" are best seen as an admission that they can't win the debate in any legitimate scientific forum where rival theories are actually tested. That doesn't mean that creationism should not be taught in public schools, only that it should be taught as a set of cultural beliefs (like the Indian legends of the monstrous reptiles or Unktehi). If it were taught, with some historical perspective, among the stories that constitute modern and traditional cultures, that would be all right.

But Sagan's story is also clearly a cultural one. And the fact that he "talks the talk" of modern evolutionary biology doesn't mean that his dinosaur story is true. For one thing, it is full of contradictions. Sagan suggests that the "instinctive fear" of reptiles shared by mammals and human beings is evidence of our deep reptilian brains, but one could argue as plausibly that we should experience an instinctive affinity and affection for our serpentine ancestors and feel a warm- (or cold-) blooded shock of recognition. If the human brain has a reptilian core, our likeliest response to our brethren serpents would be neither automatic repulsion nor attraction, but ambivalence, a combination of the two. The "ritualistic" behavior that Sagan attributes to our reptilian nature has been much better explained, I think most scientists would agree, by anthropology and the study of culture. The higher Sagan goes in the structure of human behavior, the less plausible his dinosaurian prototype becomes. Thus we are told on one page that the "R-complex" is at work in "a great deal of modern human bureaucratic and polit-

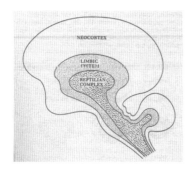

32.3
The "reptilian brain" at the core of the human brain, as depicted by Carl Sagan in *The Dragons of Eden*. Is Sagan's "evolutionary" notion that our deep reptilian brain is behind everything from aggressive behavior to bureaucratic organization any more scientific than creationist accounts of human nature?

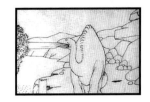

ical behavior" (63), and informed on the next page that "there is no way . . . in which the Bill of Rights of the U.S. Constitution could have been recorded, much less conceived, by the R-complex" (64). The fact that "political behavior" created the Constitution, which in turn constituted a bureaucracy, seems to elude Sagan. The further one goes with his theory of our deep dinosaurian nature, the clearer it becomes that the "reptilian brain" is simply a metaphor for the kinds of human behavior Sagan doesn't like, and the neocortex is the part of the brain that gets credit for the admirable things we do. If you happen to agree with Sagan's basically liberal politics, then this seems like pretty harmless stuff. But it hardly counts as a contribution to our knowledge of either dinosaurs or human nature.

A better way of handling the "knowledge" that both Sagan and the creationists offer is, I think, to position it in the multistory edifice that has been constructed around the dinosaur in the last 150 years. The creationists are telling a story that was first tried out by Richard Owen in his 1841 report on "British Fossil Reptiles." But Owen told the story in a much more convincing way because he was a better reader of both the fossil record and the Bible. (The biggest problem with creationists, I suspect, is not that they don't look at fossils, but that they don't read Scripture very well. They think, for instance, that a "day" for God is the same thing as a day for us. A cultural evolutionist would have to say that modern creationism is a kind of degenerate version of pious Victorian paleontology, and that it would be well served by a study of its own distinguished history.) Sagan, for his part, is engaged in the kind of sociobiological moralizing that got a well-deserved bad name during the era of rampant social Darwinism and seems to be rearing its head once again at the close of the twentieth century. The trick is relatively simple: one identifies a common human trait (aggression, ritualistic behavior, the formation of social hierarchies and bureaucracies) and traces it to its biological "cause" in our reptilian nature.[3] Human culture is reduced to a model of animal behavior, and a wide range of political attitudes (typically centered on racial or sexual stereotypes) are rationalized as "natural." For Sagan, the dinosaur becomes the image of what is foundational and natural in human behavior, what lies deepest (like Freud's id) and must therefore be both acknowledged and repressed with moral fables about the reptilian brain.

We need to figure out the relations between these two stories—the creationist myth and the neo-Darwinist "reptilian brain" fable. Cultural history is, in part, just the name of the place where competing stories can be discussed *as stories,* without needing to refute one in favor of the other, without dismissing one as obsolete, outmoded science and elevating the other to the status of final truth. The "two culture split" between science and "the humanities" has often been deplored, but it has an important role to play in serving as a check on the claims of science to an exclusive grip on "the truth" about moral, political, and social issues (see appendix B, "Science and Culture"). The dialectic between science and culture is what allows us to see an outside to science,

32.4
The dinosaur appears here as if springing up out of the modern addition to attack the traditional building. The Mercedes logo on its tail identifies it as a creature of modern corporate power, gobbling up the past. This is the *Berlinosaurus,* an appropriate monster for a city that has been tearing itself down and erasing its past for over a century. The ruined tower of the *Gedachtnissekirche* or "church of memory," is the appropriate prey for Berolinosaurus. (Postcard by Claudia Katz-Palme, collage artist, Berlin.)

32.5
Similar scenes of destructive "urban renewal" play themselves out in every German city. One can see the dinosaur here as either the crane swinging the wrecking ball or lifting girders into place for new construction. (*Colognosaurus.* Postcard by Claudia Katz-Palme, collage artist, Berlin.)

to understand it as a special form of cultural activity itself, with rituals, traditions, and superstitions. Scientific reasoning, for its part, is what allows the study of culture to be critical and historical, to be more than merely the recitation of stories and the reinforcement of tradition.

From the standpoint of cultural history, biblical creationism and Darwinism are just two stories to be evaluated and understood at many levels, not just at the level of truth claims. Darwinism happens to be widely believed and authoritative—and rightly so—in its proper domain. (The limits of that domain, however, are very unclear, as Daniel Dennett has shown.)[4] The Bible is also widely believed to be a source of considerable wisdom in its proper domain. The problem arises when the Darwinian and biblical "scriptures" find themselves on a collision course, as they do in a figure like the dinosaur. Hardly anyone believes the creationists' stories about dinosaurs, which is just fine. But almost every educated person regards some version of Darwinism as pretty close to the truth, and thinks of science (or scientific method or reasoning) as authoritative. That is the problem. It is exactly this widespread public faith in the institutions of science (and their impressive technological results) that lends credibility and authority to neo-Darwinist and sociobiological pronouncements about human nature.

Fortunately, we have created a hybrid scientific/cultural object that gives us a glimpse of the total form of our modernity. It straddles the two culture split like a colossus, forcing us to think through the interchanges between science and fantasy, nature and culture. The dinosaur is the hundred-story monster that looms next to the skyscraper of modern science and technology. At one moment it seems like an outgrowth of the skyscraper; at another, like a rival that threatens to tear the skyscraper down. As for the dinosaur itself, we have been building it up, tearing it down, and remodeling it for over a century now. It is just about complete, almost ready for re-burial. Perhaps we should take a snapshot of the whole thing before it disappears.

32.6
Every new technology destroys an older one, rendering it obsolete, archaic, and useless. The dinosaur, as metaphor for this process, overpowers the greatest modern monuments, even the Chrysler Building. Compare the fate of King Kong atop the Empire State Building. "Photosaurus" is a publicity movie for the Hulton-Deutsch Collection, one of the world's largest digital archives of photographs and film stills.

structure, energy, information

WHILE THERE MAY BE a hundred or more stories in the dinosaurian edifice, they are articulated across a series of repetitions, like the glass wall of a Mies van der Rohe skyscraper. They appear in three distinctly articulated columns that correspond to distinctive remodelings of the dinosaur (see the table in chapter 14). I described earlier the three-stage division of dinosaurology into Victorian (1840–1900), modern (1900–1960), and postmodern (1960–present) periods. The first of these periods corresponds to the creationist dinosaur image of Richard Owen and Waterhouse Hawkins; the second, to the modernized evolutionary image of the Darwinists as codified by Charles Knight and rendered as a world-picture by Rudolph Zallinger. The third phase is generally associated with the "dinosaur renaissance" pioneered by John Ostrom and promoted by Robert Bakker, which goes back to the early modern insight of Huxley and revives the bird model of the dinosaur. This image has only recently become widely distributed in mass culture, most notably in *Jurassic Park,* which has made the lively, warm-blooded, birdlike animal the "latest thing" in dinosaurology.

But it should be clear by now that the historical transformations in the image of the dinosaur have been responsive to numerous other determinations besides the internal history of paleontology, and that paleontology itself is a highly sensitive barometer of technological and cultural change. This is particularly striking if one simply looks at the most superficial "surface" elements of the dinosaur image in its public manifestations. The early dinosaur, like its cultural ancestor, Jefferson's mastodon, was principally an architectural structure. Hawkins's *Iguanodon* was a building of cement and brick with legs and ribs of iron, and represented one of the earliest uses of reinforced concrete, the technology that made the skyscraper possible. The early dinosaur was an archetype and an "ark," a framework that endured over time, like Jefferson's "ark of the constitution." The modern Darwinian dinosaur, by contrast, was seen as a living organism, an engine or machine that moved in space and evolved over time. It was a creature of thermodynamics, a motor that consumed energy, reproduced itself, and finally died out. Its image is best represented in the setting of the nineteenth-century animal landscape picture, and in the media of oil painting or cinematic animation. The jerky mechanical motions of early animation don't compromise the realism of the modern dinosaur. On the contrary, they fit with its role as a paradigm of what Walter Benjamin called "mechanical reproduction." The close association of the dinosaur with the steam engine and later with the automobile—with fossil fuels and the consumption of energy—reinforces this modern paradigm.

CHICAGO WORLD'S FAIR EDITION

PICTURE NEWS

Published by Sinclair Refining Company (Inc.), 45 Nassau Street, New York, N. Y.

KING OF THE DINOSAURS—Tyrannosaurus Rex, the most ferocious animal the world has ever known, photographed in his natural habitat at the Sinclair Dinosaur Exhibit. The Sinclair guide is pointing out to World's Fair visitors the dinosaur's death-dealing claws and enormous mouth, lined with six-inch dagger teeth. Tyrannosaurus lived 100,000,000 years ago. Sinclair has re-created this "killer of all monsters" in full life size to impress on your mind the vast age of the crude oils used in refining Sinclair Opaline and Sinclair Pennsylvania Motor Oils. It is a generally accepted fact that, by and large, the oldest crudes make the finest lubricants.

When we see the dinosaur as a product of modes of production, it becomes clear that the real revolution foreshadowed by the post-

modern dinosaur is not the "renaissance" of the bird model (which, after all, was never really lost, and was always available in Knight's early paintings), but the new age of biocybernetic reproduction, an era that combines information science and biogenetic engineering.[1] The shift is from a picture of a massive modern machine to a creature whose true identity is invisible, encoded in the strings of data we call genes. The "essence" of the animal is not in its structural "constitution" or in its dynamic movements, but in its DNA, the code which, when cracked, can allow it to be "cloned" and reproduced indefinitely. At the same time, the cutting-edge representation of the dinosaur moves from cinematic animation of mechanical models to computer animation and "animatronics," or computer-driven robots. The jerky, mechanical motions of live-action animation are replaced by the smooth, lifelike movements of the *Jurassic Park* dinosaurs; the primitive motions of *King Kong*'s dinosaurs give way to the smooth, computer-coordinated servo-motors of contemporary robotics. And the giantism of dinosaurs like General Motors and IBM gives way to downsized, innovative entrepreneurship.

33.1–33.2

From machine to cyborg: two ages of dinosaur robotics, the simple, massive motions of the Sinclair dino-robots at the 1933 World's Fair and the complex, highly differentiated movements of the Jurassic Park robots, executed by computer-coordinated servo-motors. It should be noted, however, that the development of digital animation during the production of Jurassic Park led to the cancellation of the animatronic models and threatens to render the robotics industry as extinct as the dinosaurs.

(33.1: from *A Great Name in Oil: Sinclair through Fifty Years,* © 1966, Sinclair Oil Corp.; 33.2: courtesy of Universal Studios.)

caTasTroPHe, EnTroPY, CHaos

ONE CAN SEE the whole sequence of evolving dinosaur images with special clarity if one looks at endings, at the extinction narratives that accompany each dino story. For the Victorians, for Owen, the dinosaur was an archetypal creature created by God. It had to be destroyed by a catastrophic transformation of the environment. The popular image of "antediluvian monsters" made this transformation the biblical Flood, a view perpetuated today by the creationists. Owen's extinction scenario (air pollution) was a compromise, making the dinosaur "pre-Adamite" rather than "antediluvian" but maintaining the necessity of catastrophic extinction.

For the moderns, by contrast, the extinction had to be gradual, a kind of entropy, fatigue, or energy loss.[1] Living creatures, like machines, wear out or run down. If thermodynamics was postulating the eventual heat-death of the universe, perhaps our waning sun had shone brighter and hotter during the Age of Reptiles, and the dinosaurs had died out from slow changes in the weather. Or perhaps they simply ran out of steam on their own, worn down by the weight of their own armor and overspecialization, by their sluggishness, giantism, and stupidity compared with the newly emergent mammals, who were more adaptable and especially good at robbing eggs. The end of the Age of Reptiles could be signaled, as Zallinger saw, by distant volcanoes, or by a mouse and some magnolias (see figure 31.4). His mighty saurian armada could be sunk by running out of fuel, ending up, like Disney's dinosaurs, as beached leviathans.

> **Chaos theory is not nearly as interesting as it sounds**.
>
> —STEPHEN KELLERT

Contemporary extinction scenarios have moved away from these entropic, gradualist narratives and reopened the possibility of catastrophe. The most widely publicized of these scenarios is the Alvarez hypothesis, which proposes that a giant meteorite struck the earth about 65 million years ago, raising a global dust cloud and producing a "nuclear winter" that wiped out the dinosaurs and many other life-forms as well. While the geological evidence for a catastrophe of this sort seems irrefutable, the jury is still out on whether this is what killed off the dinosaurs. The fossil record suggests that they had already been on the decline for millions of years, and may have disappeared before the meteorite hit the earth. If anything, the meteorite may simply have delivered the coup de grace.

The importance of this resurgence of catastrophe theory from a cultural standpoint is not whether the Alvarez hypothesis is finally proved or disproved, but the fact that it holds center stage in the debate. "Catastrophe" is a remarkably flexible concept, one that slides easily from scientific to cultural, political, and social connotations. Clearly it had a kind of automatic appeal to the popular imagination in the Cold War era, when the threat of something like the Alvarez meteorite seemed like a real possibility. Even within scientific discourse, the meaning of the term can vary considerably. Huxley understood "cata-

In evolutionary biology, in mathematics and increasingly these days in economics, the word "catastrophe" has acquired a somewhat technical meaning. In Catastrophe Theory the word describes not the event of common usage which could take any form, but the sequence of events leading up to and proceeding from a critical point. Catastrophe Theory is an attempt to analyze the way in which a previously stable system can reach a point of chronic instability, a "cusp" point, which leads to a total collapse of the old order (dinosaur domination) and subsequently to the emergence of a new stability of a very different kind (mammal domination).

—TOM LLOYD, *Dinosaur & Co.: Studies in Corporate Evolution*

strophism" to mean a "form of geological speculation which supposes the operation of forces different in their nature from those which we at present see in action."[2] This definition equates catastrophe with a miraculous intervention, a suspension of natural laws; it is the denouement of the creationist narrative, and the antithesis of the "uniformitarian" assumption that the laws of nature are the same always and everywhere. The Alvarez hypothesis proposes a catastrophe that is consistent with uniformitarianism. Catastrophic events do happen in accordance with the natural laws we see operating in the present (volcanic eruptions, plagues, mass extinctions or removals of populations). The arrival of Europeans in North America was a catastrophe for the Indians. Its effect was being felt in the form of famine and disease long before the genocidal frontier wars of the nineteenth century.

The issue, then, is not whether the Alvarez meteorite is the catastrophe that killed the dinosaurs, but what a catastrophe is. How rapidly does something have to happen to count as a catastrophe? Are there not different temporalities for cultural, political, and social change? For biological and geological "events"? Do catastrophes have to be perceived as such when and while they are happening? Or do they sometimes become evident only in retrospect? To what extent is a catastrophe a function not of something that is happening "out there," but of the sensitivity of our instruments of detection? (The miner's canary, remember, is an instrument to provide early warning of impending, imperceptible catastrophe.) In the debate between "uniformitarians" and "catastrophists," which side can seize the middle ground of "gradualism"? Is catastrophe to be defined by its agency or causation, so that accident, chance, or "Lady Luck" are associated with catastrophism, while the normal, automatic, predictable causal sequence is the fundamental unit of uniformitarianism?

These kinds of questions had essentially disappeared from scientific debate in the last 150

years under the twin influences of Sir Charles Lyell's geological uniformitarianism and Darwin's gradualism. They are now back on the table, spurred by information science, chaos theory, and a whole new sense of what counts as a catastrophe. It is a cliché of postmodern culture that contemporary catastrophe is likely to be unobtrusive and invisible, like the great subterranean Chicago flood of 1992 or the "industrial accident" of Don DeLillo's novel *White Noise*. At the same time, modern information systems make actual catastrophes in our world more visible, dramatic, and commonplace than ever before. Catastrophes are the junk food (and toxic waste) of everyday life in a mediatized culture of "action news" and disaster movies.

Stephen Jay Gould's theory of "punctuated equilibrium" is probably the best-known attempt to restore catastrophism to evolutionary theory in terms of chance and accident. Daniel Dennett dismisses Gould's revolution as an effort to erect a "*cordon sanitaire* between Darwinism and religion" and to bring back transcendental "Skyhooks" as explanations of natural events. Dennett contends that the slow, minute workings of algorithmic engineering (what he calls "Cranes") can still explain evolutionary processes better than Gould's ungrounded "Skyhooks."[3] This debate (which I won't try to reproduce in detail here) seems to me still caught in a division between catastrophism and uniformitarianism that is now obsolete—a dinosaur in its own way. Its dinosaurial character is best illustrated by the way our most up-to-date contemporary representation of the dinosaur (Spielberg's) completely bypasses this dilemma. Spielberg's dinosaurs are pure creations of information science, at both the level of the representation (the digitally animated image) and the level of the represented (the fictional cloned creatures produced by biogenetic engineering).[4] The distinctions between design and chance, "Skyhooks" and "Cranes," just don't operate in this world. That is why the team brought in to certify the park must include a chaos theoretician, someone who thinks about designed systems, complexity, and accident, and who is given the task of stating the "moral" of the entire film. The architectural and mechanical models of the organism give way to (and are absorbed by) informational models: the species becomes a message, an algorithm; the boundary between organism and machine, natural and artificial intelligence, begins to waver. Dragons always did stand for chaos and impending disaster, but in the new era signaled by *Jurassic Park,* chaos takes on a new meaning.

35.1
Digital Dino. A velociraptor, its skin bathed in the
beam of a film projector showing the Jurassic
Park orientation film with its explanation of the
cloning process that has brought dinosaurs back
to life. This dinosaur has its own DNA sequence
inscribed on the surface of its body. Powerful new
computers make it possible to imagine the resurrection of the dinosaur as nothing more than a
computational problem in biogenetic engineering.
These same computers make possible digital animation techniques that replace robotics as the
cinematic technology of choice. The dinosaur is
a cyborg, a computer-animated animal, in both
the story and the medium in which the story is
represented. (Film still, *Jurassic Park*.)

THE AGE OF BIOCYBERNETIC REPRODUCTION

> Whatever the social form of the production process, it has to be continuous, it must periodically repeat the same phases. A society can no more cease to produce than it can cease to consume. When viewed, therefore, as a connected whole, and in the constant flux of its incessant renewal, every social process of production is at the same time a process of reproduction.
>
> —MARX, *Capital*

WHEN WALTER BENJAMIN WROTE his classic essay "The Work of Art in the Age of Mechanical Reproduction" in 1935, the world was in the midst of deep economic depression and on the verge of war. The modern system of mass industrial production had shown its best and worst face, transforming everyday life with a host of technologies and commodities, and shattering that same everyday life with mass destruction and massive forms of social displacement and alienation. "Mechanical reproduction" (or "technical reproducibility") was for Benjamin a kind of play on words, linking the *productive* technologies and economies of the machine age (especially the assembly line) with new *reproductive* technologies such as photography, cinema, and sound recording and reproductive economies involving the distribution of images, words, and sounds to a mass public. The dinosaur images of this era, beginning with Charles Knight's romantic armored leviathans and culminating in Rudolph Zallinger's world-picture of a mobilized dryland armada, provided an image of what Theodor Adorno called the "monstrous total State" of the advanced industrial nations. In keeping with its (unacknowledged) function as the modern totem, the dinosaur image encoded radically contradictory messages.

Gigantic energy and productivity were combined with entropy and annihilation. Scientific and economic "purity" (pure research, supported by the pure gifts of big capital) was combined with connotations of impurity and contamination (disease or racial mixing), and the dinosaur's status as kitsch attraction and mass spectacle belied its claim to cultural purity.

It is tempting to simply adopt Benjamin's model of technological determination and apply it to explain the dominant tendencies in contemporary culture. We live, it is often said, in the period of DNA and the computer. Dramatic as the discovery of nuclear energy was, it was really only a quantitative extension of the age of energy—the development of a bigger productive and destructive force.[1] As we reach the end of the twentieth century, however, it is clear that biology has replaced physics at the frontier of science, and that computers and artificial intelligence constitute the frontier of technology. We could call this, then, the age of "biocybernetic reproduction" to reflect the double wave of scientific and technical innovations that have carried us beyond the machine and the assembly line, and beyond the mechanically reproduced images of photography and cinema. The "factory" in this new age might be imagined as a place where machines do the thinking, and the commodities coming down the assembly line are living creatures or organisms. As for the images, they are no longer produced by the mechanical or chemical processes of photography; they are electronic and digitally encoded strings of data that can be manipulated to produce any visual illusion that is desired. *Jurassic Park* is (among other things) a vision of this imaginary factory, where computers, biological science, robotics, and digital animation converge. It is a utopia of biocybernetic reproduction, a Disneyesque "tomorrowland" where advanced imagineering shows us the frontiers of science and technology.

There are several problems, however, with a straightforward application of Benjamin's "mode of reproduction" model to contemporary reality. The most obvious problem is that the world of "biocybernetic reproduction" is for most people an imaginary, utopian, fictional place. It is not an immediate, everyday experiential reality in the same way that the innovations of mechanical reproduction (assembly lines, automobiles, telephones, and movies) were in the modern era. The "shock of the new" that is attributed to biocybernetic technologies is highly overrated, and appears mainly in very traditional modernist forms such as movies, novels, and advertising. Computers are routinely marketed with all the rhetoric of revolutionary modernism, as if they were a technical innovation as profound as the invention of printing. But for most people, computers are simply speeded-up extensions of the typewriter, the ledger book, the mailbox, and the filing cabinet. If Melville's Bartleby the scrivener were alive today, he would be a data processor, and he would still wind up with his face to a stone wall, or a blank screen. The Internet is hailed as the gateway to a new dimension of experience called "cyberspace," and "Virtual Reality" beckons as a replacement for the mundane realm of modernity. But anyone who has spent very much time in these "new dimen-

sions" quickly discovers just how disappointing and banal they are. VR turns out to be an extension of the penny arcade or the Home Shopping Network, and Internet pornography turns out to be about as interesting as the graffiti in a public toilet. The grand convergence of computers and biology leads not to a new age of human possibilities, but to the high-tech fulfillment of a Victorian fantasy: a dinosaur theme park.

The age of biocybernetic reproduction, then, is not a revolutionary break with the past like mechanistic modernism was, except at the level of advertising and fantasy. It is rather an *evolutionary* transition, and as such it is almost by definition gradual and imperceptible in the present, seen only in the rearview mirror or in utopian projections. It is often associated in cultural history with "postmodernism," generally defined as the period since the 1960s in advanced industrial societies. If anything is clear about the postmodern period, however, it is that it was not a time of revolution, of shocking novelty or wonder, but (as Jean-François Lyotard put it) a time of "slackening"—an age of slackers and antidepressants, neo-vanguardism and reduced expectations.[2]

35.2
The birth of a cyborg. In the age of biocybernetic reproduction, the workers attending the assembly line are computer-driven robots and the commodities coming off the line are living organisms. (Film still, *Jurassic Park.*)

Perhaps most important, the age of biocybernetic reproduction is not primarily an age of "production" (or reproduction), but of *consumption* and speculative capital, as epitomized by Reagan's "age of greed." "Progress is our most important product" was the slogan of General Electric in the 1950s. Now the most important product of modern industry is the illusion of progress, the fantasy of innovation—the creation of new mass markets, new needs and desires. The "production of consumption" has of course always been central to capitalist economies. Henry Ford realized that "mass production meant mass consumption"[3]—that it wasn't enough to create an abundance of commodities, but that one also had to create a society with leisure and wealth sufficient to consume them. The age of biocybernetic reproduction might be seen as the period in which the Fordist dream of a society and culture almost completely oriented toward consumerism has come true. Symptoms of this development include the tendency for service and leisure industries to replace the production of basic materials and commodities (the new working class serves fast food at McDonald's instead of making steel) and the tendency for personal identity to be defined in terms of consumer and "lifestyle" choices (you are what you eat, what you wear, what you drive, what credit card you carry). Perhaps most telling is the perfection of "planned obsolescence" as an element of design and production. The notion of pro

JURASSIC SAFARI

Go back to a time when *Tyrannosaurus rex* stalked the earth. See this giant and eleven other life-size dinosaurs, including mothers and their young.

Watch them move, hear them roar, as the magic of Dinamation® brings these creatures to life.

FEBRUARY 25-MARCH 6
FOX VALLEY CENTER
Aurora

ducing a durable commodity that will "last forever" has become a nostalgic advertising fantasy. The reality is that the car you buy today is designed to break down the minute it is paid for, and the computer you buy tomorrow will be obsolete before you learn how to use it properly. These are not "problems" or "defects" in contemporary economic systems that need to be corrected: they are the very basis for the proper functioning of those systems. Things have to break down and turn into junk, or else "our way of life" will.

Is it any wonder, then, that the world is overrun with dinosaurs? As always, they serve as the animated animal icon of the new age, their dry bones "restored to life" in a brand new form that makes earlier dinosaurs look quaint and obsolete. Spielberg's and Robert Bakker's new bird-like dinosaurs make Zallinger's and Knight's modern leviathans obsolete, just as Knight's dinosaurs made the antediluvian monsters of the Crystal Palace look like Victorian fantasies. The small manufactory production of Waterhouse Hawkins is replaced by the Fordist mass production of Sinclair dinosaurs to prime the pump of consumption, which is in turn replaced by the biocybernetic eating machines of *Jurassic Park*.

35.3
The dinosaur is not only a figure of production and reproduction, but also an epitome of voracious consumption. Notorious for its appetite, the dinosaur is thought to be a sure-fire consumer attraction. (Compare the use of the dinosaur to dramatize the craving for McDonald's french fries). In the slow shopping days after the Christmas season, a suburban shopping mall stages a "Jurassic safari" to lure consumers into the stores.
(*Chicago Tribune* ad for Fox Valley Mall, 22 February 1994.)

36.1
Autosaurus. If the dinosaur is
the monstrous double of the
skyscraper in architecture, it
matches up with the automobile
in the world of machines.
Jurassic Park devotes an
inordinate amount of time to the
combat of *T. rex* and a park
vehicle. Meanwhile, behind the
scenes, Universal Studios'
artists make the identity of cars
and dinosaurs explicit in the
"Jurassic Parking Lot" (see
figure 36.2). (Film still, *Jurassic
Park*.)

carnosaurs and consumption

It seemed odd to be eating a creature that should, by all the laws of paleontology, have been extinct for several million years. It gave one a feeling of newness that was almost embarrassing.

—EDGAR RICE BURROUGHS, *The Land that Time Forgot*

IN JURASSIC PARK, the commodity or product that is being sold is the spectacle of consumption itself. We come to the theater to watch the dinosaurs eat, and the narrative unfolds as a series of animal and human sacrifices, offered as increasingly spectacular "courses" in the modern equivalent of the totem meal (see chapter 12, "The Totem Animal of Modernity," on the ritual of the sacrificial meal). The first course is an anonymous black worker (devoured by an unseen raptor), followed by two traditional sacrificial animals (a bull and a goat). Other victims include a "blood-sucking lawyer," a fat computer nerd, an African White Hunter/game warden, and a black technician—no one, in short, who we are really supposed to care about. Early on, the bull is fed to the velociraptors as a kind of appetizer for the spectators, who see nothing, but get to hear the roars and shrieks of a wild feeding frenzy. (Immediately after this violent meal, the director of the park informs his guests that lunch is served.) Later the goat is offered to *T. rex,* but it is beneath his dignity. Dr. Grant, in a tacit refutation of the *T. rex* scavenger theory, suggests that *T. rex* wants to hunt for his food, to confront a worthy antagonist.

The worthy antagonist turns out to be, of all things, an automobile, the Bronco in which the children are trapped when the park computers go haywire. Spielberg spends an inordinate amount of time showing the "battle" of *T.*

rex and this ersatz "off-road" vehicle, an episode that is completely absent from the novel. (In *The Lost World,* Spielberg simply inflates the automotive "cliff-hanger" sequence by giving us ten minutes of an enormous RV hanging over a cliff, held in place only by a feisty Mercedes off-road vehicle.) In *Jurassic Park,* T. *rex*'s automotive antagonist is only a simulacrum of the off-road vehicles that typically carry paleontologists on their expeditions into the bush, and suburbanites on their expeditions to the mall. This machine is, of course, a dinosaur in its own

36.2

The dinosaurial connotations of obsolescence and uselessness seem especially appropriate to the faux off-road vehicles that carry tourists through the theme park. These vehicles (conspicuous consumers of fossil fuels) are designed to awaken fantasies of wilderness safaris and big game hunts, yet the reality is that most of them never leave the highway, and they spend most of their lives in garages, driveways, and mall parking lots. ("Jurassic Parking," cartoon from Don Shay and Jody Duncan, *The Making of Jurassic Park* [New York: Ballantine Books, 1993]. Courtesy of Universal Studios Publishing Rights. ©1993 by Universal Studios, Inc. All rights reserved.)

right, partly because (like all new automobiles) it was designed to become obsolete from the beginning, and partly because this specific vehicle has been designed *never* to function in accordance with its apparent form—it has been modified to run on tracks, and couldn't operate *on,* much less *off,* any road. (According to auto industry reports, 95 percent of "off-road vehicles" never leave the road; they spend most of their lives parked in suburban garages, as monuments to advertising fantasies of family wilderness vacations, gas-guzzling testimonials to the cheap oil supply made possible by the American military adventure in the Persian Gulf.) If the dinosaur is the monstrous double of the skyscraper and the railroad, it also finds its counterpart in the world's largest consumer of fossil fuels, the automobile. T. *rex* can recognize a worthy antagonist when he sees one, so he attacks the park vehicle, chews up its tires, and pushes it over a cliff when he finds it indigestible. At this point, the park vehicle takes the place of *T. rex* as the monster in pursuit, and we are regaled with a hair-raising "chase" down the

trunk of a tree, with the monstrous eyes of *T. rex* replaced by the headlights of the Bronco glaring (in one of Spielberg's favorite "dazzle" effects) directly into the eyes of the spectator.

But the first fleshly meal actually eaten by *T. rex* is an elaborate parody of the spectacle of human sacrifice. When the cowardly lawyer abandons the children and hides from *T. rex* in an outhouse, he is snatched from his undignified "throne" by the dinosaur. Spielberg combines a standard lawyer joke and a bit of toilet humor with a visual evocation of what is arguably the most famous and memorable scene of sacrifice in modern cinema: Fay Wray tied to the altar in *King Kong*. The blonde white virgin is replaced by the "blood-sucking lawyer"; the figure of purity is replaced by the figure of contemporary corruption and professional prostitution. The ritual sacrifice of purification is parodied in a hilarious and horrible spectacle of ritual consummation/contamination in which the differences between eating and shitting, the altar and the toilet, the pure victim and the bloodthirsty monster, are systematically eliminated.

Spielberg is hard pressed to top this brilliant spectacle of the cycle of contemporary consumption in the rest of the movie, but each scene of violent death adds a distinctive new "course" to the spectacular banquet. The fat computer nerd treats the scavenging *Dilophosaurus* as a domestic pet who can be tricked into fetching a stick (this scene is probably the inspiration for the McDonald's commercial with the *T. rex* begging for french fries). He winds up "basted" in a gravy of poisonous, blinding saliva before being disembowelled. The Great White Hunter tries to play the traditional *mano a mano* stalking game with the velociraptors, for-

> **An ideal panorama of a minimally distant primordial time reveals itself to the viewer of the arcades. . . . Here resides Europe's last dinosaur, the consumer.**
>
> —WALTER BENJAMIN, *The Arcades*[1]

36.3–36.4
Two scenes of monsters approaching their sacrificial
victims. In *King Kong*, a pure white virgin is offered on the
altar to the great ape. In *Jurassic Park*, the victim is a
"blood-sucking lawyer" enthroned on a toilet. (Film stills
from *King Kong* and *Jurassic Park*.)

getting that his prey doesn't fight fair like the rhinos and lions hunted by Teddy Roosevelt.[2] The raptors are, as he notes, "clever girls" who hunt in packs. While one of them lures the hunter into a face-to-face encounter, another sneaks up on him from the side. The black technician is dismembered mainly for the purpose of bringing the white woman into the proximity of horror: his bloody arm is dropped onto her shoulder in one of the most gratuitous (and unmixed) scenes of gruesome violence in the film.

The final scene of consumption occurs when dinosaur eats dinosaur, leaving the white suburban nuclear family free to escape with their lives, chastened by the lessons they have just learned about the dangers of unbridled greed and unlimited technology.[3] But this is not the film's only lesson. The arrival of *T. rex* as deus ex machina to save the family from the raptors expresses a nostalgia for the days of big patriarchal capital, before the arrival of career women and "clever girls" in multinational corporations, before the age of bio-cybernetic reproduction transformed the family from a "natural" to an "artificial" unit. Drs. Grant and Sattler, like Cary Grant and his paleontological assistant in *Bringing Up Baby,* are a professional couple who have no time for child-rearing (at least he doesn't; Dr. Sattler spends much of the film looking wistfully at the children and encouraging Dr. Grant to take an interest in them. His whole adventure with the children in the outback of Jurassic Park might be seen as a lesson for fathers on spending some quality time with their kids.) As the family flies off into the sunset (or leaves the theater), we can be sure that they have learned that bringing up babies is their real destiny.

Or can we? Despite the liberal portions of nostalgia and sentimentality in *Jurassic Park,* the banquet is finally indigestible. For one thing, a family cannot be brought together by a film that is too violent for the children in it to see. Spielberg thought the film would be too frightening for his own children, and one of the debates over the early reception of the film was whether it was suitable for kids. So while the story envisions the reuniting of the nuclear family, its actual effect is to split it apart, and over exactly the spectacle (dinosaurs) that is assumed to be attractive to every child. For another thing, the final rescue by *T. rex* is about as plausible as Spielberg's other nostalgia film about the redemption of big patriarchal capital, *Schindler's List* (1993). In that film we are treated to the spectacle of the Holocaust overcome by the intervention of a clever industrialist who manages to save several thousand Jews by putting them to work as slaves in his munitions factory. John Hammond, like Schindler, is a clever entrepreneur who resurrects an extinct race of animals to put them to work as the main attractions in a contemporary theme park. Both movies show how to capitalize on mass death and extinction through spectacles of (respectively) rescue and resurrection. That *Schindler's List* is a true story, in contrast to the science fiction premise of *Jurassic Park,* only serves to heighten the weird unreality of Spielberg's pseudo-documentary rendering of the Holocaust redeemed by Hollywood.

Unlike earlier dinosaur narratives, however, the extinction scenario of *Jurassic Park* does not offer any way out. If earlier dinosaurs were stupid, we could hope to be smart; if they were killed by immigration, we could close our borders; if they ran out of energy, we could build new, more powerful machines; if they failed to reproduce, we could make a technology out of reproduction. But *Jurassic Park* overwhelms this sort of moral reasoning. These dinosaurs are smart and getting smarter; they are already (in Michael Crichton's novel, at least) migrating to Costa Rica; they are small, quick, and full of energy. Most ominous, they have taken control of their own means of reproduction, shattering the Japanese geneticist's bland assurance that "there is no unauthorized reproduction in Jurassic Park" and erasing any notion that an all-female animal park will contain only tractable, submissive creatures. The only extinction scenario that makes any sense in *Jurassic Park* is thoroughly paradoxical, and it is our own. The threat to human life is no longer impotence or mass destruction. No dramatic modern catastrophe looms on the horizon. The threat is the overproduction of life itself, life out of control. It is biocybernetic production itself—the whole structure of controls we have erected to rationalize and manage the biosphere, to increase fertility, enhance reproductive potency, increase the yield of agribusiness, and wipe out disease—that threatens to dissolve into a chaos of overproduction: too many people, too many environmental "side effects" of increased productivity and profitability, too many mutant viruses evolving too quickly for our slow-moving human intelligence to keep up. As always, Gary Larson portrays the situation with rigorous clarity, showing a dinosaur lecturer addressing a crowd of his colleagues with the following words: "The picture's pretty bleak, gentlemen. . . . The world's climates are changing, the mammals are taking over, and we all have a brain about the size of a walnut."

Jurassic Park is an indigestible feast, finally, because it is too smart for its own good. Certainly it is smarter than any "critique" that might be brought to bear on it. It exploits the cultural image of the dinosaur so knowingly, at so many levels of signification, that it has the effect of unveiling the totem animal of modernity, exposing its inner workings (see figure 33.2). All the strategies that have stabilized and compartmentalized the contradictions of the dinosaur—its association with pure science and impure commerce; its role as a monument to national prestige and neocolonial exploitation; its function as a figure of fertility and infertility, potency and impotence, gender differentiation and confusion; its place in parodic rituals of resurrection, consumption, and sacrifice—all these elements are brought together in a single symbolic system in *Jurassic Park*. The effect is rather like that moment when the Wizard of Oz tells the audience to "pay no attention to that man behind the curtain." And of course we pull the veil aside. Or, more precisely, a little dog does, just as the dog runs away with the bone in *Bringing Up Baby*. (Could the association of dogs with skepticism and cynicism be at work in these fictions?)[4] The traditional dinosaur could capitalize on the aura of biblical monsters, feudal romance, big game hunting, pure science, deep time, monumental museum spaces, and big bones. Spielberg's dinosaurs expend all that aura in one final comprehensive revelation. Spenser's *Fuerie Queene* brought

the sixteenth century to a conclusion with the greatest dragon story of all time, a story that had the effect of killing off the dragon for about three hundred years. *Jurassic Park* may do the same for the dinosaur at the end of the millennium.

Carnosaur is the title of a B-grade horror film produced by Roger Corman at about the same time as *Jurassic Park*. It picks up on the huge dinosaurial market that sprang up around Spielberg's film—not just the spin-offs from that movie, but the independent entries into the market—*Dinotopia, The Flintstones* movie, and so on. *Carnosaur* concerns a mad woman scientist, a biogenetic engineer who has decided to wipe out the human race by creating giant featherless mutant chickens with big teeth and green skin. She is altering the DNA of eggs at an industrial chicken farm. The eggs are hatching in fast-food chicken restaurants all over America. While happy consumers are chomping on chicken legs out front, the cooks are being devoured by dinosaurs in the kitchen. The film ends with the death of its principal human characters (including the mad scientist) and the certainty of a new reptilian world order in which human beings will be extinct. This seems to me the appropriate coda to *Jurassic Park,* and the place to draw our history of the dinosaur image to a close.

LESSONS

37

WHY CHILDREN HATE DINOSAURS

I hate you, you hate me,

Barney gave me HIV.

—First-grader's parody of *Barney* theme song

ALTHOUGH OUR HISTORY of the dinosaur is over, it isn't the end of the story. Throughout the history of the dinosaur image there has been one figure whose role we have so far taken for granted. Children are probably the principal audience for dinosaur images. Every day of the school year, busloads of children are herded into natural history museums in major cities, and in elementary schools throughout the United States, paleontology has become a semi-official fixture of the curriculum. "Dinosaur units" are now standard fare in "the majority of California school districts."[1] With the reinforcement of the toy

A VISIT TO THE ANTEDILUVIAN REPTILES AT SYDENHAM—MASTER TOM STRONGLY OBJECTS TO HAVING HIS MIND IMPROVED.

230

industry, children's television shows, advertising, and roadside attractions, the dinosaur may be the most publicized animal in children's lives.

There is a widespread assumption that all children love dinosaurs, that they find them automatically fascinating, interesting, marvelous, wonderful, and irresistible. I do not have any sociological studies or statistics to prove that this assumption is wrong, nor do I need any. The claim that *all* children love dinosaurs simply cannot, on the face of it, be true. If only one child in the world were to express indifference or ambivalence, let alone hostility, then the claim that all children love dinosaurs would be proved false. Since I have certain knowledge of one child who did not love dinosaurs (namely, myself), the common wisdom has to be wrong.

That's right. I was not one of those children who love dinosaurs. To me they always seemed a crashing bore compared with the medieval dragons, whose images were accompanied by wonderful romantic stories of courageous knights and beautiful ladies. My first introduction to dinosaurs was accompanied by a stern admonition: no stories, no fantasies; this is science. These creatures are (were) *real*. They existed a long time ago, so long ago that there were no people around to have any adventures with them, much less make up stories about them. So I tuned out of the dinosaur lessons, concentrated on King Arthur, and grew up to be an iconologist, a historian of cultural images, instead of a paleontologist. The only interesting question about dinosaurs to me was why other kids thought they were so wonderful. Did this mean that there was something wrong with me? What was I missing?

It wasn't until I saw *Jurassic Park* that I finally got the point. Dinosaurs, I realized, were just as saturated with romance and adventure as the dragons. I had just been looking for the romance in the wrong place—namely, in the real lives of dinosaurs, which, apart from occasional episodes of spectacular violence, were probably quite dull. There was romance aplenty,

37.1

The myth that all children love dinosaurs is contradicted by this nineteenth-century scene of a visit to the monsters at the Crystal Palace. (Cartoon by John Leech. "Punch's Alamanac for 1855," *Punch* 28 [1855]: 8. Photo courtesy of The Newberry Library, Chicago.)

however, in the human activities surrounding dinosaurs—in the heroic quest-romances in search of their bones, the intricate detective work of their reconstruction, the magic of their visual resurrection, the impressive temples in which they are displayed, and the endless mythologies that people spin about them. The romance was to be found, in short, in the history of the dinosaur image that you have just read.

I doubt that I am the first person in history to fail to love dinosaurs at the proper time and in the proper place (between 4 and 7 years of age, in preschool and elementary school). And even if the vast majority of children do the right thing and fall in love with dinosaurs on schedule, they also have a tendency to fall out of love with them on schedule as well. The Barney jingle, "I love you, you love me . . . " that is sung by kindergartners all over America is subjected to a hate-filled transformation within a year or two. Indeed, Barney is on the receiving end of more hostility than just about any other popular cultural icon I can think of. Parents admit to a cordial dislike of the saccharine saurian, and no self-respecting second-grader will admit to liking Barney ("He's too childish" was the response of first-graders I talked to at the University of Chicago's Laboratory School.) When Barney made a personal appearance at a suburban shopping mall a couple of years ago, the news that he had been beaten up by a teenage gang was greeted with undisguised pleasure in the news media. The audience on *Saturday Night Live* cheered wildly when Barney (standing in for Godzilla) was knocked around by professional basketball muscle-man Charles Barkley. The Barney bulletin board on the Internet consists mainly of unprintable obscenities about the dopey dino.

I will admit that Barney evokes an extreme range of emotions, from the unqualified love of the 4-year-old to the (often ironic) expressions of indifference or outright dislike by older children and adults. I think we should take

37.2
Why the intense hatred of Barney? Beneath the benign, shapeless facade, a Loch Ness monster may be lurking to lure us into the depths. (© 1995 Tribune Media Services, Inc. All rights reserved.)

Barney as a kind of weathervane of the ambivalence about dinosaurs that seems so deeply embedded in their reception throughout their 150 years of public life. It seems "built into" the culturally constructed "nature" of dinosaurs to be both monumental and trivial, awesome and contemptible, horrible and cute. In absorbing all the "cuteness" of dinosaurs, Barney seems to become a lightning rod for all the darker, more violent passions that they evoke. It's a little more difficult to feel superior to the *T. rex* or *Velociraptor,* though it should be clear that no monument, however impressive, is invulnerable to desecration or satire. At the beginning of *Jurassic Park,* when challenged by a fat little boy who doesn't see why the raptors were so impressive, the paleontologist Dr. Grant performs a demonstration on the boy's belly (with an actual raptor claw) of how the raptor would have disembowelled him and eaten him alive. The message from Dr. Grant is explicit: "Show a little respect." But the message in the boy's challenge is equally telling: kids have no respect. They do not all love dinosaurs or find them fascinating, and we should not base our educational practices or psychological theories on the assumption that they do.

What would be a better starting place? To begin with, we need to recognize the tempo-

37.3

The monster as paleontologist, shown in this still from *Jurassic Park*, in which the benign Dr. Grant gives way to his dislike of children by administering a lesson in fear and respect to the fat little boy who has dared to question whether dinosaurs were so great.

ral, transitional character of dinosaurs as cultural symbols. Lifelong fixation on dinosaurs, whether it takes the form of amateur dinomania or a professional career in paleontology, is the rare exception. Most adults go to natural history museums with their kids—or perhaps it would be more accurate to say that the kids take the adults. How many times have you heard a first-grader lecturing a parent or grandparent on the latest dino-discovery? I deliberately use the word *Brontosaurus* in conversations with first-graders to see how long it will take them to correct me on the up-to-date nomenclature *(Apatosaurus)*. On rainy Saturdays in New Haven, the curators of the Peabody Museum of Natural History know the place will be packed with kids.

We should recognize this for what it is, a rite of passage that is specific to contemporary childhood in modern societies. It was not part of anyone's childhood before 1854, it was not part of most American children's experience before World War II, and it is still not part of many children's experience in the so-called underdeveloped areas of the world. As an initiation ritual, it is a very special and recent invention. We need

37.4

Barney in Jurassic Park. Cartoon by Hickerson and Stanfill. The only thing worse than the terrifying monsters of Jurassic Park, of course, is the benign *T. rex* known as Barney.
(Copyright, 1993, Los Angeles Times Syndicate. Reprinted by permission.)

to be asking what sort of initiation is taking place in children's consumption of the dinosaur image. What cognitive skills and moral attitudes are being inculcated by the passage through dinomania? Any assumption that this process is simply "natural" or "universal" just leads us away from really understanding what is going on.

We need to begin, then, with a rather different set of hypotheses about children's (and, for that matter, adults') feelings for dinosaurs, to wit:

1. The principal affect associated with dinosaurs is *ambivalence,* a shifting complex of admiration and anxiety, identification and otherness.

2. This affect is *transitional,* subject to regular changes that may have some relation to stages in cognitive and psychosocial development.

3. This affect is not natural or innate, but part of a complex cultural *ritual* constructed by the whole ensemble of popular media images and pedagogy that influences the child's experience.

Let's see where these hypotheses take us.

"That's one of our early DNA experiments that went horribly wrong. But PBS has indicated some interest in him."

THE FAR SIDE   By GARY LARSON

© 1985 FarWorks, Inc./Dist. by Universal Press Syndicate

"If there're monsters moving in next door, Danny, you just ignore them. The more you believe in them, the more they'll try to get you."

38.1

Children understand that dinosaurs are the monsters under the bed, or the aliens moving in next door who are out to "get" them. Children also understand themselves to be monsters or aliens who would like to "get" their parents and playmates. Adults don't get this, but Gary Larson does.

DINOS R US: IDENTIFICATION AND FANTASY

> **In any case, the real truth about Dinosaurs would never be understood by anyone now; it was a secret I would keep for myself alone.**
>
> —ITALO CALVINO, "The Dinosaurs"

IT IS COMMONLY ASSUMED that the secret to children's fascination with dinosaurs must lie in some form of identification. But exactly what is identification, and how does it work with dinosaurs? One of our problems in even raising this question is that the most complex psychological account of identification at our disposal is now widely regarded as obsolete. Freudian psychoanalysis (like Marxist political economy) is generally thought to be a dinosaur. Every year a new book is published declaring categorically that Freud's "whole theory" of the psyche, the unconscious, has been disproved by modern science. We live in the age of the brain, not the mind, the age of cognitive, perceptual "skills" and "motivations," not dark emotions and irrational drives. We treat mental illness with drugs, not psychotherapy. The *New York Times* treats it as front-page news when an experimental psychologist "proves," by means of quantitative studies with subliminal imagery, that Freud's unconscious may or may not exist, and if it does, only in a much weaker and shallower form than we thought.

This continuing need to refute Freud is, of course, testimony to the continuing strength of his ideas. Popular attitudes toward Freud are as ambivalent as those about other dinosaurs: everyone knows that he "reduced everything to sex" (just as Marx reduced everything to class) and was probably unbalanced himself. Yet everyone suspects that there must be a grain of truth in what he said, or something so powerful and subversive that it must be continually opposed. Like Darwin, Freud gave us a meme—what Daniel Dennett calls a "dangerous idea"—that is so simple, memorable, and far-reaching that we can't get it out of our heads.[1] We look at Barney on the tip of the Loch Ness monster's tentacle (see figure 37.2), or on the couch getting lessons in self-esteem (figure 38.2), and we know that there is something deeply true about these pictures.

Before we descend into the deep oedipal waters where Barney lurks, however, it might be useful to scan the surface of what I will call "dinodentification." The list of cognitive skills that are cultivated by dinosaur learning in the classroom is indeed impressive. Using a cognitive approach that follows Piaget and Honig, researchers have found that dinosaur study in elementary classrooms helps children to achieve twelve distinct "instrumental goals" in learning: (1) grouping, (2) classifying, (3) seriating, (4) temporality, (5) spatial skills, (6) counting, (7) conservation (the discrimination of fact from fantasy, appearance from reality), (8) body mechanics, (9) problem solving, (10) use of fantasy, (11) communication, and (12) interpersonal skills.[2] The dinosaur is used as a kind of bait (otherwise known as a "motivational device") to lure kids into learning things that are good for them to know. "Identification" in this context is not a deep psychodynamic process, but the more prosaic activity of making sense out of the

38.2
Has there ever been a children's cuddly toy that produced so much ambivalence in adults? Did it ever occur to anyone to psychoanalyze the teddy bear? Barney is, clinically speaking, a "perverted" *T. rex*, one whose nature has been twisted from its proper character of violence and rage to peace and love.

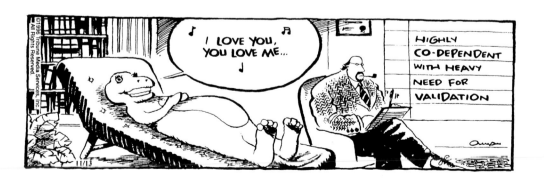

©1996 Tribune Media Services, Inc. All Rights Reserved.

238

world. Naming and classifying things, locating them in their proper places and times, deciding whether they are real or fantastic, alive or dead—all these lessons can be learned with dinosaurs. They are like a teaching machine that can't fail if the teacher knows how to turn it on. (Some teachers even testify to being skeptical about this old, obsolete pedagogical trick and then finding that it works in spite of their doubts. We obviously need some accounts of its notable failures. When does dinosaur teaching break down in elementary classrooms? Does it ever fail? I have found nothing in the literature on this subject.)

So dinosaurs provide an interdisciplinary pedagogical object that students are already familiar with: you can use them to teach math, spelling, reading, art, music, poetry, and some fundamentals of scientific thinking (the relation between fragmentary evidence and "whole" pictures, between fact and fantasy). For many children, dinosaurology provides an introduction to technical jargon and the empowerment that it provides. Adults are dutifully impressed by the pompous little pedant at the breakfast table who gleefully corrects their mistakes in dinosaur taxonomy. Of course the images and the names are probably right there on the kiddie place mat under the cereal bowl. It's not totally surprising that the tongue-twisting names are learned quickly by kids who can't remember the names of their classmates.

We shouldn't forget, however, that children can learn all of these cognitive skills without dinosaurs, and that some of them (mostly girls) aren't especially motivated by this object at all. A study by Yale psychiatrist John E. Schowalter confirms what common sense suspects: big bones are mainly a "boy toy."[3] The associations of the figure with bigness, violence, power, and aggression, the abundance of macho role models in paleontology, and the general association of science with masculinity all serve to reinforce identification in and by male children. All this is quite compatible with the dinosaur's function as a totem animal. Lévi-Strauss notes the stereotypical gendering of the totem in the "equation of male with devourer and female with devoured."[4] That doesn't mean that girls fail to play the game. Many of them have plenty of so-called "masculine" traits. Or they find an alternative "feminine" figure within the dino family—the "shy *Stegosaurus*," some graceful herbivore in skirts, or (since Spielberg) one of those raptorous "clever girls." Or they (along with a substantial number of boys) adopt a shapeless, toothless dino-security blanket like Barney, who will be whatever they want him to be. As a diverse group of walking, creeping, crawling, and (if you stretch it) flying and swimming animals, dinosaurs provide a complete bestiary for identification, all the way from the benign Barney down to Arthur Conan Doyle's representation of the pterodactyl as a "hag from hell."[5] It's the closest our children come to the traditional practice of choosing a totem animal in a tribal initiation rite.

So the "cognitive skills" that children learn through dinodentification include a lot more than counting and classifying. Among the classifications they learn is the distinction between herbivores and carnivores, the eaters and the eaten—a distinction that is routinely mapped onto gender difference.

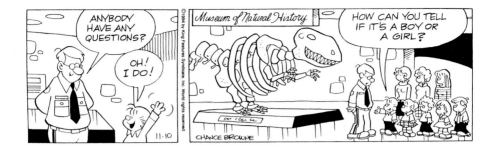

38.3

Although the dinosaur in this cartoon fulfills a common stereotype of the violent, masculine carnivore, it is actually quite ambiguous as to gender. The children and adults in this scene, by contrast, are completely unambiguous. What, then, do dinosaurs teach children about sexual identity?

(©1994 by King Features Syndicate, Inc. World Rights reserved.)

The girl in *Jurassic Park* is a vegetarian who is appalled at the idea of witnessing *T. rex* devouring a goat, a spectacle that the boy thinks will be "cool." Clearly children don't need dinosaurs to learn how to tell a boy from a girl. What dinosaurs provide is a reinforcement of common stereotypes about gender at just the age when gender identity is being formed.

The other crucial cognitive skill that is attributed to dinosaur instruction is the ability to distinguish fantasy from reality. Some children pick up this important lesson quite readily (perhaps too readily), but the research suggests that they are in the minority during the crucial age from 4 to 7 years. In experiments designed to measure children's ability to tell the difference between "real" and "pretend" images, Harvard psychologists Howard Gardner and Patricia Morison introduced three figures that they called "ambiguous exemplars of real entities" that are "remote from" children's daily experience.[6] The three entities were "dinosaur," "knight," and "Indian." Children can, of course, be told that dinosaurs are (were) real and not fantastic, but that doesn't mean they will understand the difference. For one thing, the differences "real/unreal" and "living/dead" (or "existing/extinct") are easily confused with each other, even by adults. For another, everything in children's popular culture reinforces the ambiguity of dinosaurs (along with that of knights and Indians) by romanticizing them, rendering them familiar and potent exemplars of how hard it is to distinguish fantasy and reality. (We have already noted the historical link between the dinosaur and the feudal imagery of the robber barons, as well as with frontier Indian wars and Native American totems.) If "fact/fantasy" distinctions are the cognitive skills we want to inculcate in first-graders, it is hard to imagine a more intractable device than the dinosaur for accomplishing this aim.

It's not surprising, then, that teachers themselves are often confused about their aims. Should they bone up (you'll excuse the expression) on paleontology so that they can be sure of presenting responsible, up-to-date material? Should they censor "wrong" pictures that show cave people and dinosaurs in the same period?[7] Should the creationist "antediluvian monster" and the Native American Unktehi be banned from the classroom? What, then, should teachers tell the children about the reality status of Barney, or *Dinotopia,* or *Jurassic Park?* What should they do with early, obsolete images of the dinosaur like Waterhouse Hawkins's Crystal Palace restorations? Or with the complex pre-Darwinist geology on which they are based? Should teachers simply "go with the flow" of children's interests, exploit the periodic outbreaks of dinomania in popular culture, and hope that the kids are learning some useful things? What should they do about the programming of sexual stereotypes in dinosaur images, or the tendency of some children to act out violent, aggressive fantasies in relation to the predatory figures?

I wish that I had clear, straightforward answers to all of these questions, and a lesson plan or curriculum guide to go with them, but I don't. I do think it's clear that the cognitivist account of dinosaur instruction only scratches the surface of what is happening when children encounter dinosaur images. They are learning and experiencing many other things besides cognitive skills. Some of these lessons are ones we probably would just as soon they didn't learn—the "naturalness" of being a voracious consumer, of being an aggressive predator or passive victim, a bully or a sissy. Elementary

38.4 (Overleaf)
Children empower themselves not only by imagining themselves to be dinosaurs, but by role-playing as scientific authorities, masters of a jargon that has been forgotten by their parents. What does it mean that the first introduction to science for children in the United States is generally the dinosaur lesson?
(Foxtrot ©1996 Bill Amend. Reprinted with permission of Universal Press Syndicate. All rights reserved.)

FoxTrot

BILL AMEND

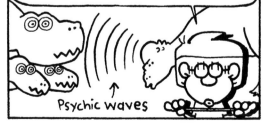

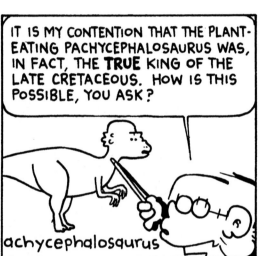

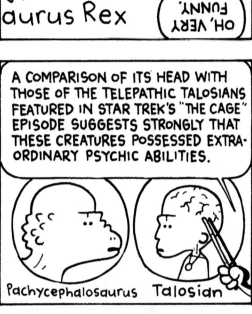

© 1996 Bill Amend/Dist. by Universal Press Syndicate

lessons in half-baked social Darwinism and sociobiology are probably no better for kids than creationist myths. And it seems unrealistic to expect overworked teachers to lead their pupils in sophisticated discussions of the relation of reality and fantasy, the split between science and culture, and the limits of scientific authority when they scarcely have time to get the volcano working in the diorama.

When I look at existing classroom practices, moreover, I'm struck by how much good sense and good will go into dinosaur instruction, right alongside the sense of mystification about what the goal is and why it seems to work. One thing we might consider is approaching elementary school dinosaur lessons as a massive research project in which the results are not yet known. Perhaps our problem has been in assuming too quickly that we know what we are doing when we "teach dinosaurs." In fact, the awkwardness of this phrase reveals an important point: we don't teach dinosaurs so much as they teach themselves. They are like teaching machines whose "lessons" have been programmed by their whole history of scientific inquiry and cultural display—the history I have been trying to lay out in this book. They express a collective unconscious and a set of ritual practices that are specific to modern culture. They are beaming a whole repertoire of messages at us that are, as yet, only partially understood.

The other crucial thing about dinosaur lessons is that they are *taught to us by children*. We need to pay attention to that crucial scene of the pedantic first-grader at the breakfast table, showing off her mastery of jargon and correcting her parents' mistakes. Dinosaurs have the effect of (to use the contemporary jargon) "empowering" children and allowing them to play the role of teacher. At the opening of the new dinosaur hall at the American Museum of Natural History in 1995, National Public Radio conducted interviews with children leaving the exhibit. After giving his assessment of the new installation, one very serious five-year-old was asked if he had any views on the various theories about dinosaur extinction. He replied that, yes, he did have views, and in fact had figured out why the dinosaurs died out. When the interviewer asked him to explain, the boy said that he was not at liberty to reveal his theory to the public at the present time.

While I doubt that this young scientist's secret theory of dinosaur extinction will shake the foundations of paleontology, perhaps this scene will reopen our curiosity about what the secret of the dinosaur is, why it has become the totem animal of modern culture, what lessons our children are learning from it, and what they (and it) are trying to tell us.

39.1
What alternative is there for a weak, puny little kid who is a failure in school and gets his lunch money stolen by the school bully every day? Imagine yourself as "Calvinosaurus!" the fiercest, biggest predator that ever walked the earth. (Calvin and Hobbes © 1990 Watterson. Distributed by Universal Press Syndicate. Reprinted with permission. All rights reserved.)

calvinosaurus: from T. rex to O. Rex

IF THE DINOSAUR IS BAIT, some children swallow it hook, line, and sinker. Psychiatrist John Schowalter notes that while most children treat dinosaurs as "a brief but useful adjunct in the developmental process," for a few "it becomes a true obsession," and threatens to become "a substitute for appropriate peer socialization."[1] Schowalter also notes the predominantly masculine pattern of identification, and the onset of "the interest in dinosaurs . . . at age four or five . . . the height of the oedipal period." The giant image of the dinosaur makes it an appropriate figure of the parents (with *T. rex* as the father, *Brontosaurus* as the mother), and the ritual "lesson" that is recited (that dinosaurs are dead) transforms them into *safe* monsters who reassure the child that someday she will change places with her parents and become a powerful giant herself. The miniaturization of the monster in toys and models reinforces this sense of safety.

The comic strip *Calvin and Hobbes* provides a vivid illustration of the way these processes might work. Calvin is an only child who clearly has problems in socialization and adaptation to school. He has a hyperactive fantasy life, one that completely overwhelms the strip in which he appears, so that part of the pleasure of reading Calvin is in guessing at just what point "reality" will reassert itself (in general, it doesn't—at least not for very long).[2] The reader/viewer of *Calvin and Hobbes* quickly gets used to the basic premise of the strip: Calvin's fantasies are the dominant reality, and what we would call "reality" is only a marginal feature. His parents are loathsome monsters, the food they serve is disgusting slime, his teacher is a troll with big teeth, and his days and nights are enlivened by intergalactic journeys, encounters with alien life forms, and death-defying joyrides on his jet-propelled sled. At the center of Calvin's fantasy life are two principal animal figures: a stuffed tiger named Hobbes, and a dinosaur menagerie in which Calvin himself is the biggest, fiercest creature of all, the "Calvinosaurus."

The salient features of Calvin's dinosaur fantasies are as follows: (1) he manages the identification of dinosaurs with parent figures who might threaten him with their size by imagining himself as a bigger dinosaur than them; (2) his identification process is double: on the one hand, he "is" Calvinosaurus; on the other, he is the renowned paleontologist who discovered and named the dinosaur after himself, much as Andrew Carnegie appropriated *Diplodocus carnegii;* (3) his fantasies are elaborated in scenes of gargantuan consumption and cannibalism (in one sequence, several tons of meat is delivered to his home by a truck; in another, he is described as being able to gobble up other dinosaurs in a single bite); (4) his identification as a paleontologist is relatively realistic at the visual level (his daydream of Calvi-

> For some time Joey continued to draw dinosaurs. Indeed, the fascination of these huge extinct animals for many psychotic children is quite remarkable. Typically they get interested in dinosaurs when they begin to guess what must happen if they are to lay to rest the ghosts of their past: that they must first exhume and put correctly together those skeletons in the closets of their minds; that they must understand what the skeletons meant when they still roamed through their lives. Freud likened the work of psychoanalysis to archaeological discoveries. Maybe the children have found a better analogy than the reconstruction of dead buildings and artifacts from buried places. Their need is to unearth something that was once very alive, very huge, and over-whelmingly stalked them.
>
> —BRUNO BETTELHEIM,
> *The Empty Fortress*[3]

247

140 MILLION YEARS AGO, THE INCREDIBLE 'ULTRASAURS' WANDER THE EARTH! SOME WEIGH OVER 70 TONS, AND EVEN THE VICIOUS ALLOSAURS ARE NO MATCH FOR THESE GIANTS!

NO! IT'S...IT'S A **CALVINOSAURUS!**

NAMED AFTER THE RENOWNED ARCHEOLOGIST WHO DISCOVERED IT, THE HUGE CALVINOSAUR CAN EAT AN ULTRASAUR IN A SINGLE BITE!

BUT WAIT! A DISTANT RUMBLING SENDS THE ULTRASAURS INTO A PANICKED STAMPEDE! IS IT A VOLCANO? IS IT AN EARTHQUAKE?

PHOOEY! I NEVER FIND *ANY*THING.

IT LOOKS LIKE YOU'VE HIT THE SEWER PIPE

39.2–39.3

Calvin has two totem animals: Calvinosaurus, who expresses all his rage and grandiosity, and Hobbes the tiger, who represents his better nature and calls him back to reality. Whether imagining himself as a monster who can devour his parents and classmates (39.2), or as a famous paleontologist who can intimidate them with his scientific prestige (39.3), Calvin uses the dinosaur as his medium for fantasies of absolute power.

calvin and HOBBES

FOR SHOW-AND-TELL, I BROUGHT THESE AMAZING FOSSILIZED BONE FRAGMENTS THAT I PAINSTAKINGLY UNEARTHED FROM SEDIMENTARY DEPOSITS IN MY FRONT YARD!

THOUGH THEY LOOK LIKE ORDINARY DRIVEWAY GRAVEL TO THE UNTUTORED EYE OF THE IGNORANT LAYMAN, I IMMEDIATELY RECOGNIZED THESE AS PIECES OF JAWBONE FROM A NEW SPECIES OF CARNOSAUR!

WHEN THIS HAPPENS, YOU CAN BE DARN SURE THAT THOSE OF YOU WHO WERE MEAN TO ME IN SCHOOL WILL SUFFER APPROPRIATELY!

I'LL EMPLOY MY RESOURCES TO MAKE YOUR PUNY LIVES MISERABLE! I'LL CRUSH YOUR PITIFUL DREAMS AND AMBITIONS LIKE BUGS IN THE DUST!

©1989 UNIVERSAL PRESS SYNDICATE

nosaurus eating the *Ultrasaurus* is interrupted by the disappointingly mundane reality of hitting a sewer pipe while digging a hole in his backyard); but (5) Calvin's capacity for fantasy is unstoppable. Even when he is confronting the reality principle, it is his tiger Hobbes who tells him about it. And when he plays his role as paleontologist in a sequence of visual realism, his *verbal* expressions become fantastically elaborate and articulate. He plays the pedantic child-teacher, seizing the power of the lecture platform and threatening to take revenge on everyone who was mean to him before he became a famous paleontologist.

Calvin's dinosaur fantasies cannot be understood without seeing them in relation to his other totem animal, Hobbes the tiger. Hobbes is the voice of Calvin's better nature. Although he is a loyal sidekick, and the only creature who is allowed to be in Calvin's secret club, he is relentlessly critical of Calvin, providing a skeptical, ironic counterpoint to Calvin's rage, anxiety, and violence-filled fantasy life. He is a boon companion on the wild rides on Calvin's sled, yet Calvin also imagines that his tiger is always lying in wait to devour him if he lets down his guard. His return from school every day is the scene of a ritual ambush, in which Hobbes springs out of hiding and absorbs Calvin in a whirlwind of violent energy. Like his namesake, Hobbes is nature red in tooth and claw, and a skeptic who loves to deflate idealist fantasies. Calvin, by contrast, is (like his great Puritan namesake) a creature of the highest idealism leavened by a hyperactive imagination. "Calvin" thus provides a kind of childish, psychotic parody of Calvin*ism*. He is caught between contradictory forces and impulses, his fantasy life a battleground of good and evil, megalomania and abject weakness, grown-up precociousness and arrested development (Calvin is a total failure in school, yet he has the vocabulary of an adult.) Like the archetypal Puritan's, Calvin's life is suspended on the border between heaven and hell, the living (Hobbes) and the dead (Calvinosaurus).[4]

The opposition of Calvinosaurus and Hobbes is one we have seen before. It is like the conflict between Cary Grant's bone and Katharine Hepburn's leopard in *Bringing Up Baby*, and it evokes the ancient antagonism between the cold and the warm, reptile and mammal, dry bones and living creatures. The reason all this is funny, and not horrifying or boringly predictable, is that it scrambles all the boundaries between the real and the imaginary that it evokes. Hobbes is just a stuffed tiger, but he is the voice of the Real. Calvinosaurus is imaginary, an utterly phantasmatic image, verging on hallucination: yet he is also scientifically constructed, certified and legitimate.

The lesson Calvin is learning from his scientific unit on dinosaurs is that science is power, the power to see that what looks "like ordinary driveway gravel to the untutored eye of the ignorant layman" is actually "pieces of jawbone from a new species of carnosaur." What is telling about this speech is that Calvin has such a mastery of the jargon of paleontological authority. He sounds as if he knows what he is talking about. And the more learned and intelligent he sounds, the crazier he seems. His perfect mimicry of the scientific persona undermines the whole notion that science is somehow antithetical to fantasy and aligned with the reality principle (see the discussion of science and "the real" in appendix B, "Science and Culture"). For Calvin (as I think for many children), science is attractive precisely because of its speculative, romantic, utopian character and its promise of power and fame. If Calvin is learning the cognitive skill of distinguishing fantasy from reality, it is in spite of his dinosaur lessons, not because of them. His total reality, in fact, would be better described as the product of two conflicting fantasies exemplified by his two totem animals, Calvinosaurus and Hobbes.

It will probably be objected here that Calvin himself is not a real but a fictional child, and we can't base any conclusions about real children on a comic strip written by an adult for adults. I think this objection seriously underestimates the power of visual-verbal fictional forms like the comic strip to give us psychological insights that can never be captured by questionnaires and interviews with real children. We might as well object that we can learn nothing about adult psychology from the characters of Shakespeare or Henry James because they too are fictional. But the crucial point is not that there is something suspect about mistaking fictional, fantasy characters for real people, but that real people are themselves constituted by processes of fantasy, which are the building blocks of identity and identification. If people could not fantasize, could not imagine and project and mimic, they would not have identities or subjectivity. They would not even be people. As for children, they do not exist in some "state of nature" that can be studied independently of what adults make of them. Childhood itself is a modern invention, one that is expanding to take up more of human life with each generation of modern culture.[5] It is well known that some professions (paleontology, for instance) are filled with romantic boys who never outgrew their dinomania.

The lesson of *Calvin and Hobbes* for teachers and psychologists, then, is to understand that the dinosaur is a good teaching machine, not because it provides a straightforward way to inculcate the "cognitive skill" of separating fantasy and reality, but because it frustrates and challenges that skill with a complex, intractable object. The dinosaur may help some children to resist bone-headed distinctions between "pretending" and "reality," and prolong their sense of wonder. It may provide an occasion for a discussion of gender stereotypes, of the "naturalness" of violence and aggression, of the role of imagination in scientific inquiry. It can offer a kind of "empowerment zone" for children in which they get to play the roles of teacher and researcher, reporting on dinosaur jokes, riddles, cartoons, toys, dreams, and stories—the whole archive of "dinosaur folklore"—alongside the scientific "dinosaurology" that some of them command. It can do this, however, only if the teacher gets over the notion that the primary or exclusive goal is to teach "correct science" to first-graders,[6] and understands that she is dealing with a hybrid object, the totem animal of modern culture, a creature that no one understands fully—least of all the paleontologists.[7]

40.1

At Dinosaur National Monument in Utah the process of dinosaur resurrection and spectacular consumption comes to a certain kind of endpoint. The bones are being left in the ground, partly exposed. (Quarry wall, Dinosaur National Monument, Vernal, Utah. Author's photo.)

TRANSITIONAL OBJECTS: FROM BREAST TO <u>BRONTOSAURUS</u>

FOR MOST PEOPLE, dinosaurs are only a phase. In rare cases, children become fixated on dinosaurs and fall into a borderline psychosis like Calvin, or find a "healthy outlet" for their obsession such as paleontology or some semi-professional form of dinomania (hobbies, collections, travel to digs). Dinosaurs are thus a later form of that class of things called "transitional objects" by the psychologist D. W. Winnicott.[1] Between the thumb and the teddy bear, the breast and the *Brontosaurus,* a whole set of objects play crucial roles in the maturation process. Security blankets and stuffed animals are the most common, and they display, according to Winnicott, a familiar ensemble of features:

> 1. They are associated with oral activities (sucking, babbling, chewing), are often adopted by the child during the weaning process, and are often used to caress the face while sucking. They are especially crucial as aids to sleep.

> 2. They are "affectionately cuddled as well as excitedly loved and mutilated" (5), serving as objects of both affection and aggression.

> 3. They seem to have warmth, life, and personalities of their own.

> 4. At some point they are cast aside, or "decathected." The transitional object is "not forgotten and it is not mourned." It is not like a fetish object that has to be repressed or hoarded.

Winnicott argues that transitional objects are crucial to human development, serving as the basic experiential bridge between subjective and objective reality, occupying a realm of illusion and play that is fundamental to "the whole cultural field" (5). Art, science, religion, and creative activities of all sorts depend upon this universal human capacity to learn and develop by playing with real objects. Both magical and scientific thinking are constructed from a repertoire of tools, technologies, and prostheses that are both "out there" in the world and serving as extensions of our inner selves, both "totemic operators" (animated beings) with wills of their own and mere instruments to do our bidding.

As a psychologist, Winnicott focuses his interest on a general, ahistorical account of the individual producer of culture. But there is clearly another route into the transitional object, and that is through cultural history, the study of the ways in which societies produce—or sometimes do not produce—a thing called "the individual." Between the thumb and the teddy bear lies the realm of history. Thumbs have been with us much longer in the evolutionary scheme of things, and are indispensable for our existence as "prehensile," tool-using animals who can grasp and manipulate things. Teddy bears have been with us since about 1901, when Teddy Roosevelt's prowess as a big game hunter is reputed to have inspired them. They are a product of modern consumer culture, a "spin-off" of fairy tales and early cinema.[2] There is nothing natural or universal about them at all, although they may occupy a niche in cultural ecology that is universal in human development. Traditional societies often assign totem animals to children to separate them into kinship or gender groupings, or

> I have introduced the terms "transitional objects" and "transitional phenomena" for the designation of the intermediate area of experience, between the thumb and the teddy bear, between the oral erotism and the true object-relationship, between primary creative activity and projection of what has already been introjected, between primary unawareness of indebtedness and acknowledgment of indebtedness (Say: "ta").
>
> —D. W. WINNICOTT, *Playing and Reality*

to give them an individualized animal identity and name. Modern child-rearing may look as if it is free of these ritual practices, giving each child a freedom of "object choice" to reflect its "individual personality," just as we provide adults with an array of consumer choices through which they may "express themselves." But this freedom is illusory: the choices themselves are programmed and restricted by gender (clothes and toys) and class (expensive and cheap), and parents who want to control their children's choices find that they are working against an international system of media images and marketing. When a Barney hand puppet becomes the security blanket of choice for an 18-month-old girl, we need to ask where the "choice" resides. There is, in fact, no determinate moment or agency of choosing, any more than there is in a traditional society where things are done because that is the way they have always been done. The difference in the modern world is that things are done because they are the newest thing and because everyone else is doing it. The "clan" associated with the totem animal is an international community of consumption.[3]

Freud traced "the return of totemism in childhood" to the Oedipus complex, seeing the ambivalent complex of love and hate, affection and anxiety that children project onto animals as a way of managing their feelings about the father:

> Little Hans was not only *frightened* of horses; he also approached them with admiration and interest. As soon as his anxiety began to diminish, he identified himself with the dreaded creature: he began to jump about like a horse and in his turn bit his father. At another stage in the resolution of his phobia he did not hesitate to identify his parents with some other large animals.[4]

It is clear, however, that the father is not the only thing that can be replaced by the large animal. Any adult (the mother, a teacher), or an older sibling or bigger classmate (like the school bully in *Calvin and Hobbes*), can have an animal "stand-in" in the child's world of fantastic, animated objects. The dinosaur's automatic identification with masculinity and patriarchy (especially the Dead White Male) does not prevent it from being reconfigured for transitions other than those of four- and five-year-old boys going through the oedipal stage. Barney is a transitional object between teddy bear and *T. rex,* an extension of the dinosaur image back into early childhood. That is why Barney is often abandoned and reviled as "childish" just at the moment the child is becoming interested in "real" dinosaurs.[5]

But real dinosaurs also turn out to be transitional objects for many children. In this role, they tend to recapitulate all the earlier functions of the transitional object in new forms. They are objects of ambivalence, of fear and ridicule, affection and aggression, anxiety and identification. The oral practices (biting, sucking, devouring) in which the first transitional object took the place of the breast give way to rituals of consumption in which the big teeth and claws, the cavernous bellies, and the voracious appetites of dinosaurs become objects of fantasy and spectacle. *Jurassic Park* unfolds as a sequence of spectacular meals. The dinner party inside the belly of the monster is the ritual spectacle that accompanies the unveiling of the Jeffersonian mastodon and the Crystal Palace dinosaurs.

The last function that Winnicott attributes to transitional objects is the movement "between primary unawareness of indebtedness and the acknowledgment of indebtedness (Say: 'ta')." (2) Perhaps the most important lesson the child is learning from the transitional object is to give it up, to give it away, to relinquish it without forgetting or mourning. A version of this process is probably being acted out in the famous "Fort-Da" game that Freud observed "Little Hans" playing.[6] In that game, the child throws away a spool attached to his chair by a thread, crying out "fort!" as it disappears from sight, and "da!" as he reels it back into view. This game of "now you see it, now you don't" has generally been interpreted as the child's way of learning by repetition to deal with the anxiety caused by the mother's absence. The ritual of disappearance and reappearance, coupled with the incantation of the magic words, gives the child a sense of power to cope with loss and frustration.

Winnicott's child is learning a more advanced lesson, the art of giving gifts and of repaying the gift with a word ("ta"). But even benign forms of generosity are, as we have seen, never pure or disinterested. The gift confers an obligation, and may in fact be a subtle act of aggression. Calvin gives his show-and-tell report on dinosaurs to the class in order to command their admiration and respect. He invites them to repay his unwanted gift by letting them become his "pals" (for just $20 per person). The gift-giving ritual for Calvinosaurus is one of bribing and intimidating others in order to make them your friends. While this is something of which we all disapprove, naturally, it is by no means an unfamiliar pattern of behavior. Thomas Jefferson's "gifts" of big bones to the natural historians of France were calculated to ingratiate and impress at the same time, as was that greatest example of dino-potlatch, *Diplodocus carnegii* (see chapters 24 and 25 above).

As important as acquisition of and fixation on the dinosaur image might be, then, it is equally important to consider the moment of giving it away, giving it up, and letting it go. Calvin is a classic instance of fixation, unable to accept the dissolving of his dino-fantasy—except under the influence of an earlier fantasy, the living presence of his stuffed tiger, Hobbes. In Calvin's case, regression to his earlier transitional object looks like a form of maturation, and his efforts to mimic rational, scientific "maturity" come off as comically grotesque.

The best example of a positive transition is the weaning of Cary Grant from his bone obsession with the help of Katharine Hepburn and her leopard. *Bringing Up Baby* traces the progression of a paleontologist from his oedipal fixation into what Freud called the "latency period" between infantile sexuality and the onset of puberty. This is what most parents will recognize as that "golden age" of childhood between 6 and 12, when many children actually like their parents, enjoy being with them, and yet are mature enough to have some independence. For Grant and Hepburn, it is a golden age of Shakespearean romance in the pastoral realm of Connecticut, a place where he has to learn to play games with a girl, even to play at being a girl, in order to grow out of his bone fetish. As the story unfolds, Grant will lose his bone, but will learn to let it go without mourning it or forgetting it. Hepburn returns it to him at the end, a transitional object that he has outgrown. She is his new object choice, along with the promise of her uncle's million-dollar gift to the museum.

Transitional objects mediate between individuals and the social, cultural reality they inhabit. Ideally, they provide a mechanism for individual maturation. They are given to us (or chosen by us) so that we can grow up by growing out of them. Sometimes we fail to grow out of them, and a transitional object turns into a fetish. The question we might ponder at this point is whether societies or civilizations adopt transitional objects in anything like the way individuals do. Is there a sense in which societies become fixated on objects and turn them into those collective, monumental fetishes known as "idols"? This thought has come to the surface most prominently during periods of major social and political revolution. The great democratic revolutions of the Enlightenment were often characterized as an overturning of the "idol of monarchy" and seen as a new stage, not just in the fortunes of individual nations, but in the maturing of the human species as a whole. Thomas Jefferson warned against treating the Constitution as an idol or sacred ark that could never be touched or altered. As a "founding father" who lived long enough to see himself canonized and idolized, he was concerned about this collective form of the Oedipus complex, and urged that the U.S. Constitution be treated as a transitional object.

The dinosaur is clearly a transitional object in the lives of many children in modern societies. The question is whether it also plays some version of this role at the level of social life and public national culture. Certainly it does not, despite its central, monumental position in the public display of natural and ethnographic history, seem anything like an idol. There is no question of treating dinosaurs as Jules Michelet wanted to treat the icons and trappings of monarchy, as idolatrous relics that had to be swept away to make room for the clean, fresh start offered by the French Revolution.[7] And yet there is a sense in which the dinosaur is, as Adorno argued, a symbol of the "monstrous total State," an ominous symbol of totalitarianism, patriarchy, and the world system of voracious, destructive production and consumption we call capitalism. "The modern economy," noted Walter Benjamin, "seen as a whole, resembles much less a machine that stands idle when abandoned by its stoker than a beast that goes berserk as soon as its tamer turns its back."[8] The gigantic skeletal structure has been linked with the framework of the modern constitution, at least since Jefferson's mastodon and perhaps since Hobbes's Leviathan (which Carl Schmitt characterized as "a combination of god and man, animal and machine").[9] As we have seen, the shattering of the monstrous skeleton has become almost as familiar a ritual as the dinner party in its belly. The spectacle of its breakup is linked with a crisis in gender roles in the first part of the twentieth century, and with a crisis in reproduction (falling birth rates in industrialized nations coupled with population explosions in "underdeveloped" areas; the danger of biological "breakouts" and plague) in the late twentieth century, the age of biocybernetic reproduction.

So if the question here is "what is to be done" with the dinosaur, I do not have an answer, except "keep an eye on it." That is, pay attention to what is happening to it, try to make sense of it. The creature has an uncanny capacity for working both symptomatically and diagnostically. It expresses the political unconscious of each era of modern life, manifesting collective anxieties about disaster and extinction, epitomizing our own ambivalence toward our collective condition. It always accompanies the disaster theme with a narrative of our own possible extinction, and how to avoid it. It has insinuated itself into global culture as the most widely publicized mythical animal in history. In the long history of mythical animals that have served as metaphors for human identity, it is the first to function as a *species* totem for the human race. It began as the totem of the modern White Male, and has evolved into the modern Other, the aliens (reptilian bipeds, of course) who have been visiting us in movies since the 1950s—or is it since the days of the dragons? So the question we must ask of it is not "what does it mean?" but "why are they here? and "what do they want from us?"

This last question is one that Calvin assigns to Hobbes. The tiger is Calvin's good nature. If we treated the dinosaur as a "Hobbes," we would not always assume that we control what it means, any more than we control our unconscious—much less that we have banished it (along with Freud) into the realm of obsolescence. We would think of the dinosaur, like Calvin's tiger, as having a life of its own, as a "companionable form" that springs surprises on us, that refuses to be controlled as a scientific object.[10] We would see it not just as a totem, but as a transitional object we might outgrow, and act accordingly. (I hereby promise that this is the last dinosaur book I will write.) In part, that would mean being willing to give it up, to get over dinomania, or to find a new way of thinking about it, one that did not imagine that its scientific importance was the sole basis for its fascination.

The future can be glimpsed at Dinosaur National Monument in Utah (see figure 40.1). There the process of dinosaur resurrection and spectacular consumption comes to a certain kind of endpoint. The bones have been left in the ground, partly exposed, on a hillside enclosed in a massive shed that bathes the fossils in natural light while protecting them from the weather. It is as if the dinosaur is being allowed to sink back into the swamp, to be buried again, to be let go without mourning and without forgetting.

Does this mean that the dinosaur has been used up, a scientific concept that has had its day, a cultural image that has been fully consumed and is now ready for the junk heap? Is it a security blanket that is about to be cast aside, a transitional object that has done its job, and is now ready for retirement? A teaching machine that has disgorged all its lessons?

Perhaps, but not quite yet. It seems clear that we still have things to learn from dinosaurs, and it is a very good bet that they will not disappear soon from popular culture. They will go in and out of style, responding to the crises of the moment. The name and the image will continue to circulate, probably more extensively than ever before. Like the medieval dragon, they have already made the transition from a real thing into a metaphor, and the next phase—the transition to a *dead* metaphor (like the leg of a chair or the eye of a needle)—is well under way. The difference is that serious research on the creatures formerly known as dinosaurs will go on, both supported and distracted by the popular hysteria that surrounds its object. Dinosaur discoveries will continue to be front-page news, and naturally I expect that my discovery of the dinosaur's totemic function will be treated with this kind of attention.

So perhaps the passing of the dinosaur will be noted without mourning or forgetting, and this, *The Last Dinosaur Book*, will be an aid to that process, a look in the rearview mirror at something that is receding into the past, but is still out ahead of us in the darkness, albeit in a different form:

Since then I had learned many things, and above all the way in which Dinosaurs conquer. First I had believed that disappearing had been, for my brothers, the magnanimous acceptance of a defeat; now I knew that the more the Dinosaurs disappear, the more they extend their dominion, and over forests far more vast than those that cover the continents: in the labyrinth of the survivors' thoughts. From the semidarkness of fears and doubts of now ignorant generations, the Dinosaurs continued to extend their necks, to raise their taloned hoofs, and when the last shadow of their image had been erased, their name went on, superimposed on all meanings, perpetuating their presence in relations among living beings. Now, when the name too had been erased, they would become one thing with the mute and anonymous molds of thought, through which thoughts take on form and substance: by the New Ones, and by those who would come after the New Ones, and those who would come even after them.

—Calvino, "The Dinosaurs"

AMERICAN MUSEUM OF NATURAL HISTORY

Barosaurus defends her young from an attacking *Allosaurus*
John Gurche 1991

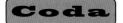

paleoart

The future is but the obsolete in reverse.

—VLADIMIR NABOKOV

41.1

Clement Greenberg called kitsch "the first truly universal art form" and urged that it be kept out of the world of fine art. Dinosaur kitsch breaks into the art world in this installation by Mark Dion. The time when dinosaurs ruled the earth is now, and their rule is synonymous with the global dominance of American culture. (Detail of 1.3.)

To THIS POINT I have been assuming that the image of the dinosaur circulates primarily among the spheres of commerce, mass culture, and science. To the extent that it penetrates the art world, it does so as "scientific illustration," and it is not generally seen as serious art, the sort of thing that could make it into the Museum of Modern Art.[1] That doesn't mean that dinosaur painters and sculptors lack skill or imagination. Waterhouse Hawkins, Charles Knight, Rudolph Zallinger, and many contemporary dinosaur artists are absolutely first-rate in their fields. But they would understand without a moment's hesitation why the peculiar status of their subject matter and their realistic style of representation prevents them from being taken seriously in the world of fine art.

The exclusion of dinosaurs from the spaces of the art world—from the studio, the gallery, and the fine arts museum—exemplifies one of the central principles of high modernism. It illustrates perfectly the difference between modernity (of which the dinosaur is the totem animal) and modern*ism* (an aesthetic of purity that rigorously excludes kitsch subject matter). This sort of purist modernism is mainly associated with the rise of abstract expressionism in American art after World War II, and with the art criticism of Clement Greenberg.[2]

Many common prejudices about the dinosaur clash with this sort of modernism. If modernism insists that the artist "make it new," creating an object that is forever fresh and self-renewing, the dinosaur is unimaginably old, a symbol of failure, obsolescence, and petrified stasis. If modernism demands the original, unique, authentic object created by the artistic imagination, the dinosaur is a mere copy of a fragment of a corpse or skeleton, a fossil imprint produced by natural accident, not by human artifice. If modernism demands the elite, refined, purified objet d'art, the dinosaur is contaminated by its status as a commercial attraction, its function as a mass cultural icon and an object of childish fascination.

The emergence of postmodernism since the 1960s has made it possible for dinosaurs to "cross the park" from the museum of natural history to the museum of fine art, from the space of mass culture to the world of elite, cutting-edge art-making. Mark Dion's multimedia installation *When Dinosaurs Ruled the Earth (Toys R U.S.)* reconstructs the dinotopia that is now available to children in the United States (and in Japan and other "developed" countries around the world) (see figure 1.3). In Dion's installation, the dinosaur is both figure and background, a multitude of objects and images in a space and the wallpapered environment in which those objects are placed. The title of the installation suggests that the time when dinosaurs ruled the earth is not just the paleontological past, but also the immediate present, when its global circulation has reached epidemic proportions. The parenthetical qualifier of the title, "Toys R U.S.," suggests that this global epidemic has its center in the United States, and in "us." The installation may be viewed retrospectively as well, as an already archaic site (like the tomb of King Tut, filled with the toys and effigies of his attendants), as if Dion were leaving a message in a time capsule for future generations to decipher.

A rather different variation on the postmodern strategy of "paleoart" is offered by Allan McCollum, an artist who is perhaps best known for his *Surrogate Paintings* and *Plaster Surrogates,* cast objects that look like blank pictures in sleek modern frames, hung in clusters like an array of paintings in a Victorian study gallery. Like Dion, McCollum is not really asking us to look at the individual objects, especially the black blank spaces inside the frames, but to look at the entire space or environment as a representation of the way we display pictures in our culture. Every picture is unique—or at least the frame is—but at the same time they are all exactly the same, epitomizing the kind of serial repetition that is characteristic of images as species or genera of artifacts. You've seen one McCollum surrogate and you've seen them all, yet none is exactly like any other. It is as if McCollum were imagining a future world in which all the pictures had gone blank, could no longer be seen or deciphered, but all remained in their positions on the walls. They hint at a world in which pictures would be fossils, traces of vanished, obsolete species. Perhaps this would be a world of the blind, in which pictures would function as sculptural pieces, and we would grope along the walls to be reassured by touch that they were still in their places. Or perhaps it would be a world in which the people were so imaginative that they could treat any blank space as a projection screen to recall any memory or fantasy they desired. We might even see here a premonition of the virtual galleries Bill Gates is installing in his electronic Xanadu in Seattle, galleries in which images from a global data base can be retrieved with the click of a remote control. In any event, McCollum's surrogates invite us to reframe the entire convention of pictorial display, to see a gallery the way an archaeologist might see an excavated treasure room, as a strange space filled with shapes and signs that may have lost their meaning, or may never have had any meaning in the first place. The effect is a curious combination of irony and melancholy, what Fredric Jameson has aptly termed the "nostalgia for the present" endemic to postmodernism.

If the surrogate pieces seem archaeological, representing cultural artifacts as if they were the unreadable relics of a past civilization, McCollum's more recent work has moved into the realm of paleontology and natural history. These copies or surrogates are not of artificial objects, but of what McCollum calls "copies produced by *nature*."[3] In *The Dog from Pompeii* (series begun 1990) and *Lost Objects* (series

41.2
What if human beings lost their ability to see images, rendering pictures obsolete? The result might be glimpsed in this installation, which could be called "fossil pictures." (Allan McCollum, *Surrogate Paintings*, 112 Workshop, New York City, 1980.)

41.3–41.4

Dogs and Bones by Allan
McCollum. A cast of the famous
"Dog from Pompeii," killed in
the eruption of Vesuvius in
79 A.D.[?] and painted concrete
casts from dinosaur thigh bones
at Dinosaur National Monument
in Utah. Who or what is the
"artist" that creates a fossil
image? Is there a form of art or
image-making that precedes the
arrival of the human hand,
namely, the formation of "natural
copies" in the process of fos-
silization? (*The Dog from Pompeii*,
John Weber Gallery, New York,
1991, and *Lost Objects* [detail of
figure 16.2].)

begun 1991), McCollum simply inserts himself into the process of reproduction or replication inherent in the natural formation of fossils. The dog is an indefinitely reproducible series of polymer-enhanced Hydrocal casts, taken from a mold that was made from a cast based on a "natural mold" left by the body of a dog that was smothered in the Vesuvius explosion of 79 A.D. The *Lost Objects* "are cast in glass-fiber-reinforced concrete from rubber molds taken of fossil dinosaur bones in the vertebrate paleontology section of the Carnegie Museum of Natural History in Pittsburgh." Fifteen different molds have been painted in fifty different colors, making "750 unique *Lost Objects* to date."

Traditional notions of the relation of copy and original, not to mention the status of the artistic "authorial" function, are clearly under considerable pressure in these works, and their effect is very difficult to pin down. In some ways, these works seem to fulfill Walter Benjamin's prediction that the age of mechanical reproduction would mean that the endless series of identical replicas would replace the unique art object with its "aura" of authorial expressiveness and tradition. McCollum makes "mass-produced" objects in a kind of art factory, like an automobile manufacturer. Yet the objects do seem to have a kind of melancholy aura, one that is increased rather than diminished by their mass gathering in the space of display. It is as if they were occasions for a double mourning, first for the deaths of the remote creatures whose traces are retraced here, and second for loss of auratic uniqueness itself, as if we were grieving over the loss of the ability to feel certain kinds of emotions. Certainly these works don't tend to provoke laughter the way the surrogates do. They are too literal in their evocation of death, disaster, and mass extinction. The dog, as the favorite domestic animal of the Romans, evokes the sphere of privacy and the everyday in the proximity of catastrophe. The bones, on the other hand, evoke the larger public spheres of the nation and the world—the dinosaur as giant "ruler of the earth," a symbol of the American nation or of the human race more generally. Taken together, McCollum's "dog and bone" series suggest a kind of symbiotic completeness in the postmodern rendering of nature.

McCollum's own remarks on the bones make it clear that a specifically national feeling was central to the production of this work:

> Sometimes I almost self-consciously functioned as an American when I was plotting out the dinosaur project. I went out to Utah to see Dinosaur National Monument, where a lot of those fossils were found that I borrowed . . . to make my molds. I enjoyed the discovery that people in Utah . . . claim dinosaur bones as their heritage. It might seem peculiar to you as a European, but responding to that as an American, I totally understood what they meant. I think from a European perspective one might think, It's not your heritage; if anything, it's the earth's heritage. (15)

The installation of these bones in the neoclassical atrium of the Carnegie Museum is for me (also an American) an uncanny resurrection of Thomas Jefferson's lost "bone room" in the East Room of the White House, as if we were privileged to go back in time and see the mastodon bones replaced by their cultural descendants, the dinosaurs.

How did the world of art come to be able to accept these strange sorts of objects in the spaces that were formerly reserved for unique, individually expressive objects? One answer is simply the appeal to a kind of period aesthetic, the "postmodern turn" that made modernism itself into a dinosaur. The exclusion of the dinosaur from the art world broke down when barriers against kitsch and mass culture were lowered. In the fifties and sixties, Jasper Johns, Robert Rauschenberg, Claes Oldenburg, and Andy Warhol had already scandalized the purists by introducing mass cultural imagery (American flags, hamburgers, and Coke bottles) into the spaces of art. In 1959, Robert Smithson became perhaps the first American artist to portray the dinosaur in a modernist idiom. Smithson (best known for his *Spiral Jetty* earthwork in Great Salt Lake) unveiled multimedia representations of "raving, multi-eyed dinosaurs and flesh-eaters" that were (according to an early reviewer) "whelped by Surrealism and primitive art" and "reared by frenzied Action painting."[4] The anthropological department of the natural history museum had long been a source for high modernism, at least since Picasso's famous cubist elaborations of African masks. So-called "primitive" or ethnographic art was a standard part of the image-repertoire and the aesthetics of both abstract painting and surrealism. Meyer Schapiro had noted as early as the 1930s that "the highest praise" one could give a work of modern art "is to describe it in the language of magic and fetishism."[5] But Smithson goes to a different department of the natural history museum—to paleontology and the dinosaur hall—in search of new subject matter.

It must be said that there is nothing particularly striking about the results. Modernist graphic styles could, in principle, incorporate any conceivable subject matter, and Smithson's *White Dinosaur* and *Blue Dinosaur* are no more

41.5

The first "modernist" painting of a dinosaur in America, Robert Smithson's *Blue Dinosaur*. According to an early reviewer, this image was "whelped by surrealism and primitive art, and reared by frenzied action painting." (Estate of Robert Smithson. Courtesy of John Weber Gallery.)

or less "transgressive" than his *Shark Man* or *Portrait of a Transvestite*. They were a kind of pastiche or synthesis of "the totemic works of Pollock . . . the stripes of Barnett Newman, together with references to Dubuffet's splayed creatures."[6] Smithson would later characterize these works as "prehistoric" in the unfolding of his own career, and treat them as unrelated to his mature work. As Caroline Jones has shown, however, they are extraordinarily interesting in retrospect as premonitions of the decisive role Smithson was later to play in reshaping American artistic practice in the subsequent decades. What is important is not so much that Smithson represents the motif of the dinosaur, but that it lures him on to go looking for artistic material in a different place, and to bring it back in a different way.

Smithson was fascinated with dinosaurs from a very early age. Raised among the New Jersey suburbs, turnpikes, and industrial swamps known to New Yorkers as "nowheresville,"

Smithson went with his father on frequent trips to the American Museum of Natural History in New York. He turned his basement into a natural history museum filled with fossils, and thought of his family as linked to the British mineralogist whose bequest founded the Smithsonian Institution. He tacked on his wall a quotation from Bruno Bettelheim that linked dinosaurs with the fantasy lives of psychotic children, and recalled Freud's comparison of psychoanalysis to archaeology (see the epigraph to chapter 39 above). He was an admirer of the paintings of Charles Knight, and saw them (as noted in chapter 21) as "modern art," not merely scientific illustration.

So the dinosaur is not, for Smithson, a symbol of the archaic as distinct from the modern; it is rather an image of the modern seen as dialectically *equivalent to and turning into* the archaic—and vice versa: "the tools of technology become a part of the Earth's geology as they sink back into their original state. Machines like dinosaurs must return to dust or rust."[7] If Smithson is the precursor of something called "paleoart," we must distinguish it sharply from what Lucy Lippard has called "prehistoric art," which attempts to revive primitive and traditional man-made art forms (Stone Age sculpture, mound building, ritualistic art) and to evoke a mystical, premodern era when, as Lippard puts it, "art and life were one."[8] Paleoart, by contrast, is an art that engages the present and future of advanced industrial societies and reframes them in the temporal perspective of paleontology and geology. It articulates the past-present contrast central to modernity in its most extreme form, fusing remote scenes of "deep time" with the immediate present. Far from evoking nostalgia for a primitive past, paleoart is engaged with technology, environmental devastation, and questions of entropy, catastrophe, and extinc-

tion. It is characterized by a corrosive, mordant irony about pretensions to human greatness.

In his 1970 film about the making of *The Spiral Jetty*, Smithson scans the dinosaurs in the Hall of Late Dinosaurs in the American Museum of Natural History, shooting them through a blood-red filter and adding a soundtrack that evokes the endless mechanical pulsations of metronomic time, with a voice-over meditation on "deep time" that seems to come from the dinosaurs as much as from Smithson himself. In the documentation of the actual building of the jetty, he juxtaposes the giant earth-moving machines with model dinosaurs. He even talks about the movie-making process itself as something "prehistoric":

> Everything about movies and moviemaking is archaic and crude. One is transported by this Archeozoic medium into the earliest known geological eras. The movieola becomes a "time machine" that transforms trucks into dinosaurs. Fiore [the editor of *Spiral Jetty*] pulls lengths of film out of the movieola with the grace of a Neanderthal pulling intestines from a slaughtered mammoth.[9]

Smithson saw, perhaps more clearly than any of his contemporaries, that this sort of perception could not be conveyed simply by representing the dinosaur in some familiar modernist medium, however abstract, surreal, or "mixed." The challenge was really to change the whole location, situation, and meaning of artistic practices and the objects of art themselves. The most dramatic outcome of this imperative was the "Earthworks" or "Land Art" movement, pioneered by Smithson, Robert Morris, Michael Heizer, Nancy Holt, and Walter De Maria, which took the artist out of the studio and into locations (generally remote and inaccessible) where "works" would be created that would only be glimpsed in the gallery through second-hand relics and documentation—bins of rocks, photographs, geological survey maps, and explanatory texts. The new American art of the late sixties and early seventies became everything

41.6
In Smithson's film about the making of *The Spiral Jetty*, the trucks and bulldozers that created it are represented as dinosaurs rooting around in the earth. The jetty is thus the track or trail of dinosaurs. (Estate of Robert Smithson. Courtesy of John Weber Gallery. Photo © Gianfranco Gorgoni.)

that high modernism was not: it was resolutely anti-optical, often providing little or nothing to "feast the eyes" of the aesthete; it was highly textual and technical, bringing the look of the paleontological workshop into the art space; and (in Smithson's case especially) it treated the industrial wastelands of contemporary suburban America as a kind of archaeological or paleontological dig that needed to be documented as if seen in the same framework as the "deep time" of the dinosaurs. Smithson's project had the same time sense as this book, which also attempts to look back at the dinosaur and its role in the modern era from a hypothetical future, in which human civilization is a relic along with the dinosaur.

It's not enough to say, then, that Smithson brings the dinosaur "into" art, as if it were just another motif to be assimilated by his style or technique. It would be more accurate to say that, for Smithson, the dinosaur swallows up modern art. Smithson incorporates art within the framework of the dinosaur by reconfiguring the space-time coordinates of the whole institution of fine art in America. In his early paintings he recognized it as the totem animal of modernity, representing it in Jackson Pollock's totemistic style. In his later work, the dinosaur sinks into the background as a metaphor and framework for the whole cultural process that will come to be called "postmodernism." In this framework, modernism will come to seem obsolete; the aesthetic of mechanical reproduction and technical innovation will be displaced by an aesthetic of biodegradability, decay, and collapse. The individual work of art will be replaced by the "non-site," the assemblage of relics and traces of a real place and time. Passaic, New Jersey, replaces Rome as "The

41.7

A characteristic "work" of paleoart is a "nonsite," an assemblage of words, images, and objects whose real "site" or point of reference is elsewhere, outside the art gallery or museum. (*Non-Site, Franklin, New Jersey*. Estate of Robert Smithson. Courtesy of John Weber Gallery.)

Eternal City," and the monuments are "ruins in reverse": half-finished highways, fountains of sewage, and idle machinery—"prehistoric creatures trapped in the mud, or, better, extinct machines—mechanical dinosaurs stripped of their skin."[10]

And the sleek modernist facade of the Museum of Modern Art, the temple of high modernism and aesthetic purity, is torn open by the dinosaurs that are filling its galleries.

41.8
The Museum of Modern Art, the last refuge of pure modernist art, violated by the figure of kitsch and mass culture. (Cartoon by Robert Morris and the author.)

42.1
The first dinosaur bone ever discovered
(by Robert Plot in the seventeenth century) was given the name of *Scrotum
humanum* in the eighteenth century, long
before the name of "dinosaur" was
invented. The name, like that of the
mastodon ("bubby teeth") is based on its
vague resemblance to a part of the human
anatomy. By the strictest rules of biological nomenclature, *Scrotum humanum* is
the true name of the dinosaur.

scrotum Humanum: THE True Name OF THE Dinosaur

IN 1993, TWO GEOLOGISTS published an article in *Modern Geology* (vol. 18, 221-24) entitled "*Scrotum Humanum* Brookes—The Earliest Name for a Dinosaur?" L. B. Halstead and W. A. S. Sargent recount the history of a bone that bears a striking resemblance to a pair of testicles at the base of a severed shaft. The bone was originally found in Oxfordshire by the natural historian Robert Plot in the 1670s, and correctly identified as the "Thigh-bone of a *Man*, or at least of some other animal." The label *Scrotum humanum* was given to it some ninety years later by Richard Brookes in an English popularization of Linnaeus, the great Enlightenment taxonomist. The labeling of the bone as an image of male genitalia was probably not meant to be taken literally. Brookes certainly knew that this was a thigh bone, and that the testicular forms were really the condyles, which constitute the stress-bearing joint at the juncture of two bones. In the nineteenth century, John Phillips correctly identified it as a *Megalosaurus* bone.

Technically, however, the name *Scrotum humanum* has a kind of validity. Halstead and Sargent note that it follows the rules of Linnaean taxonomical naming, which constructs a binomial consisting of a genus and a species name (for example, *Homo sapiens, Tyrannosaurus rex*), and meets "the other criteria governing the validity of such early names, an illustration being provided and a description and dimensions furnished." There are other equally implausible descriptive and taxonomic names (such as "mastodon," based on the resemblance of bumps on the teeth to nippled "boobs" or female breasts).

Dinosaurology is full of mistakes like this: bones attributed to the wrong animal, or placed in the wrong part of the anatomy. Richard Owen once put a thumb bone on the nose of a skeletal reconstruction. Cary Grant spends an entire movie *(Bringing Up Baby)* as a paleontologist who is trying to figure out where to put his bone. Traditional names die hard, and in fact have to be officially suppressed as *nomen oblitum* under the rules of the *International Code of Zoological Nomenclature.* Every child now knows that *Brontosaurus* has been replaced by *Apatosaurus,* and is eager to make their parents feel like dinosaurs for failing to be up-to-date about this. I've even been so bold as to suggest that the term "dinosaur" become a *nomen oblitum,* to be replaced by something like "archosaurs" or "early birds." "Dinosaur" is an obsolete name, designating two distinct subgroups (saurischians and ornithischians), and it is not a good descriptor: none of them were lizards, and few of them were terrible.

The status of *Scrotum* as "the earliest validly published generic name, and *Scrotum humanum*" as "the earliest validly published trivial name, to be applied to a dinosaur" is, of course, quite different from the status of the dinosaur's name. *Scrotum humanum* is a name that never caught on. It was forgotten until Halstead and Sargent tracked it down. Now that they've dug it up out of the natural history archives, they argue that, technically, it's not enough just to forget it again. It has to be formally suppressed, or someone might come along and insist that the earliest name for a dinosaur was *Scrotum humanum.* Halstead and Sargent therefore made a formal request to the International Commission on Zoological Nomenclature that the name be suppressed. Not surprisingly, the commission was reluctant to suppress "an unused *nomen oblitum,*" and turned down their request.

I wish to formally declare that I will be using the term *Scrotum humanum* from now on, and that my aim is to put it into circulation as the earliest validly published name to be applied to a dinosaur. I acknowledge all the semantic difficulties—the fact that the name is (like "mastodon") based in a kind of false and accidental visual resemblance, that it is a metaphor, and that it was historically never really "applied to a dinosaur," because the word and concept of a dinosaur didn't exist when it was used. Nevertheless, rules are rules, and zoology is full of strange, inappropriate names and images (like the dinosaur itself) that live on, enjoying a happy (if nominal and imaginary) existence. So until it is formally suppressed, I will insist on reminding people of Halstead and Sargent brilliant discovery. I repeat: *Scrotum humanum* is the earliest validly published name to be applied to a dinosaur.

Appendix **B**

scıence and culture

C. P. Snow long ago deplored the "two culture split" that prevents scientists and humanists from understanding one another and that makes scientific thinking incomprehensible to ordinary people.[1] This study of the dinosaur attempts to study this split, and to show how a specific scientific object has crossed the gulf between natural science and popular culture. But my aim has not been to "heal" the division between science and culture so much as to analyze the way it functions as one of the fundamental contradictions of modernity. Although I heartily approve of attempts to make scientific knowledge comprehensible to the general public, I think we need to ask ourselves why this incomprehension exists in the first place, what historical forces and developments have made science and technology mysterious to most people.

The schism between science and the humanities and social sciences has taken on an especially virulent form in contemporary academic culture. The attempts of humanist scholars to look at science as a cultural or social practice have been denounced as ignorant, malicious, and self-destructive political maneuvering. In a recent book entitled *Higher Superstition: The Academic Left and Its Quarrels with Science*, Paul R. Gross and Norman Levitt argue that a loose coalition of "postmodern" thinkers (feminists, ecologists, neo-Marxists, etc.) has launched a kind of "know-nothing" crusade against science as such. Their indictment ranges from relatively mild disputes over matters of emphasis in the work of historians of science, to outright accusations of incompetence and dishonesty, to proposals that American universities could do just fine without "traditional humanities departments," and that scientists (who are "on the whole . . . deeply cultured people") could take over the job of humanities education (243). When this academic schism is then stirred into the "political correctness" debate and linked with reactions against multiculturalism and feminism, the resulting mixture is indeed poisonous, breeding suspicion and hostility between scientists and humanists. The situation was made even worse by the widely publicized hoax of 1996, in which a professional physicist succeeded in publishing an article that mimicked all the standard clichés and myths of cultural studies of science in the journal *Social Text*. This minor scandal seemed to illustrate perfectly the ignorance and gullibility of humanities scholars when it comes to science, and to portray them as professionally derelict in failing to vet the article with a professional physicist, who would have rejected it immediately as a piece of nonsense.

There is no denying that this hoax was deeply embarrassing to many academic humanists, and there is no evading Gross and Levitt's charge that many cultural studies scholars have failed to understand the nuances of quantum mechanics, chaos theory, and non-Euclidian geometry, making impressionistic analogies between the uncertainties of modern life and (say) the Heisenberg Uncertainty Principle. The list of scientific "howlers" committed by science studies scholars does give one pause for reflection. On the other hand, Gross and Levitt provide their own set of howlers. They think that the main work of humanists is the production of evaluative statements, such as "the assertion that Racine is superior to Corneille (or Schubert to Mendelssohn)" (87), and that "the great traditions of Western humanism" (242) are the only indispensable subject matter in the study of culture. Both these claims are laughable in their ignorance and naïveté. Most of humanities scholarship is concerned with textual interpretation and historical explanation; it is not now, and rarely has been, much concerned with the evaluation or comparative ranking of the "greats," which it generally sees as a by-product of interpretation, or as itself a subject for historical analysis. Contemporary humanities scholars are concerned more with why and how Shakespeare has come to be deified than with serving as priests at the temple of bardolatry. "Western humanism" is not the unique subject matter or horizon of cultural study today. It is a historically specific and local formation within the array of human cultures, one that is constituted out of an ethnic and geographic diversity so rich that any notion of a single "Westernness" becomes conceptually incoherent.

Gross and Levitt make much of the failure of academic humanists to understand the science that they are trying to explain in terms of culture. But their own failure to understand the work of the humanities and of cultural studies is equally egregious. There is one moment, however, when they drop their cudgels and seem to admit the possibility of a middle ground between science and culture.

> Yet those who insist that science is driven by culture and by politics, by economics, by aesthetics, even by a species of understated mysticism, are not for that reason alone to be dismissed as wrongheaded. On the contrary, these assertions, if "driven" is replaced by "influenced," come near to being truisms. (234)

What is startling here is how close the great schism is to being healed. It is just a question of the difference between being "driven" and being "influenced"—a difference that unfortunately is not explained by Gross and Levitt. Can an influence sometimes become strong enough to turn into a drive? Is a weak drive the same thing as an influence? Is this a difference of degree or of kind? If science studies were to content itself with studying the influence of culture on science, would that heal the schism?

Most important, if cultural and social forces do not "drive" science, what does? Gross and Levitt do not hesitate: "science is a reality-driven enterprise" (234). The notion that "reality" might be a goal or target of science, rather than a "drive," or that it might be a set of working descriptions that science produces as an ever-changing outcome of its processes, never occurs to Gross and Levitt. Nor do they show much awareness of the fact that "reality" is a notoriously contested concept within the philosophy of science itself. It is enough for them to invoke an unanalyzed notion of "the real" as a rhetorical bludgeon to work over anyone they disapprove of.

Gross and Levitt cannot pause to deal with these hard questions because they are too eager to get back to blasting the political and academic vanity of humanists who dare to write about the historical and cultural context of science. When they calm down, they are willing to admit that a cultural account of science is at least conceivable, but they set the bar very high for achieving any results in such an inquiry: "we are saying, in effect, that a scholar devoted to a project of this kind must be, *inter alia,* a scientist of professional competence, or nearly so" (235). Alas, Gross and Levitt's wide research in humanistic scholarship seems not to have found a single honest or competent individual who meets this standard, and they claim to know with certainty that their standard "is not a dictum that sits at all happily in the minds of those thinkers whom this book has criticized" (235). It's also clear that they don't believe anyone, except perhaps a scientist turned writer like Stephen Jay Gould, ever will be able come up to their standard. They note that most scientists are too busy getting up to speed in their professions to spend much time looking at the history of what they do, much less its cultural context. Their answer is a triumphant non sequitur: culture, history, the arts are best left to amateurs.

Let me now lay my cards on the table with respect to my professional qualifications for writing a book about dinosaurs. If it has not been evident from page one, I hope it will be clear by now that I do not claim or aspire to professional competence as a "dinosaurologist," much less as a vertebrate paleontologist. My claims to professional expertise lie wholly within the realm of culture and history, particularly within that sphere of cultural history that is mediated by icons, images, symbols, narratives, visual representations and displays, and the words that accompany them. My highest aspiration to scientific competence in this book has been to get the facts straight and avoid howlers. This I have tried to do with the help of friends and colleagues whose competence in the area of vertebrate paleontology goes far beyond my own. (The usual disclaimer about any mistakes being my own responsibility still applies.) The only scientific claim this book entertains about dinosaurs is one that was made by scientists themselves for over a century: that "dinosaur" is an incoherent scientific concept, an arbitrary, artificial classification that could have been dropped without any damage to scientific thinking and that was kept alive mainly by popular interest. I recognize that this claim is now out of fashion among paleontologists and that my interest in it will be taken as a sign that I am seriously out of date.

It should be clear, then, that I have not come up to the high standard set by Gross and Levitt for competence in the cultural study of science. I wish I did meet their standards; it would have saved me a lot of time and shortened my acknowledgments page. But the question remains, does my lack of professional training vitiate the results in this book? Have I been guilty of turning cultural "influences" into "drives," or of engaging in political "vanity" by suggesting that the scientific history of the dinosaur cannot be understood fully without grasping its role in economic, political, and social history, as well as in the realms of children's fantasy and popular culture?

It's up to readers to judge whether I've gone too far in arguing that the dinosaur is a powerful cultural symbol—more specifically, a modern totem—and that its cultural status is deeply entwined with—that is, both driven and influenced by—its scientific status. I've also argued that scientists are in turn influenced—maybe even driven—by the myths, metaphors, and images that surround the objects they study. I agree with Gross and Levitt that it's not very interesting to stage these influences as a kind of political one-upmanship, where sinister ideologies are revealed to be lying behind apparently neutral and innocent scientific constructs. The "discovery" that dinosaurs have something to do with capitalism, as if this were a guilty secret rather than an obvious starting point, is no discovery at all. The question is *what* the dinosaur has to do with capitalism, *how* it becomes part of the naturalizing of modern life and the monumentalizing of states, constitutions, and individuals.

I take these as scientific questions, even though they are addressed to cultural issues. Much of what the humanist does is very similar to scientific practice. We gather data, assemble evidence, try to make arguments that are internally consistent and true. We invent technical metalanguages (linguistics, anthropology, narratology, structural poetics, iconologies) to map and describe the field of culture, just as scientists invent names and descriptions for the field of nature. It's true that we aim at a different domain of truth, more concerned with historical understanding, textual intricacy, and the analysis of human interests and passions. It's also true that we operate with different stylistic canons, and that wit, flair, an air of the daring and paradoxical, the essayistic and improvisatory, is valued (perhaps over-valued) in the humanities in a way that is rare (perhaps too rare) in the sciences. We also have a regrettable tendency (rampant as well in the sciences) to produce a lot of recycling of the already well known or self-evident, cleverly concealed by a veil of technical jargon. The amount of truly original "discovery" or important new knowledge produced in both the sciences and the humanities is relatively small.

Above all, then, the key link between science and the humanities is the production of new knowledge. Scholars who link science to culture are motivated mainly, I think, not by a desire to discredit science, but to understand it in a new way. We want to know science in a way that some scientists may not want to hear about, as a concrete social practice carried on by real people in a world of values, interests, influences, and drives. I think that inquisitive scientists—those who are faithful to the spirit of their calling—will welcome this sort of inquiry. It is, after all, about exactly what interests them, but understood in a way that they haven't had time to master.

The two culture split, then, should really be called a "two science" division, between two distinct traditions of knowledge production, one mainly centered on cause-and-effect explanations of natural phenomena, the other based in something more like reading and interpretation, the analysis of social formations, and archival recovery of the past. Each tradition has its own styles of reasoning, argumentation, and proof, and each can learn a great deal from the other about how to proceed.

The two sciences of nature and culture clearly cannot thrive by pillorying each other. Interdisciplinary study of any kind functions badly within a polarized political climate that treats honest attempts at comprehension with suspicion and hostility. Whatever we make of the "Sokal hoax," it seems clear that it did not reflect much glory on any of its participants. What are we to make of the deliberate defrauding of a cultural studies journal by a professional physicist who uses his credentials to get his clumsy mimicry of cultural studies clichés published? What does this whole episode teach us? That humanists are easy dupes who fall for the rote recitation of their favorite truisms? That they are far too deferential to scientists? That they should have rejected the essay for the worthless thing they claimed later to have known it was all along? Or is this about the acceptability of the hoax—even the bad hoax—as a literary genre?

Perhaps we should try a conspiracy theory. Is all this anger just payback for the hostility of cultural studies toward the efforts of scientists to make pronouncements about culture? The "two sciences" border is not transgressed only by humanists. Scientists—especially biologists—like to think they have a grip on the key determinants of culture, the things that really "drive" the whole sphere of social, symbolic behavior. This whole mode of explanation, especially in its sociobiological and social Darwinist guises, has received very rough treatment from the humanists, some of it regrettably abusive and polemical. I recommend, as an antidote to these anti-science tirades, Marshall Sahlins's *The Use and Abuse of Biology*, a classic exposé of sociobiology by a hard-headed cultural anthropologist who refuses to engage in moralizing or political one-upmanship. Sahlins's arguments are rarely answered by sociobiologists (and even a middle-of-the-roader like Daniel Dennett never mentions them). Gross and Levitt's fulsome praise of E. O. Wilson, the most famous sociobiologist of our time, makes sense as part of a counterattack that does not wish to name its real agenda (the stamping out of cultural studies of science, and perhaps even of the professional academic study of culture as such). Instead, Gross and Levitt declare their only enemy to be "muddle-headedness."

Let us take a cue from them and agree to make war on muddleheadedness on both sides of the two culture/two science division. Perhaps this agreement can be the basis for a negotiated peace, and perhaps the dinosaur is just the object over which we might come to some rapprochement. The dinosaur has played the role of go-between for science and popular culture throughout the modern era. Perhaps it can now take on a new role in helping us understand how something called "science" can be a practice of rational, skeptical inquiry into the real, while also being the occasion of fantasy, unbridled speculation, and utopian imagination.

Traces, Tales, and Theories

one

1. For a good survey of dinosaur images in cartoons, comics, and movies, see Donald Glut, *The Dinosaur Scrapbook* (Secaucus, NJ: Citadel Press, 1980); for early (mainly nineteenth-century) images, see Martin J. S. Rudwick, *Scenes from Deep Time* (Chicago: University of Chicago Press, 1992); on the "Dinosaur as Metaphor," see Helen Haste, *Modern Geology* 18 (1993): 349–70; for an anthropologist's view of paleontological institutions, see Brian Noble, "Dinosaurographies: The Public Politics of Monstrous Fascination" (M.A. thesis, Department of Anthropology, University of Alberta, 1994). The numerous histories of paleontology will be cited as appropriate. There is, to my knowledge, no study of literary (narrative and poetic) dinosaurs.

two

1. I'm echoing here the title of John Noble Wilford's *The Riddle of the Dinosaur* (New York: Alfred A. Knopf, 1985), the best overview of the history of scientific dinosaur puzzles.

2. The *Dinosaur Data Book* (New York: Avon Books, 1990) is a handy one-volume encyclopedia of scientific facts, and includes a chapter on popular culture.

3. *Dinosaur in a Haystack* (New York: Harmony Books, 1995), 223.

4. See Paul and Anne Ehrlich's *Extinction: The Causes and Consequences of the Disappearance of Species* (New York: Random House, 1981), 242: "Unless appropriate steps are taken soon to preserve earth's plants, animals, and microorganisms, humanity faces a catastrophe fully as serious as an all-out thermonuclear war."

5. On dinosaurs as monsters, see Brian Noble, *Dinosaurographies*.

6. Pat Dowell, "Real Man Eaters," *In These Times,* 28 June 1993, 33.

7. I'm grateful to Françoise and Claudie Meltzer for bringing this film to my attention.

THree

1. Ellis Yochelson, *The National Museum of Natural History* (Washington, DC: Smithsonian Institution Press, 1985), 125.

2. Numerous inquiries at the National Museum of Natural History have failed to turn up any further details about this story, beyond those that appear in Yochelson's anecdote. At Yale's Peabody Museum of Natural History, on the other hand, I am assured by archivist Barbara Narendra, there actually is a life-size model of a *Uintatherium* (a gigantic mammal of the order Dinocerata) made of authentic U.S. currency.

3. See Gould's remark (quoted in chapter 2) about the "cultural loops of positive feedback" that follow an "initial chaotic fluctuation."

4. See Rene Girard, *Violence and the Sacred,* translated by Patrick Gregory (Baltimore: Johns Hopkins University Press, 1977), chapter 6, for a discussion of mimetic desire. Girard's concept of a "monstrous double" is also applicable to the dinosaur as cultural icon.

5. Louis Jacobs, *Lone Star Dinosaurs* (College Station: Texas A&M Press, 1995), from promotional material.

6. Theodore Adorno, *Minima Moralia: Reflections from Damaged Life* (1951), translated by E. F. N. Jephcott (London: Verso, 1974), 115.

Four

1. Wilford, *The Riddle of the Dinosaur.*

2. Gregory Paul, *Predatory Dinosaurs of the World* (New York: Simon & Schuster, 1988), 24–25.

3. The *Dinosaur Data Book* seems comfortable with the term as well, providing an "A to Z guide" to "dinosaurologists."

4. The order of dinosaurs "would be divided in two by H. G. Seeley in 1887–1888, but in the popular imagination the dinosaurs have remained the symbols of the Age of Reptiles." Peter Bowler, *Fossils and Progress* (New York: Science History Publications, 1976), 85.

5. Technically, of course, the "proper" dinosaurs were earthbound animals. But popular folk taxonomies consistently link them with flying and swimming animals (pterodactyls and ichthyosaurs) so that "dinosaur" begins to expand into a comprehensive term for a whole parallel animal kingdom of reptilian vertebrates.

6. John Ostrom, "The Life in the Mural," in *The Age of Reptiles: The Great Dinosaur Mural at Yale* (New York: Harry Abrams, 1990).

7. Common ancestor arguments are, moreover, notoriously slippery, since all life descends, "in principle," from some common ancestor. Indeed, what is often advertised as the fundamental axiom of biology, that "all life comes from previously existing life," turns out, as Richard Lewontin has shown, to be merely a historical statement: "it could not always have been true because, after all, life originated from non-life." "Facts and the Factitious in Natural Sciences," in *Questions of Evidence,* edited by James Chandler, Arnold Davidson, and Harry Harootunian (Chicago: University of Chicago Press, 1994), 481.

8. See Scott Atran, *The Cognitive Foundations of Natural History: Towards an Anthropology of Science* (Cambridge: Cambridge University Press, 1992), on the concept of the folk taxon.

9. See Steve McCarthy, *Crystal Palace Dinosaurs: The Story of the World's First Prehistoric Sculptures* (London: Crystal Palace Foundation, 1994) on the spin-offs.

10. Spielberg's *The Lost World* (1997) emphasizes the "family values" theme relentlessly, turning the mighty *T. rex,* the lone warrior and killing machine of the modern period, into a domestic animal that gently licks the human biologist who has set her baby's broken leg.

FIve

1. My thanks to Jonathan Bordo for bringing this film to my attention.

2. Lamarckism is associated with the French biologist Jean Baptiste de

Lamarck (1744–1829). It is "now rejected as incompatible with the central dogma of molecular biology, which forbids the transferral of information from the somatic tissue to the DNA of the reproductive cells." *Keywords in Evolutionary Biology*, edited by Evelyn Fox Keller and Elisabeth A. Lloyd (Cambridge: Harvard University Press, 1992), s.v. "Lamarckism."

3. Alan Feduccia, "The Great Dinosaur Debate," *Living Bird* 13 (Fall 1994): 29–33.

4. See Elizabeth Noble Shor, *The Fossil Feud* (Hicksville, NY: Exposition Press, 1974); Charles Schuchert and Clara Mae Levine, *O. C. Marsh: Pioneer in Paleontology* (New Haven: Yale University Press, 1940).

SIX

1. These periods reflect the time span represented in Rudolph Zallinger's famous mural, *The Age of Reptiles*, at the Peabody Museum of Natural History, Yale University. See chapter 31 for discussion of this mural.

2. See Brian Noble, *Dinosaurographies*, on the dinosaur park as utopia.

3. I want to thank Bent Holm for steering me to this wonderful novel.

4. Cp. Hannah Arendt's description of "the last stage of the laboring society," which "demands of its members a sheer automatic functioning, as though individual life had actually been submerged in the over-all life process of the species." *The Human Condition* (Chicago: University of Chicago Press, 1958), 322.

seven

1. See Susan Faludi's *Backlash: The Undeclared War against American Women* (New York: Crown Books, 1991) for a comprehensive account of this phenomenon.

EIGHT

1. The best compendium of scientific dinosaur illustration is *Dinosaurs Past and Present*, edited by Sylvia J. Czerkas and E. C. Olson (Los Angeles: Natural History Museum of Los Angeles County, 1987), based on the exhibition at the Natural History Museum of Los Angeles County.

2. My thanks to Gloria Pinney for leaving a Dinosaur Cookie Cutter in my Christmas stocking.

3. The pterodactyl is not, strictly speaking, a dinosaur. It is included here as an honorary member of the group, in recognition of the folk taxonomy that associates it with dinosaurs. I use the familiar but obsolete term *Brontosaurus* instead of *Apatosaurus* for similar reasons.

4. See my book *Picture Theory* (Chicago: University of Chicago Press, 1994) for a discussion of the concept of an "imagetext."

5. For a discussion of image proliferation in terms of biological metaphors, see Dan Sperber, "Anthropology and Psychology: Toward an Epidemiology of Representations," *Man* 20 (March 1985): 73–89. See also chapter 15, "On the Evolution of Images," in this volume. See also Andrew Ross, "For an Ecology of Images," in *Visual Culture*, edited by Norman Bryson, Michael Ann Holly, and Keith Moxey (Middletown, CT: Wesleyan University Press, 1994).

6. George Gaylord Simpson, *Principles of Animal Taxonomy* (New York: Columbia Press, 1961), 16. Some biologists argue that "species" is not the lowest unit in taxonomic hierarchies, and thus that concepts such as race, breed, subspecies, and population constitute important biological taxons. And some scientists argue that all of the taxonomic levels *above* the species (kingdom, phylum, class, order, genus) no longer have any meaning to a modern biologist or paleontologist. Within another generation, I'm told, all these taxonomic levels will have gone the way of the dinosaurs. That seems only fair, since the dinosaurian suborder exists as a concept only within the very hierarchy that is now declared to be obsolete.

7. Keller and Lloyd, *Keywords in Evolutionary Biology*, s.v. "Species."

8. My thanks to Arnold Davidson, whose work on monsters and horror has been a constant inspiration during this project.

9. *The Life of Forms in Art* (1934), translated by Charles D. Hogan and George Kugler (New York: Zone Books, 1989).

10. For a discussion of Huxley's perception of the link between fossil reptiles and birds, see Adrian Desmond, *Hot-Blooded Dinosaurs* (New York: Dial Press, 1976), 42–43.

11. See Ernst Gombrich, *Art and Illusion* (Princeton: Princeton University Press, 1966).

12. *Oxford English Dictionary* (Oxford: Oxford University Press, 1971), s.v. "species."

13. See Kevin Padian, "The Case of the Bat-Winged Pterosaur: Typological Taxonomy and the Influence of Pictorial Representation on Scientific Perception," in *Dinosaurs Past and Present*, for a discussion of dinosaur images as theoretical constructs.

nine

1. See Mieke Bal, "Telling, Showing, Showing Off," *Critical Inquiry* 18 (Spring 1992), 556–94.

2. An especially effective use of a "throwback" style is that of the contemporary natural history illustrator William Stout, who employs a linear pre-Raphaelite mode that links nineteenth-century Gothicism, Arts and Crafts book production, and late Victorian children's book illustration in his book *The Dinosaurs* (New York: Bantam Books, 1981).

3. Walter Benjamin, "The Work of Art in the Age of Mechanical Reproduction." In *Illuminations*, edited by Hannah Arendt (New York: Schocken Books, 1969), 242: "Its self-alienation has reached such a degree that it can experience its own destruction as an aesthetic pleasure of the first order."

4. Greenberg, "Avant-Garde and Kitsch," *Partisan Review* 6 (Fall 1939): 34–49.

5. The history of animation, from Willis O'Brien (*The Lost World* and *King Kong*) to Ray Harryhausen (*Mighty Joe Young*) to Phil Tippett (*Jurassic Park*), is in part a history of the monstrous animal image, particularly the great ape and the dinosaur. One might look beneath the surface of the animated animal image to the supporting structure or skeleton: Waterhouse Hawkins used static iron ribs and limbs; O'Brien and Harryhausen used flexible, jointed steel "armatures" to move the body through "stop-action" animation; Tippett introduced "motion blur" in his animated dragons, made the armature visible in the robotic "Imperial walkers" of *The Empire Strikes Back,* and pioneered digital animation, in which the material model disappears altogether. The dinosaur skeleton in "Fossil Fuels," the Leo Burnett McDonald's commercial, never existed in any physical form.

6. Lizard stand-ins were used in *One Million Years B.C.,* which was one of the worst movies ever made—but this doesn't seem to be the fault of the lizards.

7. It is surprising, moreover, how much of the "real" dinosaur skeletons in museums is actually not composed of authentic fossil bones, but of synthetic cast materials.

8. The fact that most dinosaur paleontologists are actually balding, pot-bellied, middle-class professionals who lead quiet lives in the laboratory is beside the point, as is the fact that women are now entering the profession. The Indiana Jones figure persists in the popular imagination and in the fantasy lives of some paleontologists.

9. Robert Bakker, *The Dinosaur Heresies* (New York: William Morrow, 1986), 18.

ten

1. See Noble, *Dinosaurographies.*

2. My thanks to Arnold Davidson for bringing to my attention the pope-ass and the association of the monster with moral corruption, contamination, and "unnatural" hybridization.

3. The "Cookie Monster" of *Sesame Street* is an obvious candidate. But Cookie was never the central figure, and never approached the market saturation of Barney the Dinosaur, who now threatens to displace his cultural ancestor, the teddy bear, in the American nursery.

4. For "an attempt to apply the principles of evolution" (and the dinosaur image) "to the world of business and to its population of companies," see Tom Lloyd, *Dinosaur & Co.: Studies in Corporate Evolution* (London: Routledge, 1984). Lloyd argues that the "second industrial revolution" of advances in "microelectronics and biotechnology" is now making the giant corporation obsolete.

5. This is especially evident in Capek's *War with the Newts,* in which the erect reptile is the symbol of twentieth-century mass society, and in Harrison's *West of Eden,* in which the dinosaurs are associated with the devastation of aboriginal peoples by imperial conquest in the nineteenth century (see chapter 6, "Dinotopia").

6. Gregory Paul, *Predatory Dinosaurs of the World* (New York: Simon & Schuster, 1988).

ELeven

1. I wish to thank Chris Rossiter of Leo Burnett & Co. and John Moore, the creative director of "Fossil Fuels," for supplying me with the digital masters of the images in this commercial.

2. The moment is so unobtrusive, in fact, that John Moore, the creative director of "Fossil Fuels," was not even aware that it was there.

TWeLve

1. Claude Lévi-Strauss, *Totemism* (1962), translated by Rodney Needham (Boston: Beacon Press, 1963), 18.

2. The "incest taboo" is the main focus of Freud's classic (and controversial) psychologizing of totemism in *Totem and Taboo* (New York: W. W. Norton, 1950).

3. Lévi-Strauss, *The Savage Mind,* translated by George Weidenfeld (Chicago: University of Chicago Press, 1966).

4. The pterodactyl is not, of course, a true dinosaur in scientific taxonomy. It is the Dino-bird of popular imagination.

5. I owe this suggestion to Lauren Berlant.

6. Although the link of dinosaurs to "Big Science" may seem plausible, paleontology has not itself been an object of major public investment in science.

7. See Freud, *Totem and Taboo,* for a thorough discussion of ambivalence as a fundamental feature of totemism and the taboos associated with it.

8. Lévi-Strauss, *Totemism,* 13.

9. Lévi-Strauss, *Totemism,* 1.

10. Roy Willis, *Signifying Animals: Human Meaning in the Natural World* (London: Unwin Hyman, 1989).

11. Cp. my discussion of the distinction between traditional fetishism and modern commodity fetishism in *Iconology* (Chicago: University of Chicago Press, 1986), 5, 192–93.

12. Jonathan Evans, "The Dragon," in *Mythical and Fabulous Creatures,* edited by Malcolm South (Greenwood Press, Inc.: Westport, CT, 1987), 48.

13. Evans, "The Dragon."

THIRTeen

1. Evans, "The Dragon," 49.

2. See Evans, "The Dragon," 31, and Stephen Prickett, *Victorian Fantasy* (Bloomington: Indiana University Press, 1979), 79–84, on the relation of the dragon revival to dinosaur exhibition.

3. The dragon did, however, serve as a totemic clan or tribal emblem for Anglo-Saxons, Celts, Lombards, Vandals, "and other Germanic tribes," according to the Nazi political theorist Carl Schmitt, who saw the "hostile and evil" image of the dragon as a distortion of "Near Eastern and Jewish mythology." See Schmitt's *The Leviathan in the State Theory of Thomas Hobbes: Meaning and Failure of a Political Symbol* (1938), translated by George Schwab and Erna Hilfstein (Westport, CT: Greenwood Press, 1996), 9–10.

4. I wish to thank Marshall Sahlins for pointing out this parallel to me.

5. See Bruno Latour, *We Have Never Been Modern* (Cambridge, MA: Harvard University Press, 1993), for the most comprehensive version of this argument.

Fourteen

1. Owen's autocratic personality was famous among his Darwinist opponents. For a balanced account of this complex and distinguished scientist, see Nicolaas A. Rupke, *Richard Owen: Victorian Naturalist* (New Haven: Yale University Press, 1994), chapter 1.

2. Waterhouse Hawkins, "On Visual Education as Applied to Geology," *Journal of the Society of Arts* 2 (1854): 444.

3. In *The Lost World*, Spielberg's sequel to *Jurassic Park*, the obligatory multiculturalism sticks out like a sore thumb. Ian Malcolm (Jeff Goldblum) is given an African-American daughter, whose existence is left completely unexplained. She provides the "children's" interest that was supplied by the white brother-sister team in *Jurassic Park*.

4. McCarthy, *Crystal Palace Dinosaurs*, 22.

Fifteen

1. Bakker, *The Dinosaur Heresies*, 15.

2. See Desmond, *Hot-Blooded Dinosaurs*.

3. If one finds the vicious female *Velociraptor* too threatening, however, there is always the more traditional version of the feminized dinosaur, the *Maiasaura*, or "good mother lizard," hovering over her eggs.

4. "It is quite impossible," said Huxley in his lecture to the Royal Institution in 1868, "to look at the conformation of this strange reptile and to doubt that it hopped or walked, in an erect or semi-erect position, after the manner of a bird . . . " Quoted in Desmond, *Hot-Blooded Dinosaurs*, 42.

5. See Bowler, *Fossils and Progress*, for a thorough discussion of the distinction between Darwinism and notions of progressive evolution.

6. Daniel Dennett, for instance, thinks that Darwin gets the "award for the single best idea anyone has ever had," and that Darwinism (now completed with its Mendelian genetic mechanism) is simply and irresistibly true, as true as the Copernican model of the solar system, and likely to remain true in any foreseeable future. See *Darwin's Dangerous Idea: Evolution and the Meanings of Life* (New York: Simon & Schuster, 1995).

7. Sahlins, *The Use and Abuse of Biology* (Ann Arbor: University of Michigan Press, 1976), 106.

8. Richard Dawkins, *The Selfish Gene* (Oxford: Oxford University Press, 1976).

9. Jack Horner, the paleontological consultant to *Jurassic Park*, feels that the visual perfection of the new cinematic images of dinosaurs will deprive them of their mystery. The same concern could have been expressed, of course, about Waterhouse Hawkins's sculptural reconstructions: they were the perfectly accurate images of their day.

10. *Dinosaurs Past and Present*, vol. 1, 117.

11. See Ehrlich and Ehrlich, *Extinction*, xiii: "in the last twenty-five years or so, the disparity between the rate of loss and the rate of replacement has become alarming; in the next twenty-five years, unless something is done, it promises to become catastrophic for humanity."

Sixteen

1. See George Gaylord Simpson, "The Beginnings of Vertebrate Paleontology in North America," in *Proceedings of the American Philosophical Society* 86 (1943): 130–88.

2. See Joel J. Orosz, *Curators and Culture: The Museum Movement in America, 1740–1870* (Tuscaloosa: University of Alabama Press, 1990) on the relation between American cultural nationalism and natural history, particularly the emphasis on nature as compensation for the "lack of long history and a great artistic tradition" (14). See also Patricia M. Williams, *Museums of Natural History and the People Who Work in Them* (New York: St. Martin's Press, 1973).

3. Sylvio Bedini, *Thomas Jefferson and American Vertebrate Paleontology*, publi-

cation no. 61 (Charlottesville, VA: Virginia Division of Mineral Resources, 1985), 2.

4. Thomas Jefferson, *Notes on the State of Virginia* (1781), edited by William Peden (New York: W. W. Norton, 1954), 47.

seventeen

1. I'm grateful to Janice Knight and Laura Rigal for their very helpful suggestions about the significance of natural history in the Jeffersonian era. On this general subject, see John C. Greene, *The Death of Adam* (Ames: Iowa State University Press, 1959).

2. Henry Fairfield Osborn, who was to play a crucial role in the twentieth-century linkage of paleontology and politics, regarded Jefferson's pursuit of natural history as a "relaxation and satisfaction." "Thomas Jefferson as a Paleontologist," *Science* 82 (6 Dec. 1935): 533.

3. Quoted by Osborn in "Thomas Jefferson as a Paleontologist," 536.

4. See my *Iconology*, 141.

5. See Laura Rigal, "Peale's Mammoth," in *American Iconology*, edited by David C. Miller (New Haven: Yale University Press, 1993), 28.

6. *The Embargo* (1808–9) (Gainesville, FL: Scholar's Facsimiles and Reprints, 1955).

7. Rigal, "Peale's Mammoth," 19.

8. Simpson, "The Beginnings of Vertebrate Paleontology in North America," 161.

9. See Lauren Berlant, *The Queen of America Comes to Washington City: Essays on Sex and Citizenship* (Durham, NC: Duke University Press, 1996), 12, for a discussion of "the counterpolitics of the silly object."

10. Thomas Hobbes, *Leviathan* (1651), edited and with an introduction by C. B. Macpherson (Harmondsworth: Penguin Books, 1968).

11. Adorno, "Mammoth," in *Minima Moralia*, 115.

12. *The Leviathan in the State Theory of Thomas Hobbes*, 18. Schmitt argues that the "tragedy of the fate of this famous symbol" was a "result of its encounter with forces arrayed behind the traditional Jewish interpretation of the leviathan" (81).

13. In eighteenth-century France, by contrast, the concept of a "social body" had, as Michel Foucault has suggested, "ceased to be a simple juridico-political metaphor (like the one in the *Leviathan*) and became a biological reality and a field for medical intervention" ["About the Concept of the Dangerous Individual," *International Journal of Law and Psychiatry*, 1 (1978): 7]. Perhaps this is why French legal and political theory in this period tended to stress the historical malleability of even the *natural*, biological constitution, a basic tenet of Larmarckianism.

14. On the concept of a "transitional object," see chapter 40.

15. "Address to Massachusetts Citizens" (1800), in *The Jeffersonian Cyclopedia*, edited by John P. Foley (New York: Funk & Wagnalls, 1900), 195.

16. Roger G. Kennedy, *Hidden Cities: The Discovery and Loss of Ancient North American Civilization* (New York: Free Press, 1994).

17. On the "vanishing race" in American ideology, see Walter Benn Michaels, *Our America: Nativism, Modernism, and Pluralism* (Durham, NC: Duke University Press, 1995).

18. Cp. the Canadian suppression of "potlatch" among the Indians of British Columbia. See Chris Bracken, *The Potlatch Papers: A Colonial Case History* (Chicago: University of Chicago Press, 1997).

19. Howard Zinn, *A People's History of the United States* (New York: HarperCollins, 1980), 125.

EIGHTeen

1. Richard Owen, "Report on British Fossil Reptiles," *Report of the British Association for the Advancement of Science* (1841) (London: John Murray, 1842).

2. Desmond, *Hot-Blooded Dinosaurs*, 18. Cp. Bowler, *Fossils and Progress*, 86: "Owen held that his new order was the closest in structure to the mammals,"

291

another reason for thinking of the dinosaurs as the great antitype to the warm-blooded creatures. Desmond's view of the political meaning of Owen's dinosaur has been challenged and refined, but not, in my view, overturned, by recent scholarship. See Rupke, *Richard Owen: Victorian Naturalist*, 134.

3. See Adrian Desmond, *Archetypes and Ancestors: Palaeontology in Victorian London, 1850–1875* (Chicago: University of Chicago Press, 1982).

4. Desmond, *Hot-Blooded Dinosaurs*, 18.

5. Rigal, "Peale's Mammoth."

6. Desmond, *Hot-Blooded Dinosaurs*, 214, n. 8 notes the "uncanny resemblance" between the Peale and Hawkins dinner parties. There is no definite proof, however, that the Hawkins who attended Peale's dinner was the father of Waterhouse Hawkins. I'm grateful to Donald Baird for his advice on this matter.

7. See John M. Norris, introduction to *Dinosaurs Past and Present*, vol. 1, 4, for a discussion of the difference between paleontological reconstruction and restoration.

8. Before Owen and Waterhouse Hawkins, however, "visionary" paleontologists like Gideon Mantell, Mary Anning, and Thomas Hawkins had "fired the public imagination with tales of sea monsters, flying dragons, and huge land lizards inhabiting the earth before Noah" (Desmond, *Hot-Blooded Dinosaurs*, 13). These were the visions of "devout amateurs," however, who still believed that Noah's Flood was the key to extinction. The Owen/Hawkins presentation, by contrast, was certified by professional scientific institutions, and its piety was much more discreet and qualified. Owen explicitly rejected the Flood as an explanation for dinosaur extinction.

9. McCarthy, *Crystal Palace Dinosaurs*, 89.

10. Rigal, "Peale's Mammoth."

11. McCarthy, *Crystal Palace Dinosaurs*, 30.

NINETEEN

1. Louis Jacobs's *Quest for African Dinosaurs* (New York: Villard Books, 1993) provides an excellent introduction to the role of paleontology in the European colonization of Africa. Though Jacobs expresses sincere regret for the depredations of this colonial past, he has no doubt that current expeditions (like his own to Malawi) will promote national pride and prosperity, as well as the economic modernization that accompanies the oil industry's interest in sponsoring paleontological digs.

2. See Martin J. S. Rudwick, *The Meaning of Fossils* (New York: Neale Watson, 1976), 254, on "the emergence of American paleontology from its earlier quasi-colonial status into full intellectual maturity."

3. James Owen Dorsey, "A Study of Siouan Cults," *Eleventh Annual Report of the Bureau of Ethnology* (Washington, DC: Smithsonian Institution, 1894), 438–41.

4. See Robert West Howard, *The Dawnseekers: The First History of American Paleontology* (New York: Harcourt, Brace, Jovanovich, 1975), 226–27, for an account of Marsh's actions on behalf of Red Cloud.

5. Dorsey, "A Study of Siouan Cults," 393.

6. Howard, *The Dawnseekers*, 192.

7. Desmond, *Hot-Blooded Dinosaurs*, 40.

8. See Howard, *The Dawnseekers*, 64.

9. Howard, *The Dawnseekers*, 144.

TWENTY

1. Edwin H. Colbert, *Men and Dinosaurs: The Search in Field and Laboratory* (New York: Dutton, 1968), 98.

TWENTY-ONE

1. Sylvia J. Czerkas and Donald Glut, in *Dinosaurs, Mammoths, and Cavemen: The Art of Charles Knight* (New York: Dutton, 1982), describe Knight's paintings as the "first truly modern conception" of the dinosaur (1) and credit him with seeing the link with birds.

2. Gregory Paul credits Stephen Jay Gould with dubbing the "small-brained, tail-dragging reptile" of the first half of the twentieth century "the Modern Consensus." "Although paleontologists were responsible for this trend . . . Charles Knight (1874–1953) popularized it." "The Art of Charles Knight," *Scientific American* (June 1996): 86.

3. Donna Haraway, *Primate Visions* (New York: Routledge, 1989), chapter one.

4. Andrews was an archaeologist whose fame stemmed from his search for the earliest human bones, thought to be located in the Gobi Desert. He was a popular lecturer, writer, and raconteur who raised large sums of money to finance the American Museum's Central Asia Expedition in the 1920s. See Wilford, *The Riddle of the Dinosaur,* 160–66.

5. In the 1930s, the Depression begins to put all these conjunctions in a different light: the feudalism of the robber barons begins to look tawdry; it receives its first sustained historical critique in Matthew Josephson's classic, *The Robber Barons: The Great American Capitalists, 1861–1901* (New York: Harcourt, Brace, & Co., 1934); and dinosaurology goes into a scientific slump.

6. On the convergence of feudalism and technophilia, see Bill Brown, "Science Fiction, the World's Fair, and the Prosthetics of Empire, 1910–1915," in *Cultures of United States Imperialism,* edited by Amy Kaplan and Donald E. Pease (Durham, NC: Duke University Press, 1993).

7. Ronald Rainger, *An Agenda for Antiquity: Henry Fairfield Osborn and Vertebrate Paleontology at the American Museum of Natural History, 1890–1935* (Tuscaloosa: University of Alabama Press, 1991), 119.

8. *The Machine in the Garden* (New York: Oxford University Press, 1964).

9. *Walden* (1854) (New York: Penguin Books, 1983).

TWENTY-TWO

1. See Brian Noble, *Dinosaurographies,* on the idea of the dinosaur as a "shape-shifter."

2. Haraway, *Primate Visions.*

3. Rainger, *An Agenda for Antiquity,* 158.

TWENTY-THREE

1. The dinosaur's greenness may also have some connection with the development of "green politics" in the twentieth century, particularly the conjunction of early environmentalism (in which Roosevelt and Osborn played leading roles) with conservative politics. Spielberg, by contrast, is situated firmly in a liberal notion of ecotourism. *The Lost World* (1997) is basically about the ethical superiority of the unobtrusive, limited form of ecotourism, exemplified by the small expedition armed only with still cameras, to the invading army of mass tourism with its movie cameras.

2. Rainger, *An Agenda for Antiquity,* 118.

3. See Mary Douglas, *Purity and Danger* (London: Routledge & Kegan Paul, 1966).

4. Rainger, *An Agenda for Antiquity,* 98.

5. *Theodore Roosevelt Cyclopedia,* edited by Albert Bushnell Hart and Herbert Ronald Ferleger (New York: Roosevelt Memorial Association, 1941), 251.

6. I'm grateful to William Kelly for pointing out the irony of the *Barosaurus* installation in the Roosevelt Atrium.

7. Rainger, *An Agenda for Antiquity,* 119.

TWENTY-FOUR

1. Mauss, *The Gift* (London: Routledge, 1954).

2. Stanley Walens, *The Encyclopedia of Religion,* vol. 11, s.v. "Potlatch," edited by Mircea Eliade (New York: Macmillan, 1987), p. 465.

3. See Jacques Derrida, *Given Time,* I, *Counterfeit Money,* translated by Peggy Kamuf (Chicago: University of Chicago Press, 1992), especially his commentary on Mauss and the relation between mod-

ern and traditional rituals of gift exchange.

4. *Roosevelt Cyclopedia*, 553.

5. See Veblen's classic, *Theory of the Leisure Class* (New York: Vanguard Press, 1912) for a discussion of the modern versions of potlatch in late-nineteenth-century America.

TWENTY-FIVE

1. Helen J. McGinnis, *Carnegie's Dinosaurs* (Pittsburgh: Carnegie Institute, 1982), 13.

2. See Louis M. Hacker, *The World of Andrew Carnegie: 1865–1901* (Philadelphia: J. B. Lippincott, 1968), 383, on Carnegie as "an object of mingled pity and contempt" after the Homestead Strike.

TWENTY-SIX

1. Boas himself, however, was trained in physical anthropology and routinely engaged in the ritual of skull measuring.

2. See George Stocking, *Race, Culture, and Evolution* (Chicago: University of Chicago Press, 1982), 189, for a thorough discussion of this episode.

3. Lyle Rexer and Rachel Klein, *American Museum of Natural History: 125 Years of Expedition and Discovery* (New York: Harry Abrams, 1995).

TWENTY-SEVEN

1. Douglas Preston, *Dinosaurs in the Attic* (New York: Ballantine, 1988), 121.

2. Douglas Preston, "Barnum Brown's Bones," *Natural History* (Oct. 1984): 101: Osborn "shrewdly recognized that mounted skeletons of dinosaurs would bring more attention and support to the museum" than bones of mammals.

TWENTY-NINE

1. Stanley Cavell, *Pursuits of Happiness: The Hollywood Comedy of Remarriage* (Cambridge, MA: Harvard University Press, 1981).

THIRTY

1. See the discussion of D. W. Winnicott's notion of "transitional objects" (security blankets, teddy bears) in chapter 40.

THIRTY-ONE

1. I'm grateful to Jean Zallinger for granting me an interview to discuss the creation and reception of her late husband's magnificent mural, and to Barbara Narendra, archivist of the Peabody Museum, for her vast knowledge of Peabody lore.

2. Vincent Scully, "*The Age of Reptiles as a Work of Art*," in *The Age of Reptiles: The Great Dinosaur Mural at Yale*, 7

3. Henri Focillon, *The Life of Forms in Art*, 32.

4. Bakker, *The Dinosaur Heresies*, 15.

5. Scully, "*The Age of Reptiles* as a Work of Art," 11.

6. According to Barbara Narendra, the Peabody Museum's archivist, the list of requests for permission to reproduce *The Age of Reptiles* would be "endless."

7. Focillon, *The Life of Forms in Art*, 41.

8. I'm grateful to my research assistant, Sam Baker, for this insight.

THIRTY-TWO

1. Jack Hitt, "On Earth as It Is in Heaven: Field Trips with the Apostles of Creation Science," *Harper's Magazine* (Nov. 1996): 51–60.

2. Carl Sagan, *The Dragons of Eden* (New York: Ballantine Books, 1977).

3. Marshall Sahlins's *The Use and Abuse of Biology* is the best critique of this shell game, which he describes aptly as a modern form of totemism in its mapping of social onto natural differences.

4. Dennett, *Darwin's Dangerous Idea*.

THIRTY-THREE

1. See Lloyd, *Dinosaur & Co.*, on the "second industrial revolution" based in advances in "microelectronics and biotechnology" (5).

THIrty-Four

1. See Anson Rabinbach, *The Human Motor: Energy, Fatigue, and the Origins of Modernity* (Berkeley: University of California Press, 1990).

2. *Oxford English Dictionary*, s.v. "catastrophism."

3. *Darwin's Dangerous Idea*, chapter 10. For Gould's side of the argument, see "The Meaning of Punctuated Equilibrium, and Its Role in Validating a Hierarchical Approach to Macroevolution," in *Perspectives on Evolution*, edited by R. Milkman (Sunderland, MA: Sinauer Associates, 1982), 83–104.

4. The creators of the McDonald's "Fossil Fuels" commercial inform me that their *T. rex* is also a purely digital creation. There was no "object"—no skeletal model or miniature—to be photographed and then "animated." The whole thing is conjured out of digital information.

THIrty-Five

1. As Tom Lloyd points out, "the age of nuclear weapons and nuclear energy has actually strengthened the tendency toward great size in the corporate world." *Dinosaur & Co.*, 6.

2. Lyotard, *The Postmodern Condition* (Minneapolis: University of Minnesota Press, 1984).

3. David Harvey, *The Condition of Postmodernity* (Cambridge, MA: Basil Blackwell, 1990), 126.

THIrty-SIX

1. Quoted in Michael Jennings, *Dialectical Images: Walter Benjamin's Theory of Literary Criticism* (Ithaca, NY: Cornell University Press, 1987), 88. I'm grateful to Miriam Hansen for calling this passage to my attention.

2. See Haraway, *Primate Visions*, on the importance of this manly game. Spielberg repeats this motif in *The Lost World* by introducing a big-game hunter whose only fee for joining the expedition will be the opportunity to bag a full-grown male *T. rex* as his trophy. The rest of the corporate expedition to the lost world consists of a gaggle of photographers, technicians, porters, and a conspicuously long-haired, bearded paleontologist (the spitting image of Robert Bakker, I am told by a reliable source). The scene of their arrival in the lost world is like the arrival of Francis Ford Coppola's film crew in the jungles of Southeast Asia in *Apocalypse Now*, or the arrival of the filmmaking expedition on the island of *King Kong*. The scene in which this entire crew is devoured by a pack of pursuing raptors is, like Jeff Goldblum's yawn in the opening scene, a sign that Spielberg is ready to throw the whole dino-scam on the garbage heap.

3. In *The Lost World*, the explicit moral is simply "leave them alone" (but first make an $80 million film about them). The dinosaur returns to its savage condition as an untouchable taboo object, and as a commodity whose value has run its course.

4. On the cynics as "dog philosophers," see *The Encyclopedia of Philosophy* (New York: Macmillan, 1967), vol. 2, 284. The English artist William Hogarth used the dog as a symbol of his own perspective as satirist and caricaturist.

Lessons

THIrty-Seven

1. Matt Kuehl, "Fossils and Dinosaurs— A Fully Integrated Instructional Unit," U.S. Department of Education, Educational Resources Information Center (ERIC), 22 May 1995.

THIrty-EIGHT

1. See Michael Hardt's preface to *The Labor of Dionysius: A Critique of the State Form* (Minneapolis: University of Minnesota Press, 1994), which discusses the dinosaurial reputation of Marxism in the New World Order.

2. Susan L. Trostle and Stewart J. Cohen, "Big, Bigger, Biggest: Discovering Dinosaurs," *Childhood Education* 65 (Spring 1989): 140–45.

3. John E. Schowalter, "When Dinosaurs Return: Children's Fascination with Dinosaurs," *Children Today* (May/June 1979): 2–5.

4. *The Savage Mind,* 100, 105.

5. *The Lost World,* 176–77: the pterodactyls are described as "a scene from the Seven Circles of Dante," a "crawling flapping mass of obscene reptilian life" with a "mephistic" odor. Even male pterodactyls are seen as female, "like gigantic old women, wrapped in hideous web-coloured shawls."

6. Patricia Morison and Howard Gardner, "Dragons and Dinosaurs: The Child's Capacity to Differentiate Fantasy from Reality," *Child Development* 49 (1978): 642–48.

7. William H. Strader and Catherine A. Rinker urge exactly this kind of policing in their article "A Child Centered Approach to Dinosaurs," *Early Child Development* 43 (28 Sept. 1988): 65–76.

THIRTY-NINE

1. Schowalter, "When Dinosaurs Return," 5.

2. See Ellen Handler Spitz, "*Calvin and Hobbes:* Postmodern and Psychoanalytic Perspectives," *Psychoanalytic Review* 80 (Spring 1993): 55–82.

3. I wish to thank Caroline Jones for bringing this text to my attention.

4. My thanks to Richard Strier for his help in thinking through Calvin's Calvinism.

5. The infantilization of American public culture in the late twentieth century is especially notable. See Berlant, *The Queen of America Comes to Washington City.*

6. An example of how *not* to teach dinosaurs is provided by Roberta H. Barba in "Children's Tacit and Explicit Understandings of Dinosaurs," (paper presented to the National Association of Research in Science Teaching, San Jose, California, April 1995), available from the U.S. Department of Education, Educational Resources Information Center (ERIC). Barba assumes that scientific understanding is to be treated as "correct," and that other forms of knowledge are incorrect. She defines "complete understanding" as the responses that mimic what would be found in a textbook, and she scores coloring tasks on the basis of "realistic" coloring (that is, conforming to contemporary reptilian color schemes, tending to grays, greens, and earth tones). Brighter primary colors are defined as "fantasy" (this despite recent work in paleontology that suggests much less certainty about these color stereotypes). In general, this approach assumes that "cognitive maturity" is to be equated with the acquisition of standard, accepted scientific understanding. It makes no attempt to elicit the students' feelings about dinosaurs, to draw out their folk-knowledge, stories, jokes, word-play, or fantasy. It is not surprising that Barba found no significant variation in students' responses based in gender or ethnicity.

7. For an exemplary approach to children's dinosaur learning, I recommend Edith Bondi's classroom guide, "Children Appreciate Rhythm as the Repetition of a Pattern in Time" (paper presented at the New York Public Library, April 8, 1986), available from the U.S. Department of Education, Educational Resources Information Center (ERIC). Bondi's approach begins by asking children to think of ways that dinosaurs are "Just Like People"—an idea that most of them will resist, until they actually start to think about things like feet, hands, eyes, stomachs, heads, and brains. Bondi's approach stands out for its toleration of fantasy and its relaxation of the scientific imperative. Bondi admits that she doesn't know much about dinosaurs, and thinks their real interest lies in the "mystique" and the ways in which they are like—and unlike—people. She could have also asked children to list how they are not like people. Based in a theory of repetition and learning, Bondi's guide offers an interactive approach to classroom teaching that pays attention to seating, body language, varying attitudes of students, and distinctive contributions of individuals. Her drawings of dinos are also quite wonderful.

FORTY

1. D. W. Winnicott, *Playing and Reality* (London: Routledge, 1971).

2. On the invention of the teddy bear and its links with Teddy Roosevelt, see Miriam Hansen, "Adventures of Goldilocks: Spectatorship, Consumerism, and Public Life," *Camera Obscura* 22 (1990): 51–72.

3. I realize that this comparison of totem animals to transitional objects may annoy anthropologists who are concerned with preserving the distinctiveness of traditional societies. My aim here, however, is not to explain totemism by reducing it to a form of transitional object choice. It is rather to explain a specific modern object choice (the dinosaur) by reference to some (not all) of the features of traditional totemism, features that often appear in a reversed or displaced form. Thus, while the traditional totem animal could not be killed or eaten (except under prescribed conditions), the dinosaur must be brought back to life and consumed in rituals of visual restoration and spectatorship (see chapter 12 on totemism above).

4. *Totem and Taboo*, 129.

5. My parental informants tell me that Barney is being adopted (and rejected) earlier and earlier with each generation of toddlers. It is now becoming rare to find a four-year-old who has not "wised up" to the benign *T. rex*. Barney may finally displace the teddy bear and the security blanket. The only question is when the toy manufacturers will go all the way and design a "Barney Bottle" to displace the mother's breast.

6. Freud describes the Fort-Da game in "Beyond the Pleasure Principle" (1920). See *The Freud Reader*, edited by Peter Gay (New York: W. W. Norton, 1989), 599–601.

7. Jules Michelet, *History of the French Revolution* (Chicago: University of Chicago Press, 1967).

8. "Critique of Violence," in *Reflections*, edited by Peter Demetz (New York: Harcourt Brace Jovanovich, 1978), 292.

9. Schmitt, *The Leviathan in the State Theory of Thomas Hobbes*, 53.

10. The phrase "companionable form" is from Samuel Taylor Coleridge, and refers to his sense of the way some objects are not so much fetishized as treated like "friends." Cp. my discussions of the fetish/totem distinction in *Iconology* and *Picture Theory*, and David Simpson's fine book, *Fetishism and Imagination* (Baltimore: Johns Hopkins University Press, 1982).

CODA

1. For a more fully elaborated version of this discussion, see my essay "Paleoart, or How the Dinosaurs Broke into MoMA," in *Studies in Modern Art* (in press).

2. See especially Greenberg's famous essay, "Avant-Garde and Kitsch," and my essay on the modernist concept of the purified art work, "*Ut Pictura Theoria:* Abstract Painting and the Repression of Language," chapter 7 in *Picture Theory*.

3. *Allan McCollum: Interview by Thomas Lawson* (Los Angeles: A.R.T. Press, 1996). I'm grateful to Anthony Elms for bringing McCollum's work to my attention.

4. Review by Irving Sandler, quoted in Caroline A. Jones, *Machine in the Studio: Constructing the Postwar American Artist* (Chicago: University of Chicago Press, 1996). I am grateful to Caroline Jones for stimulating conversations about this topic. Much of the following material on Robert Smithson is drawn from her excellent book.

5. *Modern Art, Nineteenth and Twentieth Centuries* (New York: Braziller, 1978), 200.

6. Jones, *Machine in the Studio*, 285.

7. *The Writings of Robert Smithson*, edited by Nancy Holt (New York: New York University Press, 1979), 85.

8. Lucy Lippard, *Overlay: Contemporary Art and the Art of Prehistory* (New York: New Press, 1983).

9. *The Writings of Robert Smithson*, 114.

10. *The Writings of Robert Smithson*, 53.

APPENDIX B

1. C. P. Snow, *The Two Cultures* (New York: New American Library, 1963).

Adorno, Theodore. *Minima Moralia: Reflections from Damaged Life* (1951). Translated by E. F. N. Jephcott. London: Verso, 1974.

Alien. Directed by Ridley Scott, 1979.

Allan McCollum: Interview by Thomas Lawson. Los Angeles: A.R.T. Press, 1996.

Alley Oop. V. T. Hamlin, 1933–1973.

Altick, Richard. *The Shows of London*. Cambridge, MA: Harvard University Press, 1978.

Andrews, Roy Chapman. *The New Conquest of Central Asia*. New York: American Museum of Natural History, 1932.

Arendt, Hannah. *The Human Condition*. Chicago: University of Chicago Press, 1958.

Atran, Scott. *The Cognitive Foundations of Natural History: Towards an Anthropology of Science*. Cambridge: Cambridge University Press, 1992.

Bakker, Robert. *The Dinosaur Heresies*. New York: William Morrow, 1986.

———. *Raptor Red*. New York: Bantam Books, 1995.

Bal, Mieke. "Telling, Showing, Showing Off." *Critical Inquiry* 18 (Spring 1992), 556–94.

Bannister, Robert C. *Social Darwinism: Science and Myth in Anglo-American Social Thought*. Philadelphia: Temple University Press, 1979.

Barba, Roberta H. "Children's Tacit and Explicit Understanding of Dinosaurs." Paper presented to the National Association of Research in Science Teaching, San Jose, California, April 1995. U.S. Department of Education, Educational Resources Information Center (ERIC), sup. 418.

Barney and Friends (1992–). Public Broadcasting System, The Lyric Group.

Barthes, Roland. *Mythologies* (1957). Translated by Annette Lavers. New York: Hill & Wang, 1972.

Barton, D. R. "Father of the Dinosaurs." *Natural History* 48 (Dec. 1941): 308–12.

BIBLIOGRAPHY

Bedini, Sylvio. *Thomas Jefferson and American Vertebrate Paleontology.* Publication no. 61. Charlottesville, VA: Virginia Division of Mineral Resources, 1985.

Benjamin, Walter. "Critique of Violence." In *Reflections,* edited by Peter Demetz. New York: Harcourt Brace Jovanovich, 1978.

―――. "The Work of Art in the Age of Mechanical Reproduction." In *Illuminations,* edited by Hannah Arendt. New York: Schocken Books, 1969.

Bennett, Tony. *The Birth of the Museum: History, Theory, Politics.* New York: Routledge, 1995.

Bennett, Tony. "Regulated Restlessness: Museums, Liberal Government, and the Historical Sciences." *Economy and Society* 26 (May 1997): 161–90.

Berlant, Lauren. *The Queen of America Comes to Washington City: Essays on Sex and Citizenship.* Durham, NC: Duke University Press, 1996.

Bettelheim, Bruno. *The Empty Fortress: Infantile Autism and the Birth of the Self.* New York: Free Press, 1967.

Bird, Roland T. *Bones for Barnum Brown: Adventures of a Dinosaur Hunter.* Fort Worth, Texas: Texas Christian University Press, 1985.

Boas, Franz. *The Ethnography of Franz Boas.* Edited by Ronald P. Rohner. Chicago: University of Chicago Press, 1969.

Bondi, Edith. "Children Appreciate Rhythm as the Repetition of a Pattern in Time." Paper presented at the New York Public Library, 8 April 1986. U.S. Department of Education, Educational Resources Information Center (ERIC).

Boorstin, Daniel J. *The Lost World of Thomas Jefferson.* Chicago: University of Chicago Press, 1948.

Bowler, Peter. *Fossils and Progress: Paleontology and the Idea of Progressive Evolution in the Nineteenth Century.* New York: Science History Publications, 1976.

―――. *Life's Splendid Drama: Evolutionary Biology and the Reconstruction of Life's Ancestry, 1860–1940.* Chicago: University of Chicago Press, 1996.

Bracken, Christopher. *The Potlatch Papers: A Colonial Case History.* Chicago: University of Chicago Press, 1997.

Bringing Up Baby. Directed by Howard Hawks. 1938.

Brown, Barnum. "Hunting Big Game of Other Days." *National Geographic* 35 (1919): 402–29.

Brown, Bill. "Science Fiction, the World's Fair, and the Prosthetics of Empire, 1910–1915." In *Cultures of United States Imperialism,* edited by Amy Kaplan and Donald E. Pease. Durham, NC: Duke University Press, 1993.

Bryant, William Cullen. *The Embargo* (1808–9). Gainesville, FL: Scholar's Facsimiles and Reprints, 1955.

Bryson, Norman, Michael Ann Holly, and Keith Moxey. *Visual Culture.* Middletown, CT: Wesleyan University Press, 1994.

Burroughs, Edgar Rice. "The Land that Time Forgot." *Blue Book Magazine,* Aug. 1918.

Calvin & Hobbes. Bill Watterson. 1985–1995.

Calvino, Italo. "The Dinosaurs." In *Cosmicomics,* translated by William Weaver. New York: Harcourt Brace & Co., 1968.

Canemaker, John. *Winsor McCay: His Life and Art.* New York: Abbeville Press, 1987.

Canguilhem, George. *Ideology and Rationality in the History of the Life Sciences* (1977). Translated by Arthur Goldhammer. Cambridge, MA: MIT Press, 1988.

Capek, Karel. *War with the Newts* (1936). Translated by M. and R. Weatherall. London: Allen & Unwin, 1937.

Carmody, Denise and John. *Native American Religions.* Mahwah, NJ: Paulis Press, 1993.

Carnosaur. Directed by Adam Simon, produced by Roger Corman. 1993.

Cavell, Stanley. *Pursuits of Happiness: The Hollywood Comedy of Remarriage.* Cambridge, MA: Harvard University Press, 1981.

Chandler, James, Arnold Davidson, and Harry Harootunian. *Questions of Evidence.* Chicago: University of Chicago Press, 1994.

Clemens, Elisabeth. "Of Asteroids and Dinosaurs: The Role of the Press in the Shaping of Scientific Debate." *Social Studies of Science* 16 (Aug. 1986): 421–56.

Clifford, James. *The Predicament of Culture: Twentieth Century Ethnography, Literature, and Art.* Cambridge, MA: Harvard University Press, 1989.

Colbert, Edwin H. "The Paleozoic Museum in Central Park, or the Museum that Never Was." *Curator* 2:2 (1959): 137–50.

———. *Men and Dinosaurs: The Search in Field and Laboratory.* New York: Dutton, 1968.

Comaroff, John and Jean. *Ethnography and the Historical Imagination.* Boulder, CO: Westview Press, 1992.

Crichton, Michael. *Jurassic Park.* New York: Alfred A. Knopf, 1990.

———. *The Lost World.* New York: Alfred A. Knopf, 1995.

Czerkas, Sylvia J., and Donald Glut. *Dinosaurs, Mammoths, and Cavemen: The Art of Charles Knight.* New York: Dutton, 1982.

———, and E. C. Olson, eds. *Dinosaurs Past and Present.* 2 vols. Los Angeles: Natural History Museum of Los Angeles County, 1987.

Davidson, Arnold. "The Horror of Monsters." In *The Boundaries of Humanity,* edited by James J. Sheehan and Morton Sosna. Berkeley: University of California Press, 1991.

Dawkins, Richard. *The Selfish Gene.* Oxford: Oxford University Press, 1976.

Delair, Justin B., and William A. S. Sarjeant. "The Earliest Discoveries of Dinosaurs." *Isis* 66 (Mar. 1975): 5–25.

Deloria, Vine. *Red Earth, White Lies: Native Americans and the Myth of Scientific Fact.* New York: Scribners, 1995.

Dennett, Daniel. *Darwin's Dangerous Idea: Evolution and the Meanings of Life.* New York: Simon & Schuster, 1995.

Derrida, Jacques. *Given Time.* I. *Counterfeit Money.* Translated by Peggy Kamuf. Chicago: University of Chicago Press, 1992.

Desmond, Adrian. *Hot-Blooded Dinosaurs.* New York: Dial Press, 1976.

———. *Archetypes and Ancestors: Palaeontology in Victorian London, 1850–1875.* Chicago: University of Chicago Press, 1982.

———. *The Politics of Evolution.* Chicago: University of Chicago Press, 1986.

The Dinosaur Data Book: Facts and Fictions about the World's Largest Creatures. The Diagram Group. New York: Avon Books, 1990.

The Dinosauria. Edited by David P. Weishampel, Peter Dodson, and Halszka Osmólska. Berkeley: University of California Press, 1990.

Dinotopia: Living the Adventure. CD-ROM. James Gurney. Turner Interactive, 1996.

Dion, Mark. *Natural History and Other Fictions*. Birmingham: Ikon Gallery, 1997.

Dorsey, James Owen. "A Study of Siouan Cults." *Eleventh Annual Report of the Bureau of American Ethnology* (1889–90). Washington, DC: Smithsonian Institution, 1894.

Douglas, Mary. *Purity and Danger*. London: Routledge & Kegan Paul, 1966.

Dowell, Pat. "Real Man Eaters." *In These Times*, 28 June 1993, 33.

Doyle, Arthur Conan. *The Lost World*. London: Hodder and Stoughton, 1912.

Dragonheart. Directed by Rob Cohen. 1990.

Du Bois, W. E. B. *The Souls of Black Folk*. Chicago: A. C. McLurg, 1903.

Edelson, Zelda, ed. *The Age of Reptiles: The Great Dinosaur Mural at Yale*. New York: Harry Abrams, 1990.

Ehrlich, Paul and Anne. *Extinction: The Causes and Consequences of the Disappearance of Species*. New York: Random House, 1981.

Elsner, John, and Roger Cardinal, eds. *The Cultures of Collecting*. London: Reaktion Books, 1994.

Evans, Jonathan. "The Dragon." In *Mythical and Fabulous Creatures*, edited by Malcolm South. Westport, CT: Greenwood Press, 1987.

Faludi, Susan. *Backlash: The Undeclared War against American Women*. New York: Crown Books, 1991.

The Family of Man: The Photographic Exhibition Created by Edward Steichen for the Museum of Modern Art. New York: Simon & Schuster, 1955.

Fantasia. Directed by Walt Disney. 1940.

The Far Side. Gary Larson. 1979–88; 1990–95.

Farber, Sharon N. "The Last Thunder Horse West of the Mississippi." Illustrated by Bob Walters. *Isaac Asimov's Science Fiction Magazine* 12 (Nov. 1988): 20–44.

Feduccia, Alan. "The Great Dinosaur Debate." *Living Bird* 13 (Fall 1994): 29–33.

The Flintstones. 30 Sept. 1960–2 Sept. 1966.

The Flintstones. Directed by Brian Levant, produced by Stephen Spielberg. 1994.

Focillon, Henri. *The Life of Forms in Art* (1934). Translated by Charles D. Hogan and George Kubler. New York: Zone Books, 1989.

Foley, John P., ed. *The Jeffersonian Cyclopedia*. New York: Funk & Wagnalls, 1900.

"Fossil Fuels." Commercial for McDonald's Restaurants. Leo Burnett & Co., 1996.

Foucault, Michel. *The Order of Things: An Archaeology of the Human Sciences*. New York: Pantheon Books, 1970.

———. "About the Concept of the Dangerous Individual." *International Journal of Law and Psychiatry* 1 (1978): 1–18.

Freud, Sigmund. *Totem and Taboo* (1912). Translated by James Strachey. New York: W. W. Norton, 1950.

———. "Beyond the Pleasure Principle" (1920). In *The Freud Reader*, edited by Peter Gay. New York: W. W. Norton, 1989.

Gertie the Dinosaur. Directed by Winsor McCay. 1914.

Girard, Rene. *Violence and the Sacred*. Translated by Patrick Gregory. Baltimore: Johns Hopkins University Press, 1977.

Glut, Donald. *The Dinosaur Scrapbook*. Secaucus, NJ: Citadel Press, 1980.

Godzilla (Gojiri). Directed by Toho (Tomoyuki Tanaka). 1955.

Gombrich, E. H. *Art and Illusion*. Princeton: Princeton University Press, 1956.

Gould, Stephen Jay. "The Meaning of Punctuated Equilibrium, and Its Role in Validating a Hierarchical Approach to Macroevolution." In *Perspectives on Evolution*, edited by R. Milkman, 83–104. Sunderland, MA: Sinauer Associates, 1982.

———. *Bully for Brontosaurus*. New York: Norton, 1991.

———. "Dinomania." *The New York Review of Books* (12 Aug. 1993): 51–55.

_____. *Dinosaur in a Haystack*. New York: Harmony Books, 1995.

Grant, Madison. *The Passing of the Great Race* (1919). 4th edition. With a preface by Henry Fairfield Osborn. New York: Scribner's, 1924.

A Great Name in Oil: Sinclair through Fifty Years. New York: F. W. Dodge Co./McGraw-Hill, Inc., 1966.

Greenberg, Clement. "Avant Garde and Kitsch." *Partisan Review* 6 (Fall 1939): 34–49.

Greene, John C. *The Death of Adam*. Ames: Iowa State University Press, 1959.

Gross, Paul R., and Norman Levitt. *Higher Superstition: The Academic Left and Its Quarrels with Science*. Baltimore: Johns Hopkins University Press, 1994.

Hacker, Louis M. *The World of Andrew Carnegie, 1865–1901*. Philadelphia: J. B. Lippincott, 1968.

Halstead, L. B., and W. A. S. Sargent. "*Scrotum humanum* Brookes—The Earliest Name for a Dinosaur?" *Modern Geology* 18 (1993): 221–24.

Hansen, Miriam. "Adventures of Goldilocks: Spectatorship, Consumerism, and Public Life." *Camera Obscura* 22 (1990): 51–72.

Haraway, Donna. *Primate Visions*. New York: Routledge, 1989.

_____. *Simians, Cyborgs, and Women*. London: Routledge, 1991.

Hardt, Michael, and Antonio Negri. *The Labor of Dionysius: A Critique of the State Form*. Minneapolis: University of Minnesota Press, 1994.

Harrison, Harry. *West of Eden*. New York: Bantam Books, 1984.

Hart, Albert Bushnell, and Herbert Ronald Ferleger. *Theodore Roosevelt Cyclopedia*. New York: Roosevelt Memorial Association, 1941.

Harvey, David. *The Condition of Postmodernity*. Cambridge, MA: Basil Blackwell, 1990.

Haste, Helen. "Dinosaur as Metaphor." *Modern Geology* 18 (1993): 349–70.

Hawkins, Benjamin Waterhouse. "On Visual Education as Applied to Geology." *Journal of the Society of Arts* 2 (1854): 444–49.

Hawkins, Thomas. *Book of the Great Sea Dragons*. London: William Pickering, 1840.

Hayles, Katherine. *Chaos Bound*. Ithaca, NY: Cornell University Press, 1993.

Hitt, Jack. "On Earth as It Is in Heaven: Field Trips with the Apostles of Creation Science." *Harper's Magazine* (Nov. 1996): 51–60.

Hobbes, Thomas. *Leviathan* (1651). Edited with introduction by C. B. Macpherson. Harmondsworth: Penguin Books, 1968.

Hofstadter, Richard. *Social Darwinism in American Thought*. Boston: Beacon Press, 1955.

Horner, John R. *Digging Dinosaurs*. New York: Workman Publishing, 1988.

How Dinosaurs Learned to Fly. Directed by Munro Ferguson. 1996.

Howard, Robert West. *The Dawnseekers: The First History of American Paleontology*. New York: Harcourt, Brace, Jovanovitch, 1975.

Jacobs, Louis. *Quest for African Dinosaurs*. New York: Villard Books, 1993.

_____. *Lone Star Dinosaurs*. College Station: Texas A&M Press, 1995.

Jameson, Fredric. *Postmodernism: The Cultural Logic of Late Capitalism*. Durham: Duke University Press, 1991.

Jefferson, Thomas. *Notes on the State of Virginia* (1781). Edited by William Peden. New York: W. W. Norton, 1954.

Jennings, Michael. *Dialectical Images: Walter Benjamin's Theory of Literary Criticism*. Ithaca, NY: Cornell University Press, 1987.

Jones, Caroline A. *Machine in the Studio: Constructing the Postwar American Artist*. Chicago: University of Chicago Press, 1996.

Josephson, Matthew. *The Robber Barons: The Great American Capitalists, 1861–1901*. New York: Harcourt, Brace, 1934.

Jurassic Park. Directed by Stephen Spielberg. 1993.

Karp, Ivan, Christine Mullen Kreamer, and Steven D. Lavine. *Museums and Communities: The Politics of Public Culture.* Washington, DC: Smithsonian Institution, 1992.

Keller, Evelyn Fox, and Elisabeth A. Lloyd. *Keywords in Evolutionary Biology.* Cambridge, MA: Harvard University Press, 1992.

Kellert, Stephen. *In the Wake of Chaos: Unpredictable Order in Dynamical Systems.* Chicago: University of Chicago Press, 1993.

Kennedy, Roger G. *Hidden Cities: The Discovery and Loss of Ancient North American Civilization.* New York: Free Press, 1994.

King Kong. Co-directed by Ernest B. Schoedsack and Merian C. Cooper. 1933.

Knight, Charles. *Life through the Ages.* New York: Alfred A. Knopf, 1946.

Krauss, Rosalind. "A User's Guide to Entropy." *October* 78 (Fall 1995): 89–106.

Kuehl, Matt. "Fossils and Dinosaurs—A Fully Integrated Instructional Unit." U.S. Department of Education, Educational Resources Information Center (ERIC), 22 May 1995.

Lacan, Jacques. *Écrits.* Translated by Alan Sheridan. New York: W. W. Norton, 1977.

———. *The Four Fundamental Concepts of Psychoanalysis.* Translated by Alan Sheridan. New York: W. W. Norton, 1978.

Lanham, Url. *The Bone Hunters.* New York: Columbia University Press, 1973.

Lappé, Marc. *Breakout: The Evolving Threat of Drug-Resistant Disease.* San Francisco: Sierra Club Books, 1995.

Latour, Bruno. "Visualisation and Cognition: Thinking with Eyes and Hands." *Knowledge and Society* 6 (1986): 1–40.

———. *We Have Never Been Modern.* Cambridge, MA: Harvard University Press, 1993.

Lessem, Don. *Kings of Creation.* New York: Simon & Schuster, 1992.

———, and Donald Glut. *The Dinosaur Society's Dinosaur Encyclopedia.* New York: Random House, 1993.

Lévi-Strauss, Claude. *The Savage Mind* (1962). Translated by George Weidenfeld. Chicago: University of Chicago Press, 1966.

———. *Totemism* (1962). Translated by Rodney Needham. Boston: Beacon Press, 1963.

Lewontin, Richard. "Facts and the Factitious in Natural Sciences." In *Questions of Evidence,* edited by James Chandler, Arnold Davidson, and Harry Harootunian, 478–91. Chicago: University of Chicago Press, 1994.

Lippard, Lucy. *Overlay: Contemporary Art and the Art of Prehistory.* New York: New Press, 1983.

Lloyd, Tom. *Dinosaur & Co.: Studies in Corporate Evolution.* London: Routledge, 1984.

The Lost World. Directed by Willis O'Brien and Harry Hoyt. 1925.

The Lost World. Directed by Stephen Spielberg. 1997.

Lumley, Robert. *The Museum Time Machine: Putting Cultures on Display.* London: Routledge, 1988.

Lyotard, Jean-François. *The Postmodern Condition.* Minneapolis: University of Minnesota Press, 1984.

Marchant, R. A. *Beasts of Fact and Fable.* New York: Roy Publishers, 1962.

Marx, Leo. *The Machine in the Garden.* New York: Oxford University Press, 1964.

Mauss, Marcel. *The Gift.* London: Routledge, 1954.

McCarthy, Steve. *Crystal Palace Dinosaurs: The Story of the World's First Prehistoric Sculptures.* London: Crystal Palace Foundation, 1994.

McGinnis, Helen J. *Carnegie's Dinosaurs.* Pittsburgh: Carnegie Institute, 1982.

McGowan, Christopher. *The Successful Dragons.* Toronto: Samuel Stevens, 1983.

Michaels, Walter Benn. *Our America: Nativism, Modernism, and Pluralism.* Durham, NC: Duke University Press, 1995.

Michelet, Jules. *History of the French Revolution.* Chicago: University of Chicago Press, 1967.

Micheli, Robin. "The Incredible Mystery of Dinomania." *Money* 16 (Dec. 1987): 150–52.

Miller, David C. *American Iconology.* New Haven: Yale University Press, 1993.

Mitchell, W.J.T. *Iconology.* Chicago: University of Chicago Press, 1987.

———. *Picture Theory.* Chicago: University of Chicago Press, 1994.

———. "Paleoart, or How the Dinosaurs Broke into MoMA." *Studies in Modern Art,* in press.

Mitman, Gregg. "Cinematic Nature: Hollywood Technology, Popular Culture, and the American Museum of Natural History." *Isis* 84 (1993): 637–61.

Montgomery, Scott. "Science as Kitsch: The Dinosaur and Other Icons." *Science as Culture* 10, no. 10 (1991): 7–56.

Morison, Patricia, and Howard Gardner. "Dragons and Dinosaurs: The Child's Capacity to Differentiate Fantasy from Reality." *Child Development* 49 (1978): 642–48.

Noble, Brian E. *Dinosaurographies: The Public Politics of Monstrous Fascination.* M.A. thesis, Department of Anthropology, University of Alberta, 1994.

Norman, David. *Dinosaurs!* New York: Prentice-Hall, 1991.

Orosz, Joel J. *Curators and Culture: The Museum Movement in America, 1740–1870.* Tuscaloosa: University of Alabama Press, 1990.

Osborn, Henry Fairfield. Preface to *The Passing of the Great Race,* by Madison Grant. New York: Scribner's, 1916.

———. "Race Progress in Relation to Social Progress." *Journal of the National Institute of Social Science* 9 (1924): 8–18.

———. "What Is Americanism?" *The Forum* 75 (1926): 803–4.

———. "Thomas Jefferson as a Paleontologist." *Science* 82 (6 Dec. 1935): 533–38.

Ostrom, John. "The Life in the Mural." In *The Age of Reptiles: The Great Dinosaur Mural at Yale,* edited by Zelda Edelson. New York: Harry Abrams, 1990.

Owen, Richard. "Report on British Fossil Reptiles." *Report of the British Association for the Advancement of Science* (1841): 169–340.

Owens, Craig. "Allan McCollum: Repetition & Difference." In *Beyond Recognition: Representation, Power, and Culture.* Berkeley: University of California Press, 1992.

Padian, Kevin. "The Case of the Bat-Winged Pterosaur: Typological Taxonomy and the Influence of Pictorial Representation on Scientific Perception." In *Dinosaurs Past and Present,* edited by Sylvia J. Czerkas and E. C. Olson, vol. 2, 65–81. Los Angeles: Natural History Museum of Los Angeles County, 1987.

Paul, Gregory. *Predatory Dinosaurs of the World.* New York: Simon & Schuster, 1988.

———. "The Art of Charles Knight." *Scientific American* (June 1996), 86–93.

Peirce, Charles Sanders. "Logic as Semiotic: The Theory of Signs." In *Philosophical Writings of Peirce,* edited by Justus Buchler. New York: Dover, 1955.

Preston, Douglas. "Barnum Brown's Bones." *Natural History* (Oct. 1984).

———. *Dinosaurs in the Attic.* New York: Ballantine, 1988.

———, with Lincoln Child. *The Relic.* New York: Tom Doherty Associates, 1995.

Prickett, Stephen. *Victorian Fantasy.* Bloomington: Indiana University Press, 1979.

Rabinbach, Anson. *The Human Motor: Energy, Fatigue, and the Origins of Modernity.* Berkeley: University of California Press, 1990.

Rainger, Ronald. *An Agenda for Antiquity: Henry Fairfield Osborn and Vertebrate Paleontology at the American Museum of Natural History, 1890–1935.* Tuscaloosa: University of Alabama Press, 1991.

Reingold, Nathan. *Science in Nineteenth-Century America: A Documentary History.* Chicago: University of Chicago Press, 1964.

Rexer, Lyle, and Rachel Klein. *American Museum of Natural History: 125 Years of Expedition and Discovery.* New York: Harry Abrams, 1995.

Rigal, Laura. "Peale's Mammoth." In *American Iconology,* edited by David C. Miller. New Haven: Yale University Press, 1993.

──── . *An American Manufactory.* In press.

Ross, Andrew. "For an Ecology of Images." In *Visual Culture,* ed. Norman Bryson, Michael Ann Holly, and Keith Moxey. Middletown, CT: Wesleyan University Press, 1994.

Rudwick, Martin J. S. *The Meaning of Fossils.* New York: Neale Watson, 1976.

──── . *Scenes from Deep Time.* Chicago: University of Chicago Press, 1992.

Rupke, Nicolaas A. *Richard Owen: Victorian Naturalist.* New Haven: Yale University Press, 1994.

Russell, Dale. *The Dinosaurs of North America.* Toronto: University of Toronto Press, 1989.

──── , and Ron Séguin. "Reconstruction of the Small Cretaceous Theropod *Stenonychosaurus inequalis* and Hypothetical Dinosauroid." *Syllogeus,* no. 37. National Museum of Canada, 1982.

Sagan, Carl. *The Dragons of Eden.* New York: Ballantine Books, 1977.

Sahlins, Marshall. *The Use and Abuse of Biology.* Ann Arbor: University of Michigan Press, 1976.

Schapiro, Gary. *Earthwards: Robert Smithson and Art after Babel.* Berkeley: University of California Press, 1995.

Schapiro, Meyer. *Modern Art, Nineteenth and Twentieth Centuries.* New York: Braziller, 1978.

Schindler's List. Directed by Stephen Spielberg. 1993.

Schmitt, Carl. *The Leviathan in the State Theory of Thomas Hobbes* (1938). Translated by George Schwab and Erna Hilfstein. Westport, CT: Greenwood Press, 1996.

Schowalter, John E. "When Dinosaurs Return: Children's Fascination with Dinosaurs." *Children Today* (May/June 1979): 2–5.

Schuchert, Charles, and Clara Mae Levine. *O. C. Marsh: Pioneer in Paleontology.* New Haven: Yale University Press, 1940.

Scully, Vincent. "*The Age of Reptiles* as a Work of Art." In *The Age of Reptiles: The Great Dinosaur Mural at Yale.* New York: Harry Abrams, 1990.

Serres, Michel. *Hermes: Literature, Science, Philosophy.* Baltimore: Johns Hopkins University Press, 1982.

Shay, Don, and Jody Duncan. *The Making of Jurassic Park.* New York: Ballantine Books, 1993.

Sheehan, Bernard. *Seeds of Extinction: Jeffersonian Philanthropy and the American Indian.* Chapel Hill: University of North Carolina Press, 1973.

Shor, Elizabeth Noble. *The Fossil Feud.* Hicksville, NY: Exposition Press, 1974.

Simpson, David. *Fetishism and Imagination.* Baltimore: Johns Hopkins University Press, 1982.

Simpson, George Gaylord. "The Beginnings of Vertebrate Paleontology in North America." *Proceedings of the American Philosophical Society* 86 (1943): 130–88.

──── . *Principles of Animal Taxonomy.* New York: Columbia University Press, 1961.

Smithson, Robert. *The Writings of Robert Smithson.* Edited by Nancy Holt. New York: New York University Press, 1979.

──── . *Robert Smithson: Une retrospective le paysage entropique, 1960–1973.* Marseilles: Musées de Marseilles, 1994.

Snow, C. P. *The Two Cultures.* New York: New American Library, 1963.

South, Malcolm, ed. *Mythical and Fabulous Creatures.* Westport, CT: Greenwood Press, 1987.

Sperber, Dan. "Anthropology and Psychology: Toward an Epidemiology of Representations." *Man* 20 (Mar. 1985): 73–89.

The Spiral Jetty. Directed by Robert Smithson. 1977.

Spitz, Ellen Handler. "*Calvin and Hobbes: Postmodern and Psychoanalytic Perspectives.*" *Psychoanalytic Review* 80 (Spring 1993): 55–82.

Stewart, Susan. *On Longing: Narratives of the Gigantic and Miniature.* Baltimore: Johns Hopkins University Press, 1984.

———. "Death and Life, in That Order, in the Works of Charles Willson Peale." In *The Cultures of Collecting,* edited by John Elsner and Roger Cardinal. London: Reaktion Books, 1994.

Stocking, George. *Race, Culture, and Evolution.* Chicago: University of Chicago Press, 1982.

Stout, William. *The Dinosaurs.* New York: Bantam Books, 1981.

Strader, William H., and Catherine A. Rinker. "A Child Centered Approach to Dinosaurs." *Early Child Development* 43 (28 Sept. 1988): 65–76.

Strong, Josiah. *Our Country* (1886). Cambridge, MA: Harvard University Press, 1963.

Taussig, Michael. *Mimesis and Alterity: A Particular History of the Senses.* New York: Routledge, 1993.

Thomson, Keith. *The Living Fossil: The Story of the Coelocanth.* New York: W. W. Norton, 1991.

Thoreau, Henry David. *Walden* (1854). New York: Penguin Books, 1983.

Torrens, Hugh. "When Did the Dinosaur Get Its Name? *New Scientist* 134 (4 Apr. 1992): 40–44.

———. "The Dinosaur and Dinomania Over 150 Years." *Modern Geology* 18 (1993): 257–86.

Trostle, Susan L., and Stewart J. Cohen. "Big, Bigger, Biggest: Discovering Dinosaurs," *Childhood Education* 65 (Spring 1989): 140–45.

Tsai, Eugenie. *Robert Smithson Unearthed.* New York: Columbia University Press, 1991.

Veblen, Thorstein. *Theory of the Leisure Class.* New York: Vanguard Press, 1912.

Verne, Jules. *Journey to the Center of the Earth* (1880). Oxford: Oxford University Press, 1992.

Warner, Marina. *Managing Monsters: Six Myths of Our Time.* London: Vintage, 1994.

Watkins, Evan. "The Dinosaurics of Size: Economic Narratives and Popular Culture." *The Centennial Review* 39 (Spring 1995): 189–211.

We're Back! A Dinosaur's Story. Made-for-TV movie by Stephen Spielberg. Universal Studios, 1994.

Wilford, John Noble. *The Riddle of the Dinosaur.* New York: Alfred A. Knopf, 1985.

Williams, Patricia M. *Museums of Natural History and the People Who Work in Them.* New York: St. Martin's Press, 1973.

Willis, Roy. *Signifying Animals: Human Meaning in the Natural World.* London: Unwin Hyman, 1989.

Winnicott, D. W. *Playing and Reality.* London: Routledge, 1971.

Wolfflin, Heinrich. *Principles of Art History.* Translated by M. D. Hottinger. New York: Dover Books, 1945.

Wylie, Philip. *A Generation of Vipers.* New York: Rinehart, 1955.

Yochelson, Ellis. *The National Museum of Natural History.* Washington, DC: Smithsonian Institution Press, 1985.

Zallinger, Rudolph. "Creating the Mural." In *The Age of Reptiles: The Great Dinosaur Mural at Yale.* New York: Harry Abrams, 1990.

Zinn, Howard. *A People's History of the United States.* New York: HarperCollins, 1980.

ACKnOWLeDGments

My first thanks goes to the scientists, several of them anonymous, who read drafts of this book very carefully, pointed out technical errors, and expressed a range of responses: "brilliant although . . . I do not agree with a lot of what he says"; "I profoundly disliked this book"; "interesting and provocative"; "deeply confused"; "fabulous illustrations"; "tipsy prose poetry"; "really terrific"; "a major clash of cultures"; "hilarious"; "will upset . . . his potential readership"; "is going to create a great stir"; "ought to be publicly horsewhipped"; "perhaps a hoax." The overall impression was best captured by James O. Farlow, a geologist and co-editor of *The Complete Dinosaur Book,* who declined to write a blurb for this book and spent three single-spaced pages explaining his "deep ambivalence" about its whole conception. I've had fair warning that some scientists are going to be annoyed by this book. What I find encouraging is that so many of these same scientists evidently were not able to put it down.

The Division of Humanities at the University of Chicago provided a precious year for the writing, and Dean Phil Gossett gave me generous support, moral and financial. My editor, Alan Thomas nursed this project from its embryonic state to its present dinosaurial condition. Sam Baker provided energetic and imaginative assistance with research. Keith Thomson (whom I hope to meet someday) read every draft with a keen eye for paleontological errors; the ones that remain are my own fault. Bill Brown, Janice Knight, and Laura Rigal led me to the American theme. Jonathan Bordo brought me Northern

Theory from Canada, and Homi Bhabha provided a southerly critique. The annual meeting of the Science and Literature Society (especially Bruce Clarke and Linda Henderson) provided wonderful feedback, as did many other audiences at museums and universities from Capetown to Sydney to Berlin to New York. Barbara Narendra and Jean Zallinger opened up the utopian vista of the great Zallinger mural at Yale's Peabody Museum. Anthony Elms pointed me toward Alan McCollum, Sara Skerker suggested digging around in Robert Smithson, and Ellen Esrock made me read Italo Calvino. Marshall Sahlins gave his blessing to my totem, and Arnold Davidson gave precise definition to my monster. Chris Rossiter, John Moore, and the Leo Burnett advertising agency were extraordinarily generous with their images, as were Mark Dion, Claudia Katz-Palme, and Allan McCollum. Untold good ideas were provided by Michael Geyer, Tom Gunning, Miriam Hansen, Caroline Jones, William Kelly, Ulla-Britta Lagerroth, Brian Noble, Paul Sereno, and Joel Snyder, and superb technical assistance came from Kathryn Kraynik and Randy Petilos. If this book is beautiful, it is because of Joan Sommers' genius as a designer. If it is true, it is because Janice Misurell-Mitchell has a bone to pick with everything I say.

Page references to illustrations are in **boldface** type.

INDEX

anthropology, physical, 147, 163
Apatosaurus, 278, 287n. 3
apes, great, 164
architecture: early dinosaur associated
  with, 120, 208; Jefferson's University of
  Virginia, 122. *See also* skyscrapers
Arendt, Hannah, 287n. 4
arms race, 197
art: art for art's sake, 159; artists working
  "in the grip," 194; dinosaur images and,
  59–62; dinosaur remains compared with,
  156; elite versus popular, 183; paleoart,
  265–75; in paleontology, 55–56, 108; "prehistoric art," 272; primitive art, 270; science as, 58; throwback styles, 60, 288n. 2.
  See also modernism
artificial intelligence, 216
Artist in His Museum, 1822, The (Peale), **112**
Aryans, 150
Australian Dinosaurs (Hallett), **149**
authorial function, 269
automobiles (cars), 197, **197**, 208, **220,**
  221–23

B

Bakker, Robert: on birds as dinosaurs, 108,
  137; *The Dinosaur Heresies,* 108; in
  "dinosaur renaissance," 63, 83, 207; on
  imperial saga of the dinosaurs, 63–64; on
  modern image of dinosaurs, 104; and
  paleontologist of *The Lost World,* 295n. 2;
  Raptor Red, 41–42; on unearthing bones,
  156; visual perception and representation
  in work of, 56; on Zallinger's *The Age of
  Reptiles,* 192
Balzac, Honoré de, 54, 95
Barba, Roberta H., 296n. 6
Barney: "Cookie Monster" contrasted with,
  288n. 3; hostility toward, 232–33; in
  Jurassic Park, **235;** as perverted, **238;**
  theme song, 230, 232; as toothless, 12; as
  transitional object, 258, 297n. 5
Barnum, P. T., 120, 134–35, 166
Barosaurus lentus, 151–52
Bedini, Sylvio, 111
Benjamin, Walter: on consumption, 223; on
  mechanical reproduction, 208, 215–16,
  269, 288n. 3; on the modern economy,
  261; on one's own destruction as aesthet-
  ic experience, 60
Berger, John, 48
Berkeley, Bishop George, 129
Berlinosaurus (postcard), **204**
Bettelheim, Bruno, 247, 272
Bible, the, 202, 205
Big Bone Lick (Missouri), 116
big game hunts, 63, 142, 150, 176, 225, 295n.
  2
biocybernetic reproduction, 215–19; and
  consumption, 218; in postmodern age,

209, 217; of Spielberg's dinosaurs, 171
biogenetic engineering, 209, 213
biology: and culture, 106–7, 284; folk biology, 81; as frontier of science, 216; funding
  of, 153; sociobiology, 106, 146, 203, 205,
  244, 284. *See also* evolution; natural history; paleontology; taxonomy
bipedal dinosaurs, 23
Bird, Roland T., **49**
bird hips. *See* ornithischians
birds: as descendants of dinosaurs, 22, 25,
  27–28, 79; as dinosaurs, 108; Huxley linking with dinosaurs, 54, 104, 137, 290n. 4;
  postmodern dinosaurs and, 108, 209
Blake, William, 194
Bleak House (Dickens), 14
Blue Dinosaur (Smithson), 270–71, **271**
Boas, Franz, 163–64, 294n. 1
Bondi, Edith, 296n. 7
"bone fields," 129–30
"bone rush," 29, 111, 131, 133–34
Bones for Barnum Brown (Bird), **49**
"bone wars," 22, 134
Bowler, Peter, 109
Brachiosaurus, **76**
brain, reptilian, 199, 201–3, **202**
Bringing Up Baby (film), 174–82;
  Brontosaurus in, 174–79, **180;** dinosaur as
  totem animal in, 185; dog running away
  with the bone, 176, 226; and the family,
  225; Grant in, **174,** 175–81; Hepburn in,
  176–77; leopard in, 176, 177, 252, 260;
  skeletal reconstruction in, 278
British empire, Age of Reptiles compared
  with, 128
"British Fossil Reptiles" (Owen), 124, 198,
  203
Brontosaurus: Apatosaurus replacing, 278;
  in *Bringing Up Baby,* 174–79, **180;** in folk
  taxonomy, 287n. 3; as modern dinosaur
  image, 104; mother associated with, 246;
  Sinclair dinosaur as, **51,** 88, 167–68, **168;**
  in Zallinger's *The Age of Reptiles,* 190, 192
Brookes, Richard, 277
Brown, Barnum, 166–68; as bone hunter,
  143; as cashing in on dinomania, 12; on
  Sinclair Expedition of 1934, **166**
Bryan, William Jennings, College, 199
Bryant, William Cullen, 119
Buffon, Georges Louis Leclerc, comte de,
  112–13, 116
"Bulls Fighting" (Ward), 60, **60**
Burke, Edmund, 117
Burroughs, Edgar Rice, 114, 221

C

California, 19
Calvin and Hobbes (cartoon), 245–54, 259,
  260, 262
Calvinism, 252

culture: autonomy of, 184; and biology, 106–7, 284; cultural evolution, 147; dinosaurs as cultural symbol, 8, 18–19, 69, 72, 84, 91, 146, 282; mass culture, 63, 183, 270; and science, 164, 203–5, 279–84; for social Darwinism, 203; sociobiology, 106, 146, 203, 205, 244, 284. *See also* popular culture

Cuvier, Georges, 11, 95, 126

cyberspace, 216–17

cynicism, 226, 295n. 4

Czerkas, Sylvia J., 287n. 1

D

Darwin, Charles: on European emigration to the United States, 129; on Europeans and aboriginals, 130

Darwinism: American dinosaur bones in ascendancy of, 137; Darwinian necessity, 146; as gradualist, 213; as not necessarily progressive, 105; plausibility compared with creationism, 201–2, 205; racial theories based on, 147; rightness of, 106, 205, 290n. 6; social Darwinism, 143, 159, 203, 244, 284; "survival of the fittest," 106, 143, 146, 159; synthesizing with Marx and Freud, 107

Dawn of a New Day (Hallett), **47**

deep time, 4, 77, 272, 273

Deinonychus and Iguanodon (Gurche), **102**

De Maria, Walter, 273

democratic revolutions, 260

Dennett, Daniel, 205, 213, 238, 284, 290n. 6

Depression, the: dinosaurs disappearing as scientific object, 14, 22, 169, 293n. 5; robber barons criticized in, 293n. 5

Derrida, Jacques, 293n. 3

Desmond, Adrian, 109, 126, 134, 291n. 2, 292n. 6

Dickens, Charles, 14

dicynodont, **66**

Dilophosaurus, 71–72, 223

Dimetrodon, 190

dinodentification, 238

dinomania: age range for, 179, 232; as cyclic, 10; dinosaurs' cult status exposed by, 84; early eras of, 14; monsters and, 65–69; as obsession, 246, 256; as occupational hazard of dinosaurology, 69; paleontology as at center of, 21; as rite of passage, 234–35; science as in inverse relation to, 169; taboos and rituals at core of, 79; teachers exploiting, 241

dinophiles: as disavowing cultural significance of dinosaurs, 18; passion of, 6. *See also* dinomania

Dinosaur & Co.: Studies in Corporate Evolution (Lloyd), 289n. 4

dinosaur books, 4, 41

dinosaur collectibles: artist's installation of,

5, 265; cookie cutters, 51, **51;** as toylike and toothless, 11–12, 19

Dinosaur Data Book, 285n. 2

"Dinosaur Families" (Field Museum exhibit), 80

Dinosaur Heresies, The (Bakker), 108

Dinosauria, 23, 137

dinosaur images, 48–56; to America, 129–35; as American export commodity, 198; capitalist evolution and changes in, 100; children as audience for, 230–35; color in, 147–52, 296n. 6; as constructed, 50–52, 58, 288n. 13; cultural and natural determinants intersecting in, 107; dinosaur artists as artists, 59; dispersing through popular culture, 169; earliest compared with most recent, 54; economic cycles in speculation in, 12; evolution of, 103–9, 207–9; as imaginary, 53; as juvenilia, 60; as kitsch, 60, 62, 63; Knight's images, 104–5, 141–44; in lost world fictions, 169–73; minimal details evoking, 50–51; modern consensus on dinosaurs, 104, 108, 192, 208, 293n. 2; and modern historical crises, 19; and modernism, 60, 61, 265–66; modes of production as producing, 208; overabundance of, 4, 6; paintings, 59–60; in paleoart, 265–75; political unconscious expressed in, 261–62; postmodernist, 108, 208–9; resurrection as continuity in, 95; schematic history of, **101;** scientific illustration, 287n. 1; scientists' attitude toward, 6, 18; shifting from male hunter to good mothers, 80; sources on, 285n. 1; as stereotypes, 51; as symptoms, 184; *Tyrannosaurus rex* dominating, 10; in Victorian era, 104, 108, 124–28, 208; as vulgar, 184; what to do with obsolete, 241. See also *Age of Reptiles, The;* Barney; Crystal Palace exhibition dinosaurs

Dinosaur National Monument, 19, **44, 255,** 262, 270

dinosaurology, 21–25; as in danger of extinction, 105; in the Depression, 14, 22, 169, 293n. 5; dinomania as occupational hazard of, 69; dinosaurologists as media celebrities, 21; dinosaurs as allegories of humans in, 63–64; great schism in, 137; migration to America, 129; mistakes in, 278; as paleo-ornithology, 25; and second extinction of dinosaurs, 88; technical jargon introduced in, 239, **241;** term as questionable, 22. *See also* paleontology

"dinosaur renaissance": Bakker in, 63, 83, 207; as beginning in 1960s, 17, 24; in evolution of dinosaurs image, 104, 207; and rebirth of totemism, 83; Victorian images revived in, 104

dinosaurs: adult attitudes toward, 18, 72; ambivalence toward, 13, 82, 122, 235;

American connections of, 111–15; ancestral function of, 78–79; as an extra, 14; as backward, 197; as bestiary, 67, 78; as big, fierce, and extinct, 9–10; and birds (*see* birds); circus air surrounding, 22, 169; classic model of, 28, 192; classificatory debates over, 22, 23; creationism's account of, 199, **201;** as cultural symbol, 8, 18–19, 69, 72, 84, 91, 146, 282; as eating machines, 80; in elementary education, 9, 230, 238–44, 254, 296nn. 6, 7; as evolutionary dead end, 65; as evolutionary success story, 84; as familial, 80, 286n. 10; fascination with, 8–14; feminization of, 46, 290n. 3; footprints, **136,** 139; as gifts, 153, 156; late-twentieth-century view of, 24; as looking neat, 69; as master race, 149; mastodons preceding in cultural history, 124, 126; as modern animals, 138–39; modern consensus on, 104, 108, 192, 208, 293n. 2; moral lessons attached to, 145–46; in movies, 25, 62; nation-state symbolized by, 68; the new-model dinosaur, 24, **103;** Owen coining word and concept, 11; Owen's conception of, 124–26, 291n. 2; pterodactyls and ichthyosaurs linked with, 286n. 5, 287n. 3; as ruling class animals, 146; scientific questions about, 8; *Scrotum humanum* as earliest name for, 277–78; state dinosaurs, 19; as symbolic animals, 67; as synonym for obsolescence, 8, 12, **206;** term as a misnomer, 25, 278; term as questionable, 23–24, 105, 137–39, 282; as totem animals of modernity, 77–85, 100, 262, 282; as transitional objects, 256–63; two senses of word, 57–58. *See also* dinomania; dinosaur images; dinosaurology; "dinosaur renaissance"; extinction; ornithischians; saurischians; *and species by name*
"Dinosaurs, The" (Calvino), 41–46, 60, 77, 114, 263
Dinosaurs, The (Stout), 288n. 2
Dinosaurs Past and Present (Czerkas and Olson), 287n. 1
Dinotopia (CD-ROM), 33
Dinotopia (film), 227
dinotopias, 32–39
Dion, Mark, **5, 265,** 266
Diplodocus carnegii, 157–61, **161,** 247, 259
Disney, Walt, **42,** 167, 195
Dodge automobile company, 166
Dog from Pompeii, The (McCollum), 267, **268,** 269
Dollo, Louis, 129
downsizing, corporate, **103, 168,** 182, 209
Doyle, Arthur Conan, 85, 114, 169–70, 239
Dragonheart (film), 89–90
dragons, 86–92; Chinese, 68, 88–89; dinosaurs contrasted with, 11, 86–92, 231;

disaster symbolized by, 68, 213; *Dungeons & Dragons,* 90; as evil in the West, 89; extinction of, 85, 87; from *Historiae naturalis,* 89; as hybrids, 65, 89; images of, 54; resurrection as folklore, 88; St. George and, **86,** 89; as standing for chaos, 213; as symbolic animals, 67; Thoreau compares railroads with, 144; as totems for Germanic tribes, 289n. 3
Dragons of Eden, The (Sagan), 199, **202**
Dryptosauruses Fighting (Knight), 60, **61**
Du Bois, W. E. B., 149
Duncan, Jody, **222**
Dungeons & Dragons (game), 90

E

Earthworks movement, 273
ecotourism, 293n. 1
Edaphosaurus, 190
Eden, Garden of, **35,** 135, 199
Edsel (automobile), 197
education, dinosaurs in elementary, 9, 230, 238–44, 254, 296nn. 6, 7
Ehrlich, Paul and Anne, 285n. 4
Engels, Friedrich, 146
Enlightenment rationalism, 87
entropy, 210, 216
eugenics, 149
Evans, Jonathan, 85, 87, 90
evolution, and evolution of images: cultural, 147; dinosaurs as evolutionary dead end, 65; dinosaurs as evolutionary success story, 84; Jefferson as antievolutionist, 113, 196; punctuated equilibrium, 105, 213, 295n. 3. *See also* Darwinism; Lamarckian progressive evolution
extinction, 210–13; accelerating rate of, 109, 290n. 11; catastrophe theory of, 126, 211–13; of dinosaurs as cult object, 84–85, 88; in dinosaur stories, 42–46; in fascination with dinosaurs, 9–12; literature on dinosaurs', 27–31; Noah's Flood in, 292n. 8; Osborn on dinosaurs', 145, 149–50; Owen on dinosaurs', 125–26, 196, 210; public thinking it understands dinosaurs', 25; sexual and reproductive anxieties associated with dinosaurs', 80; theories of dinosaurs', 145; in Zallinger's *The Age of Reptiles,* 195–96
Extinction: The Causes and Consequences of the Disappearance of Species (Ehrlich and Ehrlich), 285n. 4
Ezekiel, Book of, 95, 126

F

Faerie Queene (Spenser), 85, 226–27
Fall of Man, The (van der Goes), **35**
family, the: dinosaurs as familial, 80, 286n. 10; as endangered species in *Jurassic Park,* 181, 184, 225

Fantasia (film), **42**, 167, 195
fantasy: and biocybernetic reproduction, 217; in *Calvin and Hobbes*, 246–47, 252, 253; as defined in this study, 53; dinosaur learning as teaching children to identify, 240–41; *Dungeons & Dragons* as, 90; off-road vehicles as, 222
Farber, Sharon, **26**, 29–31, 42, 46
Federalists, 119
feminism, 46, 279, 280
Ferguson, Munro, 27
fetishes, 17, 78, 260
feudalism, 143, 293n. 6
Field, Marshall, 153
Field Museum of Natural History (Chicago): "Dinosaur Families" exhibit, 80; Knight's *Tyrannosaurus rex* and *Triceratops* painting, **140**, 142; in modern paleontology, 111; Sue (*T. rex*), **154**; totem poles in, 76
films. *See* movies
Flintstones, The (television program and film), 33, 227
Flood, the, 134, 135, 210, 292n. 8
Focillon, Henri, 54, 187, 192, 193
folk biology, 81
folk taxonomy, 23, 87, 286n. 8, 287n. 3
Ford, Henry, 218
Ford Edsel, 197
Fort-Da game, 259
"fossil feuds," 22, 29
fossil fuels: automobile consumption of, 222; dinosaurs associated with, 88, 208; in *King Kong* remake, 173; Sinclair advertising of, 167
"Fossil Fuels" (McDonald's commercial). *See* McDonald's "Fossil Fuels" commercial
fossil record: dinosaur decline indicated in, 211; in evolution of dinosaur images, 103, 104; as fragmentary, 4
fossils: the "bone rush," 29, 111, 131, 133–34; "bone wars," 22, 134; as few compared with replicas, 2; North American "bone fields," 129–30; seismic imaging of, **105**; as source of dinosaur fascination, 48. *See also* fossil record
Fossils and Progress (Bowler), 290n. 5
Foucault, Michel, 64, 291n. 12
Fox Trot (cartoon), **242**
Frank, Robert, 194
Frankenstein, 63, 95, 184
french fries, 80
Freud, Sigmund: on cigars as cigars, 177; "dangerous idea" of, 238; as dinosaur, 107, 237; on Fort-Da game, 259; on latency period, 179; on Oedipus complex, 258; *Totem and Taboo*, 289nn. 2, 7; on totemism, 82, 289n. 2; tricameral model of the psyche, 201; for understanding dinosaur fascination, 107
frontier, American, 121
frontiersmen, 30–31

G

Galton Society, 149, 163
Garden of Eden, **35**, 135, 199
Garden of Paradise (imitator of Hieronymus Bosch), **36**
Gardner, Howard, 240
Gates, Bill, 266–67
gender: in *Bringing Up Baby*, 174–79; carnivorous and herbivorous dinosaurs encoded as difference in, 78; in children's identification with dinosaurs, 246; dinosaur images shifting from male hunter to good mother, 80; in dinosaur learning, 239, 240, **240**; dinosaur stories as gendered, 45–46; in image production, 54; in interest in dinosaurs, 9; *Jurassic Park* dinosaurs as female, 9, 78, 46, 226; *Maiasaurus* as "good mother lizard," 80, 290n. 3; male hysteria, 182, 183; male potency, 150, 168, 182; masculinity associated with science, 239; in totemism, 239. *See also* women
George, St., **86**, 89
Gertie on Vacation (film), **144**
Gertie the Dinosaur (film), 25, 62
giantism, corporate, 25, **103**, 167, **168**, 209
gift-giving: children learning, 259; gift and giver identified in, 157; potlatch, 155, 160, 163; reciprocity requirement, 160, 259; in traditional cultures, 155–56. *See also* philanthropy
Gilded Age, 14, 157, 177
Girard, Rene, 286n. 4
Godzilla, 63, 197–98
Goes, Hugo van der, **35**
Golden Calf, 17
Gombrich, Ernst, 54, 108
Gould, Stephen Jay: on the archetypal fascination with dinosaurs, 9–10; on commercialization of dinosaurs, 25, 82; on the modern consensus on dinosaurs, 104, 186, 192, 293n. 2; on punctuated equilibrium, 105, 213, 295n. 3
Grant, Cary, **174**, 175–81
Grant, Madison, 149, 163
Gray, Richard, **154**
great apes, 164
Greenberg, Clement, 62, 143, 265, **265**, 297n. 2
green politics, 293n. 1
Gross, Paul R., 279–84
Gurche, John, 60, **102**

H

Hadrosaurus: Hawkins's painting of, **35**; Hawkins's sculpture of, **133**, 134; as New Jersey state dinosaur, 19, **133**
Hallett, Michael, **47**, **149**
Halstead, L. B., 277, 278
Hamilton, Alexander, 119
happiness, pursuit of, 177–78

of, 277, 278; Peale's skeletons, **112**, 117, 124, 126–28, 134; as preceding dinosaurs in cultural history, 124; as symbolic political animal of the United States, 119, 124

Mather, Cotton, 120

Mauss, Marcel, 155, 157, 160

McCarter, John, **154**

McCay, Winsor, 25, 62

McCollum, Allan, **114, 139**, 266–70, **267, 268**

McDonald's "Fossil Fuels" commercial, 70–75, **72, 74**; animation in, 288n. 5, 295n. 4; dinosaur as totem animal in, 79–80, 84; *Jurassic Park* scene as inspiration for, 223; *King Kong* contrasted with, 173; totem poles in, 74, **75**, 84, 164, 289n. 2

mechanical reproduction, 208, 215–16, 269, 274, 288n. 3

Megalonyx jeffersoni, **123**

Megalosaurus: in Dickens's *Bleak House*, 14; Hawkins's reconstruction of, **50**; *Scrotum humanum* as from, 277

memes, 106

Metropolitan Museum of Art (New York City), 59

Michelet, Jules, 261

Mighty Joe Young (film), 288n. 5

migration: in dinosaur extinction, 145, 150; Osborn on immigration, 149–50

mimetic desire, 17, 286n. 4

miscegenation, 149

Model of Stenonychosaurus and Dinosauroid (Russell and Séguin), **3, 40**

modernism: as aesthetic of mechanical reproduction, 274; Cubism, 59; dinosaur images as out of step with, 60, 61, 265–66; modernity contrasted with, 265; primitive art as source of, 270; Smithson's *Blue Dinosaur*, 270, **271**

modernity: childhood as modern invention, 253; on dinosaur extinction, 210; dinosaurs as emblems of, 67–68; dinosaurs as gray-green in, 147; dinosaurs as modern animals, 138–39; dinosaurs as totem animals of, 77–85, 100, 262, 282; the modern consensus on dinosaurs, 104, 108, 192, 208, 293n. 2; modernism contrasted with, 265; as oedipal phase of history, 179; schizosaur as totem animal of, 145

modernization, 67

monsters: antediluvian monsters, 88, 104, 134, 195, 210, 241; and dinomania, 65–69; dragons as, 90; Hobbes's *Leviathan*, 120–21; as hybrids, 65, **68**; natural monsters, 67. *See also* dragons

Moore, John, 289n. 2

Morgan, J. P., 14, 144, 153

Morison, Patricia, 240

Morris, Robert, 273, **275**

movies: animation, 62–63, 170, 208, **214,**

288n. 5; comedies of remarriage, 177; dinosaurs in, 25, 62. *See also by name*

multiculturalism, 147, 280

multinational corporations, 181

museum gift shops, 10

Museum of Modern Art (New York City), 275, **275**

museums of natural history. *See* natural history museums

mythical creatures: dragons as, 88; images of, 54–55; unicorns, 53, 54, 67, 88. *See also* dragons

N

Nabokov, Vladimir, 265

National Film Board of Canada, 27

National Museum of Natural History (Washington, DC): in modern paleontology, 111; the *Stegosaurus* made of money, 15–18, 286n. 2

Native Americans. *See* American Indians

natural history: and American nationalism, 112, 290n. 2; methods of, 52; morals drawn from, 146; visual and pictorial construction in, 59. *See also* natural history museums

Natural History Museum of Los Angeles County, 287n. 1

natural history museums: children as visitors to, 230, 234; dinosaurs and totem poles as marquee attractions of, 84; dinosaur skeletons as casts, 288n. 6; first wave of dinosaur displays, 17; gift shops, 10; Peabody Museum of Natural History, 104, 187–97, **188-91**, 287n. 1; Peale's museum, **112**, 117, 120, 128, 134; picture windows in laboratories, 21; private philanthropy as supporting, 153. *See also* American Museum of Natural History; Carnegie Museum of Natural History; Field Museum of Natural History; National Museum of Natural History

nature: capitalist values projected upon, 146; and culture, 58–59, 62. *See also* natural history

neocortex, 201, 203

New Jersey, 19, **35, 133**

New Mexico, 19

new women, 46

Nineteenth Amendment, 177

Noah's Ark, 199

Noah's Flood, 134, 135, 210, 292n. 8

Noah's second Ark, 195, **195**

Noble, Brian, 65

Non-Site, Franklin, New Jersey (Smithson), **274**

Notes on the State of Virginia (Jefferson), 112, 113, 122

nuclear family, 181, 184, 225

nuclear winter, 211

socialization, 246

Social Text (journal), 280, 283–84

sociobiology, 106, 146, 203, 205, 244, 284

Sokal hoax, 280, 283–84

specialization, in dinosaur extinction, 145, 150, 210

species: as basic classificatory unit, 53, 287n. 6; etymology of term, 55; in nature and art, 58–59

Spencer, Herbert, 159

Spenser, Edmund, 85, 226–27

Spielberg, Stephen: ambivalence toward dinosaurs, 69; animation in films of, 171; as cashing in on dinomania, 12; as imagineer, 97–98; on the monster breaking out of the museum, 121; *Schindler's List*, 121, 225. See also *Jurassic Park; Lost World, The*

Spiral Jetty (Smithson), 270, **271**, 273

state dinosaurs, 19

Stegosaurus: as feminine, 239; in Larson cartoon, 197; as modern dinosaur image, 104; as ornithischian, 23; papier-mâché model of, 15–18, 88, 286n. 2; in Zallinger's *The Age of Reptiles*, 190

Stenonychus inequalis, **3**

Stout, William, 288n. 2

Strong, Josiah, 150

Stubbs, George, 60

stuffed animals, 256

Sue (*T. rex*), 41, **154**

Surrogate Paintings (McCollum), 266, **267**

"survival of the fittest," 106, 143, 146, 159

symbolic animals, 67, 77, 88

T

taboos, 78, 79, 80, 82, 185

taxonomy: cladistics, 87; Dinosauria as problematic term, 23, 137; folk taxonomy, 23, 87, 286n. 8, 287n. 3; Linnæan naming conventions, 277; objectivity of order achieved in, 57, 58. See also species

technical jargon, 239, **241**, 283

teddy bears, 257

Tennyson, Alfred, Lord, 88

Texas, 19

thermodynamics, 208, 210

Thompson, Daniel Varney, 192

Thoreau, Henry David, 144

throwback styles, 60, 288n. 2

Tiebout, Cornelius, **119**

Tippett, Phil, 288n. 5

Totem and Taboo (Freud), 289nn. 2, 7

totemism: dinosaurs as totem animals of modernity, 77–85, 100, 262, 282; dragons as totems for Germanic tribes, 289n. 3; gender in, 239; getting over, 107; Lévi-Strauss on, 58, 77–78, 82–83; naturalizing culture as, 106–7; as obsolete notion, 23, 82; schizosaur as totem animal of moder-

nity, 145; taboos associated with totem animals, 78, 80; totem animals for children, 257–58; the totem meal, 80, 100; traditional totem animals, 79; transitional objects and totem animals, 257, 297n. 3

totem poles: in American Museum of Natural History, **162**, 163, 164; in Field Museum of Natural History, **76**; in McDonald's "Fossil Fuels" commercial, 74, **75**, 164; in natural history museums, 84; in potlatches, 155

transitional objects: Barney as, 258, 297n. 5; constitutions as, 260; dinosaurs as, 256–63; *Diplodocus carnegii* as, 160; Godzilla as, 197–98; Jefferson's bone collection as, 122; and totem animals, 257, 297n. 3

Triceratops: Knight's painting of *Tyrannosaurus rex* and, **140**, 142; as modern dinosaur image, 104; as ornithischian, 23

Tweed, Boss, 131, **134**

"two culture split," 203, 279–84

Tylor, E. B., 82

Tyrannosaurus rex: as big, fierce, and extinct, 10; Brown finds first, 166; dinosaur imagery dominated by, 10; father associated with, 246; first complete reconstruction, 150–51; in *Jurassic Park*, 71, **73**, 182, 221–23, 225; in *King Kong*, **170**, 171, 173; Knight's painting of *Triceratops* and, **140**, 142; in *The Lost World*, 80, 286n. 10; in McDonald's "Fossil Fuels" commercial, 70, **72**, **75**, 80, 173; as modern dinosaur image, 104; Paul's image of, 54; as saurischian, 23; Sue, 41, **154**; in *We're Back! A Dinosaur's Story*, 14; in Zallinger's *The Age of Reptiles*, 190, 192

U

unconscious, the, 237

unicorns, 53, 54, 67, 88

uniformitarianism, 212–13

Unktehi, 131, 184, 241

V

Veblen, Thorstein, 156

Velociraptor: in *Jurassic Park*, 67, 78, 182, **214**, 225; as postmodern dinosaur, 104, 182; as saurischian, 23

Verne, Jules, 114

Victoria, Queen, 98

Victorian era: on dinosaur extinction, 145, 210; dinosaur images in, 104, 108, 124–28, 208; the Gilded Age, 14, 157, 177. See also Crystal Palace exhibition dinosaurs

Vietnam War, 17

Virginia, University of, 122

Virtual Reality, 216–17